MAGICAL KNOWLEDGE

BOOK TWO

THE INITIATE

BY JOSEPHINE MCCARTHY

SECOND EDITION

TaDehent Books
Exeter
2020

Copyright 2020 © Josephine McCarthy

All rights reserved

Without limiting the rights under copyright reserved above, no part of this publication may be reproduced, stored in, or introduced into a retrieval system, or transmitted, in any form or by any means (electronic, mechanical, photocopying, recording or otherwise) without prior permission of the copyright owner and the publisher of this book.

First edition published by Mandrake of Oxford, 2011

Second edition published by TaDehent Books 2020
Exeter UK

ISBN 978-1-911134-50-3

Cover image by Stuart Littlejohn
Typeset by Michael Sheppard

Dedicated to Josephine Stockdale, my greatest teacher.

Contents

Introduction   **1**

1 Accessing the Inner Worlds   **3**
    1.1   Accessing beings: making a contact 6
    1.2   Human inner contacts 8

2 Practical methods for working with angelic beings   **11**
    2.1   So how and why do we work with them? 14

3 Working with deities: pitfalls and approaches   **19**
    3.1   Forms of deity 20
    3.2   Working with the deity 21

4 Working with ancestors   **27**
    4.1   Time jumping 29
    4.2   Family ancestors 30
    4.3   The ancestral vision 31
    4.4   The family 34
    4.5   Guarding the children 35
    4.6   Tribal ancestors 36
    4.7   Cultural ancestors 39
    4.8   The vision of Tin Hinan 40
    4.9   Practical use of ancestral work 41
    4.10   Time and intention 42
    4.11   Interactions with ancestors 43
    4.12   Vision of meeting the ancestors 45
    4.13   Dynamics 46

5 Accessing and working within the Faery Realm   **49**
    5.1   Short vision for accessing the Faery Realm 50
    5.2   Longer vision of the Faery Realm 51
    5.3   Work 54
    5.4   My own discovery of faeries 56

	5.5	Magic, faeries and sex	60

6 Polarization: magical dynamics and partnerships — 65
- 6.1 Polarity within magical partnerships ... 68

7 The physical implications of practising magic — 75
- 7.1 Treating impacts ... 76
- 7.2 Working with balance ... 78
- 7.3 Food ... 80
- 7.4 Practicalities while working ... 81
- 7.5 The effects of inner contact on the endocrine system ... 83
- 7.6 The future ... 88

8 Inner landscapes of the people and the land — 91
- 8.1 Energetic load-sharing: a short look ... 96

9 Magical protection: working methods — 101
- 9.1 So when do you use banishing and talismans? ... 102
- 9.2 House protection ... 105

10 Sigils and seals — 109
- 10.1 Angelic and demonic sigils ... 109
- 10.2 Deity sigils ... 112
- 10.3 Magical seals ... 113
- 10.4 Platonic solids and geometric shapes ... 116
- 10.5 Mandalas ... 118

11 Inner world parasites — 121
- 11.1 Dealing with and removing parasites ... 123
- 11.2 Emotional parasites ... 125
- 11.3 Sexual parasites ... 125
- 11.4 Magical parasites ... 126
- 11.5 Parasites of the dying ... 128
- 11.6 Minor parasites ... 129
- 11.7 Removing parasites: practical application ... 129
- 11.8 Summary ... 131

12 Removing ghosts and other unwelcome guests — 133
- 12.1 Types of hauntings ... 134
- 12.2 Land-based entities ... 136
- 12.3 Possession of a house by demonic forces ... 139
- 12.4 Possession from an object ... 141

13 How to deal with simple magical/psychic attacks — 143

14 Dismantling Hermetic or Kabbalistic curses   147
    14.1   What is a Hermetic/Kabbalistic curse? 148
    14.2   How do curses affect the victim? 149
    14.3   So what about protection? 151
    14.4   Dismantling the curse: working methods 154
    14.5   What do they look like on the inner? 156
    14.6   How are curses taken off? 157
    14.7   What is the cleanup procedure? 159

15 Short tour of the Tree of Life without Kabbalah   161
    15.1   So what actually is the Tree of Life? 162

16 The Structure of the Abyss without Kabbalah   167

17 The eighteenth-century pattern of initiation in Britain   175
    17.1   The Walk of Initiation at Stourhead, Wiltshire 176
    17.2   The Stourhead initiation 177

18 Working with Sleepers   183
    18.1   So what are sleepers? 183
    18.2   Are the sleepers still active? 185
    18.3   Communing with sleepers 188
    18.4   Vision for contacting a sleeper 192
    18.5   The future 193
    18.6   Bridging 194

19 Death and Birth   199
    19.1   Death 200
    19.2   So what happens when a person dies? 201
    19.3   The death vision in detail 202
    19.4   The Bridge 205
    19.5   The Plains 206
    19.6   The Mountain 207
    19.7   The awakening into rebirth 209
    19.8   Practical working methods 210
    19.9   Physical practicalities 211
    19.10   Birth 212

20 Using tarot as a working tool   215
    20.1   Layouts 217
    20.2   The use of tarot in healing 222
    20.3   The health layout 225
    20.4   Making a contacted deck for magical seership 232
    20.5   Minor layouts 235

20.6	Creating your major cards	235

21 Working methods for leading group visions/workings 239
    21.1   Contacts 240
    21.2   Energy dynamics 241
    21.3   Reality or imagination? 242
    21.4   Snatched energy 243
    21.5   Different strains for different places 244
    21.6   Picking up maps from written visions 245
    21.7   Clearing up 246
    21.8   Creating a vision from a personal experience 246
    21.9   The vision of the goddess Tefnut in Ethiopia 247
    21.10 The vision of Metatron and the Abyss 250
    21.11 Vision of the elders 252

22 The inner aspects of consecration 259
    22.1   Born or touched 259
    22.2   Pros and cons 260
    22.3   Physical and magical effects 263
    22.4   Training versus nature 264
    22.5   Lines 266
    22.6   What is the future for such consecrations? 266

23 Afterword 269

A The directions in Western magic 271
    A.1   Background 271
    A.2   The magical directions 273
    A.3   The current magical use of the directions 274
    A.4   Nineteenth-century Europe 276
    A.5   The sixteenth century 289
    A.6   The modern structural approach 296
    A.7   Dynastic Egypt 297
    A.8   Right hand path, left hand path 316

B The Book of Death 325

Introduction

Once you have been initiated into or have been working at any depth in a magical or spiritual line, there are certain things that will start to happen to you: the inner contacts will begin to include you in their job listings and things will be put in your path for you to sort out. If you decide to be totally self-serving, then this peculiarity will fade off and they will eventually leave you alone. Just bear in mind if you do that, they will also leave you alone when you don't want them to.

But if you rise to the challenge, then more things will be put in your path and the tasks that will be thrown your way might have no connection to the stream of magic/spirituality that you are initiated into or working on. You become a worker in their eyes and they will give you jobs: they don't care what robes you wear or who's books you read.

This book is about methods, approaches and techniques that can be used regardless of what tradition you are from, as it is a book that shows you the world from the back door: a view into the boiler room of the universe. This is where adepts work from, whether they are Western Mystery adepts, Mystical Christian adepts, or Pagan adepts. It doesn't really matter because once you get past the surface details, the skills and techniques are more or less the same, and the beings that you will encounter are most definitely the same.

Instead of taking you by the hand and spoon-feeding you details, visions and a step-by-step guide, which is a stage you should be past now, these chapters look at potential pitfalls and suggest good working methods, approaches and how to tackle common problems. There are practical parts where you are shown how to develop certain tools, but in general the idea is to move beyond the beginner shuffle and progress to more advanced working methods.

Introduction

Once you have got your head around using working methods without specific structures (i.e. traditions) then you start to look at the tradition that you are an initiate of in more depth. You start to see the inner pattern that holds that tradition together and the blueprint of the structure that was used to build it. Once you look at a tradition this way, you start to see its strengths and weaknesses, and it begins to expose the reasons why certain things within that tradition are the way that they are. It helps you to understand the best way to work within your tradition, and the most positive way to move forward with the work as a part of the new generation.

A tradition that grows as a result of the magical development of its initiates and adepts is a tradition that will survive the many ups and downs that all magical and spiritual groups go through. The more balanced a tradition, the less infighting, power games and glamour it expresses and that balance comes from the maturing of the skills of the adepts over time and sometimes generations. It also encourages offshoot development which keeps the original group healthy by pruning and by satellite development instead of mummifying and degenerating the line of magic as a result of no innovation.

> What is a magician?
>   'One who does magic' is the Magician's reply.
>
> What is a magician?
>   'One who stands at the centre of everything' is the Developing One's reply.
>
> What is a magician?
>   'One who reflects the golden rays' is the Foremost One's reply.
>
> What is a magician?
>   'One who is I,' replies the Divine.

Chapter One

Accessing the Inner Worlds

Making contacts without the use of temples, rituals and patterns

Magical and spiritual traditions have developed working structures over hundreds of years to enable the practitioner to gain access to the inner realms in one form or another.

Without inner access, most magical work is pointless as it is not 'plugged in' or connected. The outer ritual must have an inner mirror, an inner connection through which power, contact and action can flow. Some traditions and working methods dispense completely with the outer ritual/action and focus purely on the inner structure/action. Some use a mixture depending on the desired outcome. There are traditions that work with only outer ritual and evocation methods, using complex patterns, rituals, incantations and sigils.

The less inner work that is done in a temple/lodge, the less power manifests and therefore the more fragmented the practitioners and work become. This usually manifests in ego squabbles, tantrums, power games, sexual manipulations etc., which are all symptoms that something is badly wrong with the inner power structure.

Over the years various methods of accessing the Inner Worlds (also known as astral travel) have developed and have matured according to the consciousness of the people involved and the consciousness of the culture of that time. As our minds have become more pliable, so our inner abilities have become more flexible and able to 'imagine.' TV, computers, phones, and internet have all changed how we perceive communication and how we use our imagination. This in turn has changed how we use our inner abilities and how our imaginations work in a visionary sense. Magical working methods have to catch up with this change and flex accordingly.

1. Accessing the Inner Worlds

There is also a movement that has been developing in the magical community over the last hundred years or so to move away from ritual structures, deities, temples, etc. and move back towards nature, the land, the Faery Realm and the ancestors: returning to the garden. Unfortunately a lot of those movements have fallen back upon the need for structure and have mirrored the ritualist groups in one way or another using directions/attributes/priests/magical sigils/patterns etc. We have been civilized for so long it is as if we have forgot how nature actually works, and how we can attempt to work naturally within the inner structure of nature.

So, if you want to access the Inner Worlds but do not wish to continue using the age-old patterns, then what do you do? You cannot just sort of float around in the Inner Worlds hoping to bump into someone: that is just silly and dangerous.

In Western culture, using drugs to catapult yourself into the Inner Worlds is also not that bright, unless you know exactly what you are doing and where you are going. Really the only safe way to work in the Inner Worlds using drugs is if you are working within a cultural/religious structure that is designed for such use i.e. shamanic/native cultures.

Hallucinogenic drugs strip a layer of protective skin from the consciousness and allow you to see and access places that you would normally be blocked from seeing (for your own good usually). When you go magically into vision, you develop inner 'muscles' (for want of a better description) that uphold and protect you as you work. If you bypass this natural but lengthy process of strengthening by using drugs, you are often thrown straight to the threshold of your existence. This means you come face-to-face with the angelic being that straddles life and death, which often presents as a large many-headed snake being with many eyes (sound familiar to all you acid/ayahuasca/DMT heads?).

An inner adventure without complex rituals, sigil patterns, drugs or annoying drum-banging sessions: what do you do? You go back to the source of humanity itself.

For those who have done magical/spiritual inner work, you will have your own version of the Void. This is a deeply profound place from which all flows and to which all returns. And if this is a place from which all comes, then everywhere in the Inner Worlds is connected to this place: therefore everywhere can be accessed from this place. All elements also flow from this place, and the Void is within all elements: hence the use of an element (fire, water, earth, air) as an access point to the inner worlds.

To work in this simple form, the practitioner must have good mental focus: there is no pattern/temple or easy visual aid to fall back on. As you start the vision to access the Inner Worlds, you must be clearly intent on where you are going. That intent is the key to everything: the mind is the car that takes you there and it has a route finder if you know how to use it.

The key to this method is the ability to go into the Void and be there in total stillness and focus. That ability frees up the mind and strengthens the inner focus that enables the imagination to open the door to anywhere. Going into the Void creates stillness and allows the mind to disconnect from the outer world. From that point of stillness, the intent of place can be focused without interference. As soon as the mind connects to that place, the practitioner steps out of the Void and begins to walk towards their intended destination.

Even if you are trying to gain inner access to an outer place that you know well, it is good working practice to still go through the Void. This creates an inner discipline and also creates the inner stretching that is necessary for such inner work. This practice also replaces the need for lengthy patterned visions or preparations.

For example, say I wish to access an ancestral sacred site near my house from an inner point of view. I can choose to access it as it is now, i.e. the inner expression of the site complete with the inner contacts there, be they faery/land/elemental beings, or I can access it back in time when it was used by my ancestors. What matters is the clear intent when stepping into the Void. At first, spend time in there stretching, dropping the daily life and returning to an eternal stillness. That frees the spirit and allows it to flow naturally between the worlds.

Another good stretching method is also taking your time getting there once you step out of the Void. Don't step out of the Void straight into the middle of where you want to be. Step out onto a road or walkway and take a little time walking there. This inner

1. Accessing the Inner Worlds

dynamic in important for the success of the vision/contact, but also has a protective effect on the body: it doesn't get so impacted if you take your time.

When you have finished with the contact you don't have to spend as long going back as you did getting there. What is important is that you make sure that you are clean and balanced before stepping back into the void to get home. If you have worked at healing someone, clearing someone, bridging death, or connecting with beings in the Abyss, then the chances are you are pretty gunked up and need a clean up. Use something that is within the realms of that vision: a stream, river, hot springs, etc. and take a bath/wash.

Once you step back into the Void, let the vision fall away from you and feel your earthly self reemerge before you step out of the Void back to where you first started.

1.1 Accessing beings: making a contact

Making an inner contact from scratch, without the interface of a temple/ritual/structure or pattern, can be quite daunting to someone who does not have a natural ability to connect with inner contacts. Usually inner interaction with a power site will also connect the practitioner to a contact. However, there is an interesting way of working that reaches out for an unknown contact in a place: it is almost like 'feeling' for a connection. The method relies once again on a sense of stillness and connectedness: this developing awareness helps to filter out parasites and other undesirables, enabling the inner senses to be selective and discerning.

You can either go into the Void with the specific intent of connecting with a particular being/person at a set place/time, or you can go into the Void with the intent of connecting with a particular type of being. If you do not know the contact but wish to reach out for one then you have to use the method of 'homing in on a beacon' in the Void. This entails going into the Void/stillness with some intent, e.g. to meet an ancestor, then reaching out in the Void for a time in that ancestor's life when they cried out to the universe for help, or when they mediated a great deal of power. The cry for help creates a beacon that lights through the worlds and attracts the attention of

1.1. Accessing beings: making a contact

beings that flow in and out of the Void in service. You can pick up on that beacon and appear before that ancestor, but you must be prepared to help them.

If you are looking for an inner teacher who is connected to magic/ritual/spirituality then you must use those patterns, which is a totally different story. But if you are wishing to reach back before such patterning, then you can use the beacon method.

All in all, it is always about intent, not allowing self-limitation, and developing total focus. With these skills you can more or less go anywhere and connect with anyone. This is the reason why mystical sects and powerful magical groups insisted upon physical discipline, self-sacrifice, aestheticism and meditation: these skills develop the ability to focus with intent, to not be fragmented by desires (which is a great protection from parasites) and to not be easily frightened.

We do not have to join a monastery for twenty years hard labour, but we can use our everyday life with intent to develop and hone such skills for inner use: it just takes more self-discipline and awareness of everything that is around us. This in turn heightens our abilities to connect with inner contacts. The more you stretch out your everyday awareness of who is around you, the more you become aware of beings in the Inner Worlds. We spend so much of our time cut off from each other and closing our personal space that we slowly end up closing off our inner ability to commune with consciousness: thus when we reach out to inner contacts, it is a terrible struggle.

Learning how to be open, to have thinner barriers around us without being eaten alive by every draining person and parasite, teaches us to be able to flow through the worlds and be receptive to the slightest whisper from inner contacts while retaining our energetic health and integrity.

A different method of passing into the inner realms and making contacts is to pass through the Void with the intent of going to an Inner Temple, the Abyss, the Desert of the Tree of Life, or the great Inner Library. All of these places are human constructs of consciousness from millennia ago and have been used by magical workers of many different traditions for hundreds if not thousand of years. Because they are well-trodden paths, as soon as you focus that intent within the Void and step out, you will find yourself before that inner structure.

Gaining access is a different matter and depends largely upon your intent. If you are allowed into these places, you will make contact with the beings and adepts that work there. Again, the whole story is about discipline of the mind, focus and intent. Discernment is also a necessary quality to have when working in vision. You wouldn't trust a stranger in the street, but people seem to think that because a being manifests itself in the Inner Worlds, it must be powerful, wise and willing to communicate with you. That is a fantasy and it would be far better and much more productive to simply use your common sense. Parasites abound in the Inner Worlds just as they do in the outer world.

1.2 Human inner contacts

There are a variety of different human inner contacts, but the most common ones are people who became true adepts in their own lifetime and upon their death chose to stay in the Inner Worlds as teachers rather than come back into the cycle of life and death once more.

Being a true adept means that a person has let go of their mortal existence and has allowed true spiritual maturity to flow through them: they are spiritually as well as magically adept. It does not mean that they are all knowing/all powerful, but they carry less shit than the rest of us. The further and longer they spend in this inner state, the less connection they have to everyday earthly existence. Most inner adepts quickly let go of their life pattern and do not hold the personality with all its inherent failings any longer. However, this is not always the case.

There are some magical adepts who have learned to navigate death properly, and have chosen to stay in the Inner Worlds as a contact or teacher. They are often still heavily connected to their magical group/lodge/order and can often try hard to continue to wield power in the outer world through their priests and priestesses. They retain their personality, with all its problems and issues, but it slowly begins to distort.

1.2. Human inner contacts

As they move further into death this can become a problem, as they lose full understanding of the earthly life without losing the wish to have power in that realm. If the person was unbalanced in their earthly life, then that imbalance can sometimes get a little worse as the person becomes more desperate to cling to power.

In between those two extremes are a wide variety of people working as inner contacts and teachers, some with good intent, some with bad, and some unconditionally. With this in mind, if you make or pursue contact with an inner teacher, use your common sense and discernment. Choose an inner teacher in the same way you would choose an outer teacher, although often inner teachers, as with good outer teachers, find you when the time is right.

They stay with you only as long as they can teach you something, and when you have learned what they had to give you, they tend to boot you out. This is good and healthy. Any teacher, inner or outer, who holds onto you or allows you to cling to them, is not the sort of teacher that you need.

Some lodges work with specific inner adepts who were once outer adepts in the order. This is a classic mistake as the adept is approached in vision as the personality they were before they died. To work in this way limits both the adept and the group as the adept is constantly trapped in the dressing and knowledge that they had in life. The adept needs time after death to drop the outer pattern of their life, which then allows the deeper part of their consciousness, which has many lifetimes of knowledge, to surface and get to work. Once they return to the lodge, they are often not recognized for who they used to be, but who they are now.

Finding these inner contacts often happens by accident after you have screamed at the universe begging for help. The universe usually let you hang a while, just to cook, before you are connected with help. The more you do inner work in the flavour of service, the more help seems to reach out to connect with you, but you do have to ask. And then there are the junction points in life: times when people and power seem to all come together at the right place and you connect deeply with them.

There are also inner human contacts that are alive in their own space, working in service. Just because you make a connection with

1. Accessing the Inner Worlds

someone in the inner realms does not mean they are dead: it might mean they are in the inner realms too, and your paths have crossed.

These people are in their own place, doing their own tradition, and offering help/contact to those who need it. There are also the ones who reach out from curiosity, and the usual rules apply: be wise about those with whom you choose to connect. But useful stuff can flow back and forth between cultures and traditions.

There are also human contacts who are in their own place and their own time, reaching through the Void, out of time, for contacts, or offering help as an inner contact. At first when you make an inner contact it can be difficult to discern who is what from where and when. But as the contact deepens and you get to know each other, it then slowly becomes clear who is what.

The more you work and the more experience you gain, the more you will be put into the path of others that you can help. When someone cries out for spiritual help, that cry echoes throughout the Void, and as you pass through the Void during your meditations, you hear them or are drawn to them. If that happens, then follow the call and step out of the Void in the direction of the call.

Be aware that when you do that, the person or group that sent out the call may not be aware that you are also human in your own time and place. They might expect you to be all knowing/all powerful and ask impossible things of you. Don't go into lengthy explanations that you are actually from Michigan and work in an office: that would freak them out. Just quietly do what you can and ignore the rest before gracefully pulling away from the contact. Always disconnect from such contacts by going back into the Void to rebalance yourself.

Chapter Two

Practical methods for working with angelic beings

In magical work, you will come to a point where the need to work with angelic beings cannot be avoided as they are the threshold keepers, the bridges, as it were, to certain forms of power. There are many different approaches to working with angelic beings and most of these tend to be a part of a religious/magical system.

The most common approaches to angelic beings in the western world are Kabbalistic, Christian and Islamic. The pagan systems tend to reflect these three monotheistic systems usually with a bit of Greek or Egyptian mythology thrown in for good measure. In ritual magic the Kabbalistic and Greco-Roman are the most commonly used approaches, using the names, attributes etc as a precursor to invocation.

Some magical systems simply invoke these beings, and when they are successful the beings emerge into this realm and look at the magician. The magician looks back and the angelic being waits for the working request. Nothing happens except that the magician, in terror and awe of the immensity and power of this being, freaks out and begins frantically waving their arms about in a futile attempt to create a banishing sigil. Usually though, if a person doesn't know what they are doing, nothing tends to happen other than a puffed-up ego and some rather impressive recitation.

Certain magical systems have tight structures for working with angelic beings which filter the power, and shape it to the needs and wants of that group. This is probably a safe if ineffective way to work with angelic beings and while not an awful lot can be done, not a lot of damage can be done either.

2. PRACTICAL METHODS FOR WORKING WITH ANGELIC BEINGS

The exception to that rule is pure Kabbalah: the system is tight and heavily filtered, but can, when used properly, bring immense amounts of angelic power into our world. Luckily such a system takes a lot of time to learn and practice, which filters out most idiots. There are however, the occasional 'high-level' Kabbalists who still use these beings to carry out their own personal agendas.

So can you work with these beings without all the names, rituals, patterns, etc.? Well, the answer is yes. It's not easy, but it does allow the worker to interact with an angelic being without the human-made filters or bindings: you have to rely totally on the angelic being to create its own filter so that its power will not destroy you.

Before we go any further, let's go over some basic facts: Angels are not fluffy light beings: They are immensely powerful, large and strange-looking beings often presenting with many heads, many eyes, loads of wings, sometimes in a serpent shape, sometimes half-beast, and sometimes as cubes or spinning Wheels of fire. Their voices are powerful enough to destroy buildings or kill people.

Angels are hive beings: they are often made up of many fragments which are all the same being. All of the parts together make an archangel. When we humans work with angelic beings, often what we are working with is a fragment or tiny part of that being. That is all our feeble bodies can handle without self-destructing.

Angelic beings have no emotion: they do not discern 'good' or 'bad,' they simply do their job. If their job is to destroy, and you point them at a city, they will destroy it, if you ask in the right way. (That's the knack, knowing how to ask: it's like trying to get spending money out of a parent...)

They do not have a wide range of perception: they basically see only what they are programmed to see. What this means is that they have a needlepoint type of consciousness that tends to do one thing or one stream of actions, and do it extremely well. They do not understand or perceive much out of their field.

There are many orders and types of angelic beings. Some work closely with humanity, some work occasionally with humanity, some stay well away, and some are not even aware of our existence. An angelic being is the threshold for the consciousness of a planet, it is the threshold for the consciousness of a grain of sand, a puff of air, a tornado, an animal, a tree, a rock...hopefully you get my point.

There are certain angels, usually named angels, who have been magically bound into service over the centuries or even millennia. Regardless of what their bound action is, they are dangerous as they are operating from a standpoint of human manipulation and not their true purpose.

The binding of angels (it happens with demons too) stretches right back to Mesopotamian and Egyptian magic, and it is also used in Tibetan Bon magic: it is powerful, dangerous and corrupt. A lot of the named angels that appear in Kabbalistic magic have been bound into human service as temple guardians, providers of power and as assassins. To sidestep this problem, it is better to work with angelic consciousness without using a name/presentation: go deeper to the source of angelic consciousness without human form and you will begin to touch upon clear, true angelic power.

As an adept gains more magical knowledge, they will come across bound angels more and more. This is an attempt to put the adept in the path of work, and they will be expected to recognize the bindings and take them off. It's a hell of a job, but well worth it if you or a group succeeds (although the physical fallout afterwards really sucks and can last weeks). Then you get to see and interact with true angelic power.

Without an angelic threshold, nothing can pass from formlessness to form, nothing can manifest in our physical world. We pass through angelic consciousness when we are born and we pass through them again when we die. We perceive this as seeing them helping us and they work in every aspect of life and death. They are the thresholds of power in the temples, and the threshold of power within our bodies.

They do not do your gardening for you, nor do they do marriage counselling. If someone is advertising that they counsel marital problems with the help or channelling of angels the person is either a con artist or a naïve person who is being played with, probably by parasites. Do remember that many other beings cross-dress either to get what they want or just for the hell of it. Faery beings in particular have a twisted sense of humour, and will pluck an image from your head and dress like that. Parasites will dress like angels if that gets you

2. PRACTICAL METHODS FOR WORKING WITH ANGELIC BEINGS

to open up your energies for 'healing': there is always some hapless New Age victim who has more money than sense.

2.1 So how and why do we work with them?

Working with angelic beings can be useful in many instances: the most obvious is within death or birth. They can also be worked with when tackling demonic powers, heavier intelligent parasites, when bringing through deities, lifting death curses, building or dismantling sacred buildings, communing with Divinity, searching for the balance of the scales, and for the passing on of consecrated lines. Basically if the work is heavy dude stuff (that is, of course, a technical description!) you pull in the angelic beings to help you.

There are magicians who use/invoke bound angelic beings to gain personal power. This creates an inherent weakness in the magician, both emotionally and magically. If you draw something from outside yourself to make you more powerful then you have failed: you are drawing on a power that is not yours, so you are in fact, not more powerful, just more dependant. That creates a major weak spot in the person and the magic.

The best and most profound way to work with angelic beings is to keep it simple and powerful. First off, you need to be focused because there is no ritual to tune you and hold you. You also need to be clear about whom you are trying to reach and why: make sure you get the right angelic being for the job. For example it will do you no good whatsoever to work with the angelic being of water to lift a curse placed by a fire priest. You need to use appropriate angels to do the job, which means you need to know your angels, and you need to know the structure of what it is you are working on.

So you need to know your elements (each element and direction has an angelic being), know your thresholds, and be simple and clear about your intention. Most of the angelic beings that are taught about in Kabbalah and Christian mythology will not be of much use to you in that their functions are not really the sort of skills that can be used by us: they are often bound into skill areas that are dangerous and nasty. But there are a few that can be useful, and these are the ones we work with: hence it is important to know your angels.

2.1. So how and why do we work with them?

The way to reach an angelic being is the way that it is possible to reach most things: going through the Void. Most people brush the Void off as some benign concept, not fully understanding what it is or what it does. They prefer instead to reach out for complex, glamorous and overstuffed visions.

The Void is within everything and is the basic root of everything: therefore it can be an access point to virtually anything. All that is necessary is absolute concentration and focus. You go into the Void with specific intent, shedding your surface life and allowing the eternal you to expand to the surface. Once you are in that totally still place and the focused intent is held, the contact emerges through the Void.

Before we go any further, another point I would like to make about the use of the Void is that because you shed your earthy existence when you go into the Void (which should be a daily maintenance exercise) you are far more able to work face-to-face with an angelic being: you are not bound by the limits of your earthly life if you drop it when you go in. This is why, when you first approach the Abyss, you are asked by the angelic being if you are willing to give up your life. You have to have that clarity: you must cling to nothing and be able to let go of everything.

Going into that timeless space puts you back closer to your natural state, which is a formless, powerful soul. You can take much higher levels of power impact in such a state without doing too much damage to yourself.

You reach out in the Void for that angelic contact and when it emerges before you, you step into it. There are two ways of working with these beings: one is to work within the being, which appears as the being working within you, with its arms through your arms, etc. The other way is to step through this being, and to emerge out the other side with a fragment of that being coming with you as an ally or coworker.

When you step into these angelic beings, it is a good idea to stop for a little while and stay in their energy. It allows you to acclimatize to their power and allows them to get a good grasp of you and what you are about. Show them in your mind what you wish to achieve, and the tools that you need to do the job will emerge out of the being

2. Practical Methods for Working with Angelic Beings

for you. Just make sure you leave those 'tools' behind when you have finished: they are a fragment of a fragment of the being itself, and you do not want those hanging around your consciousness afterwards.

Once you have established contact and you are ready for work, step with the being out of the Void and off to where you are going to work. When you have finished, you reverse your action and go back into the angel, remembering to release all the fragments and tools that came with you. Then you step out into the Void for rebalancing before stepping out from the Void back into your earthly life.

When you have worked with such powers, your body will of course have some impact. If you have worked through the Void and trusted their filters, you will not be seriously damaged, but you will have some physical impact that will need rest and maybe even treatment. Sometimes if you work inside archangelic beings it can knock the deeper part of you off-balance and the best way to be 'put back' is to be treated by a cranial osteopath.

If you have a homeopath who understands inner work, then that will be good also. The reason for the homeopath needing to understand inner work is that when you do such deep inner work it changes you at profound depths and changes how your body responds to things. Homeopathic remedy pictures become meaningless and the choice of remedy has to be made using different tools and a different way of thinking.

After a powerful working with these beings, rest is the best thing. And do not eat meat for a few days if you are a carnivore: the life that the animal led will impact you for a few days. Passing through an angel can heighten your inner senses for a while and everything can become loud or bright, and your 'sight' can become a great deal stronger. Sometimes the opposite happens and it feels like you have a bag on your head for a few days: everyone's body reacts differently, but it sure does react!

One thing to be careful of when you begin working with these beings: do not become carried away by the power that you have access to. Most silly egomaniacs tend to be blocked from working with these beings by nature of their inability to be disciplined. But any worker can get sucked in if they are not careful, particularly when you realize just what potential level of power you are accessing. I

2.1. So how and why do we work with them?

have seen some great priests destroyed or turned into parodies of themselves by grabbing power from, or abusing the power of these beings.

Just remember when you work with these beings it is always best to work in service for others or for the land: unravelling, unbinding, opening gates, etc. If you instigate a new action using these beings, then you are starting a new pattern of fate and because you have used these threshold beings, the pattern is powerful: the backlash could be immense.

Chapter Three

Working with deities: pitfalls and approaches

If you are working in the realm of magic, no matter what form you use, at some point you are going to work with a deity or deities. Different traditions have different approaches and all have their strengths and weaknesses. The one approach we will not go into is the psychological approach (that the deity is only a creation of man and we work with the idea of a god to explain things). The reason for not looking at this form of deity work is that it falls more in the realm of therapy that it does magic.

One method of approaching this type of work is the devotional form, where a priest or priestess aligns themselves with, or is initiated into, a steam of magic associated with one deity or a close family of deities. This is where the act of magic moves closer to a religious movement, so that spirituality and magic becomes a combined path.

The relationship between deity and priest/ess is often structured and intense: the priest/ess is required to maintain certain devotions, tasks, and emotional/sexual restrictions. The deity patterns will often dictate how the priest/ess conducts their daily lives, and whom they socialize with.

In today's pagan community, it also affects how the priest/ess dresses, acts, does magic, etc. It can become an all-consuming identity. The deeper octave of this is when the priest/ess opens themselves up for the deity to step into and co-habit their body. This is done for a few moments at a time, although some particularly strong and stupid ones do tend to carry around destroying deities for a few months or years. This can have a little bit of a toll on the human body, to say the least!

3. Working with Deities: Pitfalls and Approaches

But that form of devotional service, to me, is more religious than magical (which is a system that magic grew out of). When you work magically with a deity or deities, another approach is more one of working colleagues who are better qualified than you, like working with elders, only stronger. Deities are by nature polarized consciousness and the nearer to humanity they are, the more polarized they become.

3.1 Forms of deity

There are many different forms of deity. Some are divine expressions of the land that flow through a semihuman form (taken from their environment and our consciousness). Then there are the polarized parts of Divinity that appear in more or less the same expression all over the world: they do not appear similar because they are all from one place or people, it is more likely that they are similar because that is what people see when they go into the inner world.

Some are the Divine expression of the people, and some are ancient ancestors/kings/queens/elders who have become deified over thousands of years.

If for example a major priest or adept opts out of the circuit of death to become an inner contact, then sometimes that contact becomes more than the original person: their human form becomes a conduit for a greater power which in turns becomes a deity expression either by virtue of its actions, or by the reflection of the people they serve.

So before you go to work, know who and what it is you are working with. The reasons for this are many: if you are working with a polarized form of Divinity, it/he/she will have a set repertoire of skills, powers and needs in return for help. These forms of deity are the most powerful and have to be worked with most carefully. They will often want devotion and allegiance: there you have to decide if you want to be a worker or devotee.

If you want to be a worker, then you have to justify your wants and needs to the agenda of the deity. They will not just do what you want, rather they will do what you need to accomplish your work provided the work fits with their ethics and actions. In return, they will often put things in your path that they want you to work on.

When you are working with a deity that is an expression of the land/people, it/he/she will have a narrow view of the world and they will only be able to operate within that view and that environment. If you want something that is within their field, then they will work with you if the time/place/action is right. They will often not work with you for things that do not serve/help/feed them. They are there to keep a balance of sorts in that land: if your actions fit that, then all is good, if not, you will be told to piss off.

The gods/esses that have developed out of ancestral consciousness or an ancient king/queenship are interesting to work with as they are closer to humanity and have a deeper understanding of what our tiny minds are about. The only problem with that is if you get one that is not a 'goodie.' Now, you cannot go by their historical myths: I have repeatedly found with these types of deities that they often got bad press by later generations, or that their identities were often false. Many times the fluffy bunny deities turn out to be just downright evil (in the nicest possible way of course).

You have to work with them to find out who they are and what they are really like. The relationship will often be one of: if you do this for me, then I will do this for you. Just be careful what you get sucked into and don't get glamorized, and ignore the promise: if you do this I will give you endless power...uhuh...

One interesting aside when working with this type of deity is hearing their version of history. They will often want to tell you about their time, what happened, who they were and what they did. It can make a lot of nonsensical myths suddenly make perfect sense, and the sense often resonates with what is happening magically today. Power works in octaves: what was happening to them is probably happening now in some way, and the lessons they learned can help us too.

3.2 Working with the deity

Overall, working with deities is powerful and interesting, but can be dangerous both physically and spiritually. You have to use your common sense and remember that you are a worker: by doing so,

3. Working with Deities: Pitfalls and Approaches

you opt out of the often unhealthy role of devotee which can become a relationship that ultimately weakens you.

If you work with deities for your own personal power/gain, you will do pretty well up to a point, but the limits are put in place by you and the deity. If it is solely for your needs, then the power that will be raised by the deity will be only enough for one person at the end of the day. If you are working in a wider service, then you will be given the power you need to do your job and the harder/more dangerous the job, the more power flows into you.

By being a worker as opposed to a devotee, there are fewer limits on whom you can work with and when you work with them. You work with them when there is need and the rest of the time you get on with you magical life and they get on with theirs. There is none of this getting up at four a.m. to feed raw pigs' liver to the sacred cat after banging a gong six times while standing on your head: life is a little too short for that.

Just be aware that if you work with a variety of deities, that you do get some that don't like each other (their powers clash) and it can turn into a workplace filled with bratty hormonal temperamental gods who refuse to work with you if you work with 'that one': a little discernment goes a long way.

When you work with deities, there are many different ways that you can practically work with them to achieve things. You can work with them in vision, you can work with them through images or places, you can raise them to work in the room with you, or you can be a complete idiot and bring the deity into yourself to achieve something.

When I was young and stupid, as opposed to now where I am old and stupid, I had the bright idea of bringing Kali through. At first I had the intent to bring her through into a painting. I set about preparing, pulling the power in, setting it all up, and then I began the weave that brings the Goddess through. I painted her, but she wanted a sculpture of herself to move into. So I began the sculpture. By this time I had already been working for twelve hours, but I could not stop. I worked through the night and the Goddess flowed into me as I worked. I held her in my body for about twenty-four hours while I worked and then finally bridged her into the sculpture and painting.

3.2. Working with the deity

The day after the working I got sick. Then I got sicker. Then it turned into scarlet fever and I became dangerously ill. I went bright red (the colour of Kali) before then developing rheumatic fever. It took six weeks to recover and stop peeling, but the illness left permanent damage.

I got the message: yes you can bring a deity through, yes it hurts and does damage when done properly but without a structure for it to flow through.

As usual I learned the way I have always learned: when they say don't press the red button, I invariably do. It was an important lesson though, and it taught me a lot about Kali. By having her flow through me, I felt her at her depth and felt all the parts of her that are not written about or expressed in images. I learned to work with her properly from that experience and I think it was invaluable. I would go through it again, but this time I would have antibiotics on standby!

Over the years, many things have dawned on me since that silly weekend, and I slowly learned how to work sensibly and powerfully with deities without trashing myself too much.

The painting that had Kali in it ended up to being too much for the house and anyone who went anywhere near it. It had to eventually go into the fire to release the power within it. Interestingly from an astrology point of view, that was the beginning of my Pluto transit. Dude, I know how to blow up in style!

Discernment is a really good skill to have around deities: the closer they are to humanity the less likely they are to tell the truth if they do not get their own way, and they will try and manipulate you to get what they want. Boundaries have to be drawn from the earliest days.

The other really important thing to be aware of is that if you feed and water the deities, they will get stronger. Again the closer they are to humanity, the more they mirror the needs of a human: they want food, water, trinkets, power and sex. Be careful what you give them because certain power/energy can dictate how they react to certain situations. Look into their history and you may find clues regarding how they eat/act.

The most fascinating way to work with a deity is to reach for the old gods which means going down into the part of the Abyss where

3. WORKING WITH DEITIES: PITFALLS AND APPROACHES

the older deities sleep. As newer gods and goddesses emerge and work with humanity, so the older gods sink down into the land to sleep. You can reach them either by going deep into the Underworld, or by going down the Abyss to where their power is asleep.

The ancient gods that worked with other forms of humanity also sleep there and the beings that you can meet and work with become fascinating. Sometimes they want you to go down to them to work with them and learn from them. Sometimes they want you to bridge them so that they can rise out of the Abyss and walk once more upon the surface of the earth. That takes a lot of hard work but is also a form on service.

Some of the ancient gods are still in our realm simply because their images are still here and their temples till exist, even if they are in ruins. Just that image and Inner Temple bridge allows their power to stay with humanity, so it is much easier to reach and work with them. That is why it is so easy to work with the Egyptian or Tibetan gods: they are still in our minds and landscape.

The much older gods who no longer have images or temples in our world are harder to reach and nearly always have to be accessed through the Underworld or the Abyss. When you work with these ancient gods, be aware that their relationship with humanity was probably different to what we expect today, in fact they might have even worked with a different form of humanity and not understand us at all.

They might ask you to do things that are way off our radar or repertoire of actions and if that happens, you have to just say no. You will have to teach them about your form of humanity and what our culture finds acceptable and not acceptable. So when the deity offers you limitless power in return for the decapitated heads of the men of the tribe of whatever, you have to politely point out to them that we don't really do such things anymore (unless you are a far right wing Republican, in which case it might be plausible).

The skills and knowledge that they can bring to us are interesting and useful, and the view of modern humanity can be useful to them. I think they mostly look around at our world and decide that the pit of the Abyss, with all its demons, is probably a safer place to be.

3.2. Working with the deity

At the end of the day, you shouldn't really need to use deities that much: it's like taking an anti-aircraft missile to crack a nut. Depends really on what you are doing and what you want to achieve.

Chapter Four

Working with ancestors

As soon as we pass into the inner realms, the little things with which we surround ourselves fade away. Our excuses to ourselves, our fantasies and our deliberate blindness all fall away, leaving us no option but to see ourselves as we truly are. This is not a spiritual revelation that happens overnight. It is a slow but steady awakening from which we cannot retreat.

We gradually begin to see the true consequences of our actions, be they good or bad, and we are unable to turn from them. 'Sorry' is a word that does not exist in the Inner Worlds. If you cause something to happen, you and you alone are fully responsible for the full unraveling of the consequences of your action. No matter how long, how many lifetimes, how many regrets you have. It is not a punishment, merely a cause and reaction. It is the natural law of power and balance.

Ancestral work is one of the hardest things to do, mainly because of the emotional baggage usually passed down through families, but also because of the energetic dynamics of the work. When you do ancestral work, you are not truly working with an individual but a whole genetic line that flows through both the past and the future.

Modern concepts of ancestral work are taken from tribal and shamanic practices without the accompanied wisdom of land, beings and power. Tribal ancestral work consists of working or communing with a being that is not particularly your ancestor, but is a composite being made up of human, faery and land consciousness. Most ethnic shamans or tribal magicians understand this without rationalizing it, because the consciousness of the people is such that it operates from within a holism.

A land spirit connects with a human at birth, and the tribal consciousness is woven into the child from the moment it draws

4. Working with Ancestors

breath. So when the person dies, the consciousness of that land being is still there and operating within the structure of the human identity. It is this being that is worked with as an ancestor within a tribal cultural setting. It is not masquerading as an ancestor: rather, it upholds part of who that human was in one life, echoing the soul that has since moved on.

Sometimes, the person themselves waits at the threshold of death: not moving all the way through death to rebirth allows the ancestor to continue communion with his family and tribe. This quickly becomes unhealthy, though, if the spirit refuses to move on and is holding onto lifetime grudges, wants or ambitions. Sometimes they wait for a while, until they have achieved something in service for the tribe, and then they move on.

A second form of ancestral contact is working with ancestors within the world's many ritual burial mounds. In this case, the ancestor is still present in a spirit form for us to work with. They are there to do a job within a certain span of time, usually connected to the welfare of the land. The greatest tragedy occurs when archaeologists, in their pursuit of the past, hack into and remove the bodies of these sleepers. When a body is removed from its ritual sleeping place, the interaction between the sleeper and the land is ended.

So what are sleepers and how do they get there? A sleeper is a person who has opted to step out of the cycle of birth and death to act as a threshold or inner contact between the tribe, the land and the Inner Worlds. The death would have been a ritual slaying with the permission of the victim. Please note that later sacrifices, like those found in Central America were a degenerate form of this tradition, and forced sacrifices are relatively modern in history. What we see in the Inca culture for example are the twisted remnants of what was once a sacred Mystery.

The ceremony of ritual slaying would make sure that the spirit of the person did not pass on, but stayed within the body that was usually, but not always, buried in the earth. A mound was built around the sleeper: it was revered as a sacred place. The seers of the tribe would establish contact with the sleeper and the sleeper would guide the tribe by acting as an intermediary between the inner contacts, the deities, and the people.

Some sleepers were there as guardians of the land. Their spirit would guard the land or sacred enclosures, keeping the land healthy and strong. It is ironic that in today's world, which has the most need of these sleepers, we dig them up and stick them on public show. Not only is this a terrible indignity, but it strips the land of the interaction between humanity and the sacred earth. All inner protection that the land and tribe jointly enjoyed is destroyed out of greed and curiosity.

4.1 Time jumping

The most common form of ancestral work is working with the ancestor in their own time. You are not working with a dead person who is hanging around just for you to contact them. You are reaching out of time, passing through timelessness to connect with a person in their own life. Such work affects all the generations that come after that person.

This dissolving of the barriers of time is the key to ancestral work. So what is time? It is a condition that is bound by substance, movement, gravity. Our everyday life on the surface of the planet is bound by a series of rhythms and cycles. These cycles denote time, a linear time that starts at A and finishes at B. We accept this as a whole reality: the 'be all and end of life.' And with that acceptance comes the concept that life has no inner pattern or existence outside the physical body. And if we look at the world simply from that physical plane, then it is not that far from the truth.

But the world is not just a physical plane. There are many levels of consciousness, many forms of existence and energies that exist without physical expression that we can perceive. The physical substance is merely the outermost expression of being: the end of the line, so to speak. Once you stretch beyond the physical substance, to the inner consciousness, then gravity and time have no meaning. They are simply laws that govern substance, but they do not govern reality.

Stepping out or beyond the base physical reality frees a person from the bonds of time. It allows them to experience the true expression of consciousness without its strictures of substance.

To step out of time, you must take your consciousness beyond the world of substance. Doing that is simpler than it sounds. Tuning into the inner flame and passing through the flame into the Void obviates time immediately: allowing you by the power of disciplined thought to move freely through time. This is not a theory. It is an active working technique.

4.2 Family ancestors

Next comes the question: why would you do ancestral work and what you would use such a working for? Working through and with your ancestors is probably one of the most profound and powerful ways to work on tribal/family issues. It is also an effective way of working on one's own internal issues beyond the usual mundane gripes that we carry.

When you trace back and work with an ancestor, you are given the opportunity to interact and transform the negative and difficult patterns that become so entrenched. These patterns trickle down through the generations and affect everyone in their path.

As the generations flower, the original situation that manifested the pattern is forgotten, but the effect still lives on from generation to generation. Simply finding the original cause of a family pattern of behavior can go a long way towards healing that pattern.

The other great joy of this particular work is that it often uncovers surprises. It is work that is often undertaken by people who have no real idea of who their family is. It enables them to track back through their line and reconnect with their ancestral and tribal line. No matter how fast we live and how independent we consider ourselves, there comes a time when the rootedness of blood becomes important.

The following vision takes you back through your line to a place within the history of your family: to a point in time where you can interact with and learn from your ancestors.

It is a vision that should be done more than once, so that it builds in power and connection.

4.3 The ancestral vision

Light the candle flame and watch the flame for a few seconds before you close your eyes. See the candle flame before you with your inner vision and be aware of the breath of life that flows through the candle flame: the divine flame that manifests on the edge of the Void.

With your inner vision, see the room in which you sit fall away and you find yourself out in a field of grasses and flowers. Beside you are a knife, a fire, and a bowl of water. You will see the sun rising before you in the east. Be aware of that direction and of the west behind you. Be aware of the north and south, of the earth below and the stars above. Be aware of yourself sitting in the center and within your center is the sacred flame of all being.

In your inner vision, pick up the knife and slice across your hand causing blood to flow. Hold the blood over the bowl of water and allow your blood to mingle with the water. When your hand stops bleeding, hold it near the fire to cleanse the wound.

A crow circles above you and then dives down, hitting the bowl of water causing it to spill onto the ground. The liquid flows out of the bowl and creates a stream of blood and water that flows off into the distance. The stream grows and grows until it becomes a river that you fall into and the current pulls you along. You allow the current to carry you as the water flows over your face. The taste of blood reaches your lips and the water gets deeper and deeper as you are pulled along.

When you feel that you are about to drown, your hand touches a branch and you hang onto it. Hauling yourself up out of the water, you see that you are hanging onto an old gnarled tree that is bent over and many of its branches are trailing in the river. Pulling yourself out of the river, you roll on the grassy bank and rest.

As you lie steaming in the sun, you hear voices in the distance. Something within you recognizes the voices, even through the language may be strange. You get up and walk towards the voices, pushing through taller and taller grasses as you go. The surrounding trees seem to bend down to join the grass, creating a wall of green that you must push through. As you emerge on the other side, you

4. Working with Ancestors

will see a person standing in a clearing, looking around as if they have just heard something.

Approach this ancestor carefully, taking in the situation around them and acting accordingly. Commune with your ancestor, and tell them about yourself and your world. Ask the questions that need to be asked. Offer help and advice where you can, and be of assistance to your ancestor should they need it.

At the end of the interaction, step back and tell them that they will be remembered in the future. Allow the ancestor to walk away from you and wait until they have vanished. Then it is time to push deeper into the forest as you reach further back through time.

The further back you go, the denser the forest will be. The journey starts to take its toll on your body and your muscles begin to feel as if you have carried heavy weights. Push yourself forward until you reach a clearing in the trees.

As you emerge from the forest, you will see people sitting around a fire. Go and sit with them quietly and watch the flames. One of those in this gathering looks at you intently, and recognizes you as someone from the future.

The seer looks around the group for someone who is connected to you. When the seer recognizes which member of their community is your ancestor, the seer stands and walks towards you. With one arm outstretched, he or she asks you to follow as they turn and leave the fire. You are led a short way to a tent or structure and told to wait.

The seer leaves, and then returns shortly with someone at their side. This person is told that you are here and that you wish to commune with them. The seer places a hand on your head, and a hand on your ancestor's head. He or she acts as an interpreter between you and your ancestor.

When the communion is over, the ancestor leaves and the seer turns to talk to you. The seer tells you of the tribe and its problems, and asks you—as a person of the future—if you have any advice that you can give. Do your best to answer honestly and clearly. If you do not have an answer, then you must say so.

In return, the seer offers you advice for your life or family. Take the advice into your heart where you can unravel it and make it

4.3. The ancestral vision

appropriate for your own time. The seer then places a hand over your eyes. Through the hands of the seer, you are empowered with the seer's sight. The landscape and way of life is revealed to you as you look around. The seer also looks into you and sees your world.

When the time comes to leave, you begin to feel tired. Your body feels so tired that you can hardly stand up. Finally, your legs give in and you lie down on the soft fresh earth. Sleep comes heavily upon you and you drift in a state of total relaxation. The seer stays beside you and sings a lullaby to you in a language that your body understands, even if you do not.

The earth seems to cover you over and the grass grows all around you. A feeling of deep peace descends upon you as you lie in communion with the earth. You become aware of a presence beside you, as though it flows from the earth that is all around you.

The presence touches you deeply and you begin to weep tears of love and compassion. The presence is your first ancestor, the source of all patterns that run through you. You merge and mingle together as one, feeling the planet turn through time as you lie in union.

Your tears reach the surface of the earth and become flowers, turning their faces to the sun and blossoming. All awareness of your time-bound life falls away and all you are left with is the timeless union of blood within the earth.

As you lie together with your first ancestor, you hear a voice calling out your name. The sound echoes through the earth, vibrating within the rocks and causing you to stir. You want to reach out for the sound, but you need help.

An instinct deep within you causes you to push your hand and arm up through the earth to the air. Your arm emerges out of the rich earth and grasps onto someone's hand. That someone pulls on your arm, pulling you out of the earth.

As you emerge, you find yourself standing before a future ancestor, someone from your own future who has reached through time to commune with you. Be with this person: pass on all that you can. The future ancestor looks deeply into you and sees a pattern within you that you were not aware of. It is something that you acquired in your present life and it can affect generations to come.

4. Working with ancestors

They reach out to help you with this pattern and you must choose to allow them to assist you with the letting go and recognition of what that pattern might be.

Visions of scenes within your life, issues that you cling to and emotions that are becoming difficult parade before your vision and the future ancestor helps you to look at these objectively. Your body feels the transition as you let things alter and change.

Before you can commune further, the future ancestor falls back into a mist and vanishes from your sight. You hear the flow of the river which rages like a torrent all around you. You look down to find yourself standing on an isthmus, almost surrounded by the water that flows on all sides.

The water laps around your feet and pulls at you to leave. Reluctantly you dive back into the river and swim towards the setting sun. As you swim, you become aware of fires that burn on both sides of the river. Some are bonfires lit for the ancestors, and some are natural fires.

The flames build up around you until it seems that you are swimming through fire: the fires burn around and within you: cleansing and purifying you as you reach back to your own time.

You emerge out through the central flame and find yourself back in the room where you first started. You take you seat and look at the central flame. Around you, you see the rivers of water and blood flowing into and out of you, vanishing off into the far distance. When you are ready, open your eyes and look at the central flame.

4.4 The family

A major part of ancestral work is bound up with our present day families. When you care for an elder or child within the family, you are caring for the family ancestors. All those who have gone before live on in one way or another through our lives. A thread of their experiences and patterns are carried down the line of blood and will be passed onto the future generations. It is our responsibility to make sure the right patterns carry on and that unhealthy ones are brought to conclusion in our lifetime.

One of the many ways to do this is through the children: protecting them magically as they develop and ensuring that old patterns are not repeated. Often just the sense for a child that they are totally safe from all things is enough for them to have space to blossom and grow to their full potential.

The following vision is one for working with the children within your family. It is something that I have used for many years with my own children and my family's children. I do it periodically as a form of service to my family.

4.5 Guarding the children

This is a vision of ancestral responsibility, the sharing of the burden of protection for the future generations. It is usually conducted within your own family or tribe and must not be done with any other family group without permission.

Light a candle and close your eyes. See the flame before you and see a flame deep within you. The more you focus on the inner flame the more it draws you inward until you find yourself in the Void that is at your centre.

As you stand in the stillness and silence that is within, you hear a baby cry. The cry gets louder and louder and pulls upon you, urging you to step forward. You recognize something within the cry and something within you tells you that a child of your blood cries out in the dark for protection.

Stepping forward you pass over the threshold of the west and find yourself stood before the bed or crib of a child. The child is crying and is distressed. You sense danger around the child: either inner or physical danger, maybe even serious sickness.

As you look at the child, you see a pattern of energy that you recognize: the child feels a little like you. You realize that this child is of your family or tribe, and that you have responsibility as an ancestor to protect them.

Reach out your hand and place it lightly on the child's head or shoulders. When you have established the contact with them, feel for the child's inner flame, seated deep within them. Cup the child's inner flame in your hand carefully and respectfully.

4. Working with ancestors

Now feel the deep inner peace that always visits you when you reach into your inner flame. Allow that peace and stillness to flow over the child as you mediate silence from the eternal inner flame: the flame of Divinity.

The child begins to settle down and fall asleep. You, as ancestor, stand guard over the child as they sleep. As you watch the child slumber, a song rises up from deep within you and you begin to quietly sing. The child relaxes more and more as you sing, and the sound carries around the room creating a pattern of protection that swirls around the child.

Faery beings from outside creep closer to listen to the song and you also become aware that all the creatures around the building are listening to your voice. The song tells of the child's heritage, the blood of the tribe and the gifts that the child can carry forward for the future.

You begin to get tired and just as your eyes begin to close, you feel a hand on your shoulder. Another ancestor of your blood stands beside you and offers to take over to watch as the child sleeps. You may or may not recognize them.

The ancestor takes position beside the child and begins to sing as you quietly back out of the room. Turning, you find yourself on the threshold of a wall of fire that is the threshold of the Void. Stepping over the threshold, you suddenly remember a time when you were a small child and you were frightened. You remember a sensation of someone coming to watch over you or protect you and you remember your fear being taken away. When you are ready, pass through the Void back into the room where you first started and blow out the candle.

4.6 Tribal ancestors

When I talked earlier about the blending of a land spirit and an ancestor, I suddenly realized that this was probably the basis for a lot of localized legends of strange-looking humans that would help the community.

When I lived on a reservation, I did come across all sorts of stories and legends that are based in the land there. Although the

4.6. Tribal ancestors

local tribes did not come from this particular patch of land, (they were previously living about sixty miles south) they would go to the area once a year in gathering to hold ceremonies and reunions.

While in sweat one evening, I had a vision of a great spider that was busy weaving the lodge. I talked to her and asked her who she was. She told me she was the Tou'piah, or great grandmother. I thought this strange, as this particular tribe does not look well upon spiders: they are seen here as bad. I told her this and she just laughed and then became serious.

She showed me another version of herself, as an old woman and went onto tell me about how the local Jesuits did horrific damage, as everywhere else, but that they had also managed to change the beliefs of the local tribe. She was sad that her descendants had inherited such mistruths as traditional facts. I told her there was nothing I could do about it: I was a guest in the lodge and it was not my place to interfere.

After the sweat, I told the medicine man who had led the sweat what I had seen and heard and he nodded sadly. I described the old woman and he told me that was the original matriarch of the family who owned the lodge. She had died in her early fifties and had been a strong protector of the traditions and songs of the family. I asked him about the local fear of spiders and he shrugged saying that he was not from here, and his tribe saw spiders as powerful medicine. So I have to assume that the great grandmother was raised before that particular propaganda was pushed about by the Jesuits.

After that encounter, she would appear whenever I sweated in that lodge and she would show me things that were about to happen. The only problem was the images she was showing me were presented in a way that I could not do much with the information unless a person connected to that happening was in the lodge.

Once I was sweating and I suddenly saw a head-on collision between a car and a truck. I was so shocked and it was so real that I started to panic. After that sweat round, I went to the spring to try and calm down. I told the sweat leader what I had just seen. He asked me if I recognized anyone or even knew the car. I told him that the car was familiar but that was all.

4. WORKING WITH ANCESTORS

I knew the Tou'piah was frustrated with me because I didn't recognize the people in the car. Later I found out that the doorman's (the man who guards the entrance of the sweat lodge) family had been in a head-on collision with a truck just at the time we were sweating. The spirits of the lodge were trying to help but there was too much of a disconnection for it to work.

And this is the problem today: too much disconnection. The tribal disconnection was done deliberately. I hadn't realized this until that point in time. I had always thought that the Catholic Church pushed aside the tribal culture just out of ignorance and saw it as mindless stupidity. But after what I had experienced in the lodge, I wasn't so sure about that any more. It seemed to me after living and working with tribal people that their power had been specifically and deliberately dismantled.

By simply turning spiders into bad things, they singlehandedly disconnected the local tribe from their ancestral contacts. None of the tribal people in the lodge, other than the medicine man, had any contact with the Tou'piah. If anyone had natural sight, they would shun such a connection away immediately out of fear. Clever.

Usually what has been told to us to avoid (spiders, the Underworld, the dark, etc.) are all powerful things that should be explored. Working with and for tribal ancestors becomes a task of not only protecting the family and unravelling past patterns, it is also a task of reeducating us away from religious propaganda and allowing the spirits and ancestors to speak once more.

If you are from a tribal community, one of the ways forward for this path is to visit the graves of the community that went before you. Be with them, talk with them, take them gifts of food/herbs/stones and establish a connection with the continued line from past to future.

This is also something that can be done if you wish to respect and acknowledge the ancestors of an area where you live. I visit the local graveyard regularly here and commune with the ancestors here. They guide me in many things and I am grateful for their contact. In return I keep their memories alive and tend their resting places.

4.7 Cultural ancestors

In Algeria is the ancient city Abalessa, former capital of the Hoggar region. In Abalessa there is the tomb of the famous Tuareg queen Tin Hinan (she who came from far away).

There are legends in Libya that Tin Hinan was an Amazon queen, and that the Amazon warriors were heavily established in North Africa a long time before the Amazons of Northern Turkey. The Berbers, of which the Tuareg (aka Imuhar) are a tribe, call themselves Amazigh in their language. There is definitely a strong similarity between the words Amazon and Amazigh.

Women in Tuareg society are the holders of property and power. It is a matriarchal society in which only the women are literate and they are the keepers of history through stories and poems. They were also fierce warriors and the first Arab invasion in A.D. 700 was fought off by a band of warriors, male and female, led by a woman.

To the Berbers, Tin Hinan is their mother, their founder: indeed even today she is still called 'mother of all.' She became the Mother Protector, first ancestor, to the Berber people and her tomb is still a place of pilgrimage and worship.

So great was the respect of the tribes for this woman that her tomb was never desecrated: she was buried with multiple gold and silver bangles, and her body was covered in precious jewels. When the tomb was finally excavated by westerners, not only did they find this fabulous wealth, but they also found evidence that the tomb was used for healing sleep and visions by the local tribes.

People would travel great distance to lie by her tomb and sleep with her. Their dreams would be recounted in poems that would be passed down the generations of women.

This is a wonderful example of true ancestral work. And because there is such a long tradition of work with Tin Hinan, it is a line of consciousness that we can tap into, respectfully, to learn about how to honor our own ancestors and the land.

4. Working with Ancestors

4.8 The vision of Tin Hinan

Light a candle and close your eyes. With your inner vision see the candle flame and as you watch the flame, it grows into a fire. The room in which you are seated falls away and you find yourself seated around a camp fire at night with a group of women. They are wrapped heavily with many layers of dark cloth to protect them against the fierce sun during the day and the harsh cold of the desert night. Their faces bear the marks of tattooing and as you look at their tattoos you realize that one of them can see you.

The rest for the women is over and someone calls for the night march to resume. Some of the women grab torches from the fire and hold up the fire to light the way for others. As the women walk through the dark they sing a song which tells you the history of their first queen: their mother.

You walk with the women, listening to their songs until the dawn begins to awaken. Your feet are heavy from walking, and the dawn pulls at you to sleep. One of the women puts a hand to your back to keep you walking and you struggle to continue against an overwhelming urge to sleep.

As the sun rises, you see a large mound ahead of you and upon the mound sits an ancient brick structure. The women snake up the mound and enter a low doorway one by one, extinguishing their flames before they enter. When it is your time to enter, you stop and take off your sandals before entering the gathering place.

All of the women sit, laugh and unwrap leaves which they hand around to each other. Someone hands you a small bunch of leaves and motions for you to chew them. They taste bitter on your tongue and yet the bitterness is refreshing after the desert.

A strange but pleasant feeling flows over you and your tired feet and your muscles relax as the magic of the leaves unfolds within you. Without thinking, you lie down and close your eyes. You become aware that the other women are also lying down and preparing to sleep.

Immediately sleep pulls you deeply and you begin to dream. You are pulled through the floor into a tomb with a woman lying as if asleep on a beautifully carved wooden bed. Flowers and jewels lie all around her and a bone knife has been laid beside her. Her robe reaches down to the floor and you instinctively kneel and touch the hem of her robe.

Her power flows through her robe and into you, filling you with a sense of awe. She is a queen, an embodiment of the Goddess, and as such you know that you must give her a gift: something worthy of a great queen. You hold out your hand and whatever appears in your hand you must be willing to give her. You lay the gift at her feet and a guardian steps forward out of the dark shadows to place a hand upon your shoulder.

The guardian tells you that this place is sacred to all women: this is the tomb of one of the great sleeping queens. The guardian instructs you to lie down and he places a hand over your eyes.

You immediately fall into a deep and refreshing sleep. As you sleep, you can feel hands massage you and heal you. Old wounds and old illnesses surface and then vanish under the powerful touch. A deep peace descends upon you as you join in sleep with all the great sleepers hidden around the world.

The sleep reaches through time, and every time that you have ever closed your eyes and gone to sleep, you realize that a part of you has unwittingly come here. In future, you will be able to reach this place in your sleep if you wish, so that you can lie with the great queen and bathe in her healing power. In return you must always remember her and keep her name alive.

Now it is time to return. Someone calls your name and you find yourself waking from a deep healing sleep. You remember the candle flame that is before you and you remember the room in which you are seated. When you are ready, open your eyes.

4.9 Practical use of ancestral work

Connecting with the old ancestors can be useful from a learning point of view. Learning to work without temples, priests/esses and deities can be difficult when we come from a culture that is based around hierarchy, temples and worship.

But the old ancestors did just that: the ordinary people of the land thousands of years ago worked from a premise that anyone can leave an offering for the Earth Mother, that everything around them was sacred and therefore there was no use for a temple, and that Divine Being was everywhere and in everything: every rock, spring, tree and mountain was sacred and treated as such.

This is no revelation, but we have, as a magical community in the west, taken that knowledge and then fashioned robed rituals, hierarchies, priesthoods, temple spaces, etc., in an effort to give a familiar form to an ancient magic.

But to connect back through thousands of years to a pre-temple people who lived without such structures is really useful. Some of the most powerful magical teaching acts through resonance: that is to say, being in the same space, working alongside someone allows magical knowledge and power to pass from one spirit to the other.

So to go back through time and work alongside someone who is partaking of such magic is powerful. Being in the middle of a working teaches us much more than reading about something. It also puts many things in context and a new understanding begins to dawn. Going back through time in vision takes discipline and focus. You have to be sure you are not going to be disturbed (turn your phones off) and not be tired. Don't drink coffee too close to the working (coffee blocks some inner powers) and obviously don't drink alcohol for a few hours before working.

4.10 Time and intention

Do you have to specify a time to reach back to ancient workers? Basically, no. The intention to go back to before temple structures will open out a certain pathway for you to walk. Then what will happen is that your spirit is drawn to the most powerful happening around that time period. This is the easiest way to stretch back. When there is a powerful magical happening, it sends out ripples throughout time, and your spirit can home in on it like a beacon. You do not need to know what time you are in, you are not there to prove a point.

Picking up on the power beacon along with the intention is usually enough to take you to where you need to be. The other signal that flows out through time is the magical request. I am sure you have also done this at some point in your life: called out to the universe for help. When this happens and if it is powerful enough, the call flows through time and as you pass through the Void with your intention of going back through time, the call echoes through the Void and you pick up on it. Just be aware that when this happens, you are not a tourist: you will be expected to help in what may be a difficult and dangerous situation.

The method of passing through the Void with the intent of time jumping is a good, clean, clear way of working that protects you from all sorts of nasties and will also help your spirit to become more pliable while staying intact. We will look at this in more depth in a moment.

4.11 Interactions with ancestors

So how do you behave with these ancestors? What or who do they think you are? If you are stretching back beyond temple structures, be aware that you are going pretty far back and that the concepts, magical ways, culture and even physical make-up will be different. Be careful about how you present yourself: by this I mean be focused, clear and simple in how you envision yourself, for this is how they will see you. If you are festooned with magical baubles, talismans and protective spirits, they will think you are a lunatic at best, and a danger at worst.

Present yourself in a simple way, i.e. in a simple physical form, with a clear heart. Also be aware that past ancestors are not New Age fluffy pink nice old grannies. Life has always been tough and full of people with greedy agendas, so be on your guard and use your common sense. If they have sent out a calling beacon for help then you are less likely to trip up and bump into shamans looking for an easy target. They will be glad of the help and in return will forge a good contact with you for knowledge exchange: remember that this is always a two-way street.

If you are going back by focusing on a burst of power (i.e. a powerful event that you can be drawn to) be a little careful until you know, by the feel of it, what that powerful event was. Make sure for example that it was not some massive slaughter for sacrifice or war. You could end up becoming someone's dinner! You do not have to

4. WORKING WITH ANCESTORS

take all that is offered, you do not have to give all that is demanded and you do not have to do what is requested if you do not think it is right. If you have landed somewhere in time where you feel you are way out of your league, break the contact, leave the room and go take a bath.

An ancient working space is useful as a focal point to access back through time so. So before trying to do this work in vision, it is helpful if you are able to physically go to one of these spaces (an Iron Age fort, a stone circle, a sacred hill, an ancient burial, etc.). If you are unable to go to one of these sites then choose one that you feel a deep connection with: learn about it, fix its qualities in your head and put up a picture of it so that you see it regularly.

For example, there are a few ancient sites close to where I live, so when I am working with ancestors I reach out through the Void for contacts or power surges that are connected to one of those sites. They may end up coming from somewhere else, but they have a connection to that site, or were visiting it at some point. It is a good way of working in the early days of time jumping as it gives focus and roots to the work connection.

As the work deepens, you become used to trotting back and forth and then experimenting wider, so that your range opens out. It often happens through inner necessity rather than idle curiosity.

Once you have made an inner connection with your outer site it is time to go to work. Choose your working element (stone, bowl of water, flame) and keep that candle/stone/water bowl only for this work. Place your element before you and prepare yourself for work. If you are using fire then light your candle. The easiest way to build up this work is as follows:

Prepare for work with an element (flame or bowl of water, etc).

Still yourself and move through the element into the Void, the place of nothingness from which all things flow forth and to which they return. Spend time in the Void connecting to the sense of nothing, stillness and silence. Be aware of flowing through all things in this place. Focus on looking for a power burst or call connected to a site you have been working with and when you sense it, turn towards it and step out of the Void.

See yourself stepping into mist and walking towards the power source or call. When you meet the ancestors, commune with them and do what they need. When you have finished use the fire (ancestors often reach for contact in front of a fire) as a focused doorway back into the Void: from the Void step back through your element into your working space to conclude your visit.

The following vision can be used to approach ancestors at a sacred place if you haven't been able to establish a call.

4.12 Vision of meeting the ancestors

Still yourself by going into the Void: spend some time in the stillness, being aware of yourself as a timeless being, as a being of service. Be aware that you can pass through all structures, all time, all places: your consciousness has no boundaries.

Stepping out of the Void you find yourself walking through a mist which obscures everything around you. Hold to a clear intent to reach the sacred place you have chosen to visit. The sacred space you have chosen emerges out of the mist and you walk to the centre of it. You can see nothing beyond the sacred enclosure, as the land is surrounded in thick mist.

Using your inner vision, you stand up with your arms outstretched, and begin to turn. You turn and turn, with the mists swirling around you, allowing the power of the Void to flow through you and out into this most sacred place. As you turn you begin to feel an immense build-up of power swirling around you, and you feel the power of the Underworld beneath your feet flowing up through your body to the stars, and the power of the stars flowing down into the Underworld. You turn in the centre of this flow of power, acting as a fulcrum of power as it flows through the worlds.

You hear a voice calling out and you begin to slow your turning until you come to a stop. The power slows down and as you look around you see many people stood in a circle. One who is sighted sees you and comes forward to you. At first they think you are a land spirit, but you must tell them that you are a person from another time who wishes to learn from them and also help them.

4. Working with Ancestors

The sighted one asks you what you need to learn and you commune with this elder to learn what you need for your service. In return, you tell them things of the future that will assist them in their spiritual lives. You can also act as an inner contact or worker for them, assisting them to heal or work on someone, or to act as a death worker for someone who is dying or recently dead. They will show you what they need from you.

When you have finished you withdraw from the group, walking into the centre of the space and stilling yourself. Be aware of the Void and of stillness. See yourself passing from the sacred space into the Void, letting all the work you have done fall away from you, and allow yourself to rest for a while in the stillness.

The knowledge that you were given lies within you and will surface when needed, but for now it passes from your mind as you drift in the stillness and silence. When you are ready, step out of the Void and back into the room where you first started. Focus on the element before you as you slowly come back to consciousness and when you are ready, open your eyes.

4.13 Dynamics

The dynamics of ancestral connection is always a two-way affair. At this stage of the work it is about service as well as learning, and time jumping is a major part of this service. We are bound by time only by virtue of our physical existence. As soon as we pass into the inner states of consciousness, then the mind has no time boundaries and we can flow back and forth. In practical terms, working through time can be hard on the physical body and you must be ready for the impact exhaustion afterwards.

The further back you go in time, the harder it can be to understand what the contact is trying to communicate. This is mostly because our consciousness is so different from the consciousness of the ancients. Just the speed at which we think and process is far in excess of the processing abilities of our ancestors. But then again they have a deeper and more anchored sense of connection from which we can truly benefit.

4.13. Dynamics

Our inner abilities have a great deal more elasticity than the people who went before us. This has accelerated over the years so that, within just two generations, the work has become far more pliable: magical work that we now find fairly easy was a terrible struggle for those working only a hundred years ago.

To go back in time we have to be aware of the subtle as well as obvious differences and adjust our communications accordingly. Because of our flexibility in working with power, which is probably a side product of our modern existence, we can often do tasks that the ancients would find incredibly difficult. When we appear in a certain time in a sacred space, that time is often determined by a call from the ancestors who reach out to the Inner Worlds for help. That call for help flows through the worlds, and as we reach back for that ancestral contact, it puts us both on the same frequency. Our spirits respond to the call (hence the hearing of a voice as we turn in the centre of the sacred space).

The need for working with ancestors seems to take on a natural flow of its own. There are tides within the land, tides within the races of people and tides within families that sometimes all come together to create a porthole for working. You will be pulled in dreams, thoughts and ideas, and that is when you know it is time to do this work.

It can also be important to tune into this work at certain times of the year, like the solstices or equinoxes. Learn to trust your inner instincts with the work: if it is right you will be almost obsessively drawn to the work. If it is not the right time, you will not be able to get it together to get the work done, regardless of what the New Age reconstructionalist calendars tell us. This is all about learning to tune into to the tides, to the inner natural patterns and to the voices of all those who work around the world in and out of time. Every person who makes that step to inner service becomes connected at a deep level. The more you work the more you become aware of them in their own time and place, doing similar work to yours. It is a bit like being a part of a large insane family!

As you work more and more through time you will find that some of the other workers begin to appear in your own work as inner contacts, appearing at a time when you need help or guidance during

4. WORKING WITH ANCESTORS

a healing or working. The call for help, when it is truly needed, never goes unanswered.

Chapter Five

Accessing and working within the Faery Realm

The Faery Realm is a part of our world, overlaid and hidden within the landscapes that are all around us. Some magical streams of work ignore this facet of inner work which is a shame and a great loss: we are surrounded by many orders of beings and all of them and us have a part to play in the great scheme of things.

A simple way to access the Faery Realm is to look at the landscape around in which you live. You can access the Faery Realm via a hill, a forest, a rock or a spring. Once you are in the Faery Realm, the central point of focus is usually the crossroads at which is a standing stone, which is actually the Goddess in one of her most powerful forms.

This way of accessing the Faery Realm is not the only way by any means, but it is simple, effective and has no baggage attached to it. It is important however that the first doorway to the Faery Realm is connected to the land upon which you live. The reason for this is that the contact needs to be real, connected and able to flow in a two-way relationship. Connection with the Faery Realm means working with the land, birds, animals and plants that are all around you regardless of whether you live in the country or a city.

Connecting with faeries brings about a relationship that is interdependent and active. They will want you to do things for them and the land. In return they will work with you, help you and teach you many things. They often want feeding, entertaining and companionship. You cannot do this if you are working in a way that is not connected to your everyday existence.

Look for an access point around you that you can build upon. Use the following two visions to build up the inner connection point

5. Accessing and working within the Faery Realm

for faery contact. From that connection point flow many paths within the faery realm, which take you to many different forms of contact, beings and landscapes. I use the Void as a threshold to many different places, including the Faery Realm, because it is a clear, clean place of peace, which puts us in a better frame of mind to meet other beings. The second vision takes you through a more traditional access route through the upside-down tree: an ancient and powerful image that is found throughout the British Isles (e.g. Woodhendge).

5.1 Short vision for accessing the Faery Realm

Use a flame, bowl of water or a rock as an elemental focus. Be aware of yourself passing through the element into the Void where you allow your daily life to fall away and a sense of stillness to wash over you. Take your time to feel yourself expand in all directions, feeling yourself reach out while breathing through the Void.

When you are still and calm, step out of the Void, seeing yourself walking upon a path that leads to a hill, a large rock or a tree. As you get closer to the access point you see a small crack in it that you hadn't noticed before and you squeeze yourself through, passing into a dark damp tunnel with a faint light at the end. As you walk in the darkness you become aware of many eyes watching you, and many whispers surrounding you, but you cannot hear what they are saying.

You emerge into the light of a grassy plain with a low hill in the distance and a standing stone at a crossroads up ahead. Walk up to the standing stone and place you hands upon it. You will feel it breathing under your touch and you become aware that the stone is a living being. You prick your finger and place a drop of your blood upon the stone and a drop of your spit in offering: in response the stone begins to change shape. The stone becomes a woman who sings in many tones at once, as if calling.

Many beings approach from the four pathways in response to the call and you see faery beings of all shapes and sizes approaching you warily. They stop at a short distance and wait for what you have to say. Commune with them, offer them a gift of your service and listen well to their reply. If they ask you to do something, then make sure that you are willing to do it in your own world, as they will hold you to your promise.

They offer you a gift in return and you also commune with the woman. When you have finished, return the way you came, and when you emerge out of the rock/tree/hill, see a misty area in the path and walk into the mist. It will take you back into the Void. Be still in the Void for a little while, remembering what you have just done and when you are ready, open your eyes.

5.2 Longer vision of the Faery Realm

This vision is a vision that you can use regularly to connect with the Faery Realm and build a relationship with the beings of that world. It goes down through the Underworld (its back door being in the Abyss) and gives you access to a much older ancestral faery consciousness. Once you have been to this place by the 'front door,' it is then interesting to access it by going down the Abyss to the place where this consciousness now rests. It is important to note at this point that faeries are not cute little half-dressed prepubescent Victorian constructs, they are strange, often wild-looking beings of various sizes from little to extremely large.

Sitting quietly, be aware of the inner flame that burns deep within you. As your awareness of the flame builds, reach within you and bring out a fragment of the flame, holding it before you. The fragment of flame lights up the space in such a way that you can see things that were previously hidden.

As you look around with your inner vision, you see an opening in the floor that falls down into the Underworld. The fragment of flame plunges down the hole and you follow. As you fall, you become aware of many different scents that you recognize. They all evoke emotions, and yet the precise memory of these familiar scents evades you.

Deeper and deeper down you fall, twisting around the directions as you pass roots, earth and stone. The flame falls below you and lights your way and in the dim light you become aware of beings falling with you, keeping you company as you pass through the earth and into the ancient Faery Realm. The beings that are falling with you start to shout loudly that they are nearly home. You begin to

5. Accessing and Working within the Faery Realm

pass tree roots as you fall and finally you pass tree trunks. You fall through a forest of upside-down trees and emerge in a strange land of great beauty. The friends that fell with you land beside you gently. Before you can speak to them, they vanish leaving you alone.

All around you is grass and flowers. Many trees hang down from the sky, reaching for the grass. The light comes not from the sky, but from the ground below your feet. In the distance there are many hills and standing stones. One particular stone stands out for you and you set off walking towards it. Faint singing whispers all around you and as you listen, you hear that the song is advising you where to go.

On your chosen path, there is a stone blocking the pathway. Something tells you, deep within you, not to walk around the stone, but to touch it. Reaching your hands out, gently caress the stone, which moves under your touch. A wild power emanates from the stone and you realize that this stone is special. Before you can draw breath, the stone transforms into a tall muscular woman who blocks the path.

Her eyes bore into you, seeing everything that is hidden within. She looks at your intentions for seeking the Faery Realm. She looks for a deed that was done without selfishness. If she is happy with what she has seen, she opens her arms to you. Her body scent evokes memories, long since forgotten, of your babyhood. The nurturing of the mother's breast flows from her as she invites you to embrace her.

Stepping forward towards her, you pass through her and she vanishes. The mother of all being has awoken you to life and you now see the landscape through different eyes. All the plants, trees, flowers and bushes show themselves to you as tall beautiful beings that uphold the earth. Many creatures dart in and out of the forest that has appeared all around you.

The stones move and breathe as many strange and wondrous faery beings tend them. All around you is vibrant life in balanced communion. Reach down to the earth and scoop a handful up. The scent of earth is that of the Mother who stood in your path. The scent of nurturing fills you and you lie down on the earth to embrace your Mother.

All of the faery beings lie down with you and each one places an arm around another until one of them places an arm around you. The

5.2. Longer vision of the Faery Realm

spirits of the plants, trees, flowers and stones all participate in until every living thing is joined, united in honoring of the Mother. A sense of communion and family flows strongly through you as you realize that all the beings assembled are truly your brothers and sisters.

A gentle rain starts to fall. The community of beings starts to separate and enjoy the soft falling water. The faery beings dance with the raindrops, and all the plants and trees open themselves out to receive the life giving water. The rain falls all around you and also falls through you. Much that is incoherent, unbalanced, suppressed or inappropriate is washed from you by this rain. What falls from you is taken up by the earth and transformed.

When the rainfall stops, a hand reaches out from the earth, holding something out for you. The hand of your first ancestor holds out your imbalances: they have been transformed by the rich earth. Opportunities for learning from what you have relinquished are offered to you. Take the offering and place it within you, where it will unfold slowly throughout your life.

The assembled faeries are beginning to dance through the forest and they call upon you to join them. Holding out your arms, you follow, dancing and singing as you pass ever deeper into the forest. Someone grabs your hand and dances with you. A faery being has chosen you as a companion and should you choose to upkeep this friendship, it will be your companion throughout life.

As you dance, your faery companion asks about your life in the surface world. It asks you what you eat, how you play, where your favorite tree is. In turn, you can ask about life in the Faery Realm.

A call sounds out and the dancing stops. Your companion tells you that it is time for you to leave the Faery Realm and return to the surface world. The assembled faeries accompany you back to the tree, and ask you to return to them again. They tell you that when you return, all you need to do is call out your name when you have jumped from the tree. Your companion will hear your call and will come to greet you. They will escort you to the many places within the Faery Realm and teach you about their world.

Your companion offers you a gift as you prepare to leave. It is something from the Faery Realm that will help you learn more about nature in the surface world. In return, you must make the gift of a

5. Accessing and working within the Faery Realm

promise to the assembled faeries. Whisper your promise, and the faeries will whisper it back to you.

Now it is time to leave. You jump up into the tree, catching onto a tree branch as you start to climb. Carefully climb through the branches until you reach the hollow trunk. Many of the faeries climb with you as you enter the tree hollow and ascend to the surface world. The fragment of your flame is hovering at the roots of the tree, guiding you back. The closer you get to the surface world the more you begin to be aware of the pollution, both physical and psychic of the world in which you live.

The faeries who climb with you begin to sing sad songs as they climb, telling of all the terrible things that have happening on the surface of the earth. It is only then that you realize the faeries are carrying work tools. They tell you that they are going out into the surface world to tend what is left of the flowers, the trees and the creatures. They advise you on how you can help on your own land—small things that you can do to help these beings in their never ending work.

Finally, you emerge back in the surface world, back where you first started. The fragment of inner flame returns back to its source deep within you, and you feel its refreshing power flow through you. Remember the promise that you made, and remember the ways that you can help maintain the land where you live. Also remember the gift that was given to you, and the friends that you made. You can return to the faery realm, back to your friends, whenever you feel it is appropriate.

To complete this vision, if you are indoors, go outside. Take off your shoes and feel the earth beneath your feet. If you are in a city, find a park or a patch of wasteland that has grass. Remember the scent of the Mother and those powerful beings that are the plants and flowers. Honor them quietly.

5.3 Work

Once you have established contact, you will find that things start being put in your path, sometimes literally! If you need something for your work, it will start to appear around you if you truly need it.

5.3. Work

The more you work with the local tree, rock, spring, hill etc., the more of a conversation will seep into your dreams, visions and waking life.

You will start picking up instincts regarding 'good' areas and 'bad' areas, places that need cleaning up either literally or from an inner point of view. Follow your instincts, listen to the voices within you and go with those feelings. You will often be asked to pick up litter, move rocks, clear springs, walk hills, sing, dance, put out honey, fruits and nuts for the faeries and birds. You also may be asked to change how you feed yourself and what you drink.

The processes that happen from faery work can totally transform a person's life for the good, and often bring us much closer to the land and creatures that live on and in that land. You will learn to heal creatures, how to feed and guard them, how to birth faeries and live among them whilst living in the human world.

Faery work is entwined with the environment: they are one and the same thing. So once you have gotten over the 'tourist' agenda and are ready to go into the Faery Realm to work rather than gawp, you will be offered many jobs that really need attending to.

These 'jobs' take many forms including the unwinding and dismantling of religious patterns: pre-1800 Catholic and Anglican churches in Europe tend to have ritual bindings and pinnings in the foundations that trap beings within the land and block access for faeries to the surface world: they hold the ancient powers down so that they cannot be tapped into. This is often displayed in churches by images such as St. George and the Dragon, St. Patrick and the serpent, St. Michael and the dragon, etc.

When the Romans came, they used Apollo to suppress, pin and block the dragon power of the Bright Goddess in the British Isles, just as they had done at Delphi. Ancient Britain was a place of oracles, warriors and druid priests who worked with the weather, and the Romans wanted to pin and control that power just as they pinned and controlled the oracle at Delphi and other places of power. Later this pinning method was absorbed into the Early Roman Christian church: the pin became the cross of Christianity and the sword of the saints that pinned the ancient dragon power down through rituals designed to destroy or imprison that power forever.

5. Accessing and working within the Faery Realm

Churches were built upon sacred enclosures, groves were cut and mounds were dug up. This ritual entrapment also blocked a lot of faery access to the surface world. It did not stop it by any means, but it did interfere with the natural balance of power and order, leaving the land unbalanced and disconnected. Dealing with this disconnection is one of the most common requests voiced by the faery beings of the land of Britain. The other is sweet food, which of course is an energy source!

Song is another faery request that is often put to humans. Music and song have great power: we are creatures of spiritual harmonics, as are faeries, angelic beings, and the land itself. The harmonics flow back and forth, energizing, strengthening and balancing the land. The best way that we can contribute on an external level is to play natural instruments (rather than recordings of psychedelic trance stuff) and to sing with a clear heart. Words are irrelevant—it is the sound that draws all consciousness to the fire to listen.

It is a bonding mechanism and also a healing tool in a non New Age sense: sometimes beautiful tones cross all war lines, all mountains of adversity and all manner of hatreds.

5.4 My own discovery of faeries

When I was a kid, I was very much the loner. I was way too weird for other kids to want to play with me and I wasn't interested in the things they were interested in. My idea of heaven was to spend all day outside in the woods alone, hanging out with the trees and the creatures.

I had a rough mountain pony called Topper (because no matter how bad other ponies were, he could top that). He had one wall eye (blue eye) and a mean temper. He bolted when he got bored and loved to suddenly break out into a flat out gallop and then just as suddenly slam on his brakes and put his head the to the floor. I would, of course being bareback, slip down his neck every time and land flat on my back in the mud. He loved it: what power!

So everyday I would spend a couple of hours trying to catch him until one day I decided not to chase him, which was what he wanted, but to sit quietly in the forest where he had dumped me and wait for

5.4. My own discovery of faeries

him to come to me. Day after day I would sit among the fallen trees and thick broom bushes, laying back in the weak European sunshine, and wait for the brat to get bored.

During that time I began to watch the squirrels and the birds. I loved talking to them in my mind and I would hold long imaginary conversations with them. Once such day I was deep in conversation when I saw a wild rabbit. I had never seen a wild rabbit before and I was fascinated.

During my childhood the government had seen fit to release a disease that would wipe out the rabbit population which had grown out of control. The rabbits often died a terrible agonizing death and I can remember when I was young, about 5 yrs old, seeing the last death throws of a rabbit in the road. My father covered my eyes and told me not to look.

To see a wild healthy rabbit in the late sixties/early seventies was rare. I watched him, thinking he was the most beautiful thing I had seen. Something happened at that point in my life, that instant. Something opened deep inside me and I looked around and saw just how beautiful everything was in this forest. Everything had life, a bright dazzling life that just was bursting with something that I didn't even have the words for.

That day I felt like I had seen God for the first time. I was nine years old and everything I touched, the trees, the plants, even Topper spoke to me in a silent voice that made me feel like I was hearing for the first time. It was that moment that I became aware that there was something else in that forest with me: something that was not bird animal or human. I could feel it, I could hear it, but I didn't know what it was.

Later that day, I went home and was busy watching my mother. She would often be gone for long periods of time so when she was around, I would sit and watch her: sort of filling myself up with her. I started to try and tell her what had happened that day, but it blurted out in a clumsy way.

I didn't have the words in my brain to describe what had happened. But what I did get was that I thought there was something else there in the forest with me that day. Could it be a ghost? No she replied, it sounds like they were faeries. She told me next time I went

5. Accessing and Working within the Faery Realm

out to the forest with topper and took a pack lunch, I should share some of it with them by leaving them the best and sweetest foods on a tree stump.

I did just that. Then I hid to watch and see if I could catch a glimpse of them coming to get their food. I had put out some grandma buns (my grandmother's special recipe) and some plot toffee (a bittersweet toffee made with dark treacle and made only in the months of October and November), my favorite. But alas, no one turned up except an excited crow. I kept waving him off the food and he would just caw at me.

I was so disappointed. I so wanted to meet with the faeries. I told my mother of my abysmal failure and she smiled a wide smile. "No Josie, they don't eat like we do, they take the strength out of the food and leave what's left for the creatures. And you can't see the faeries with these eyes: you have to look at them in a different way. They don't have bodies like we do, they are like Adam and Eve were before God gave them skin and threw them out of the garden. The faeries were never bad so they didn't get skin and they are still in the garden."

But I wanted to see them! I did learn to feel them however. One of my favorite games as a child was the Mayday precession. It was something we did every year where I lived and we would all have a large picnic afterwards. And I loved to recreate it. I would get our family statue of the Virgin Mary and dress her up in flowers with a flower crown. I would place her on a book and parade around the garden with a sheet tied around me like a robe and in my arms was the flowered Virgin resting ceremoniously on my father's history book. I sang the old may song to her as I paraded with my two bemused cats following me with suitable dignity. "Oh Mary we crown thee with blossoms today, Queen of the Angels and Queen of the May."

And something else followed me, I could feel them. Something that liked what I was doing and sang with me. And that feeling of companionship grew. And it also saved my life many years later when as a teen I was walking through a dark alley and was told by them urgently to run. I ran like the wind. I found out the day after that the Yorkshire Ripper grabbed a student from that alley around the time

5.4. My own discovery of faeries

I was walking through there, and he tortured and killed her. It could have been me.

They began to talk to me, to tell me about the trees and the wind and the horses. None of it was like conversation talk, it was not like talking at all. It was something else. At the time I wrote a poem about them which didn't survive the ravages of time, but one line I can remember from it is "hear the whispers, mumbles and cautions, silent eyes that watch and wait." That was probably the best description that I could give. Wherever I went I could hear them and feel them, and they gave me a knowing.

And they taught me how to talk to birds. My mother knew how to talk to birds and it was not unusual to have a wild blackbird furiously banging on our window in the morning as it looked for my mother.

Since that time I too have tended to birds, both wild and exotic. Some have come to me with terrible injuries and the faeries have always helped me to find the way to treat them and get them better.

When I was in my early twenties, I went through a phase of thinking that my childhood interactions with the faeries was just the imagination of a lonely child. I even went back to my forest as a young adult, just to look and convince myself that it was all in my head. The place, which I called the Blue Lagoon, had seemed to me in my childhood to be a deep wild forest with a beautiful lagoon and some mysterious ruins.

When I returned I found a small patch of woodland with a dirty pond full of trash and the remains of an old house: nothing romantic at all. At that point I stopped putting out food for the faeries (something I had done ever since that wonderful day) and began an inner fight with myself. It didn't last long. And they won.

Faeries are a part of everyday life, particularly if you live out in the country. I lived for a few years on the edge of preserved wilderness in West Montana and faeries really make their presence known there. They come in a variety of shapes and sizes there, some look human whereas others have no human features or shapes at all. I lived near a place where two mountains come together and form a strange-looking canyon. A powerful underground river rushes out from the side of the mountain and falls many feet before it carves a path through the forest and valley.

5. Accessing and working within the Faery Realm

Working in that area, by the falls, is powerful: the spirits of the land and the Goddess are apparent there. It is on tribally protected land which ensures that there will never be buildings there, and that the spirits of the land will be undisturbed. I went to the falls often and it was my favorite place to do a Faery Realm meditation.

But look around you, even in the city. They are there and would really benefit from contact. Feed them, tend them and tend the birds and animals around you. None of them are pests, they are all creatures in balance.

5.5 Magic, faeries and sex

There is a whole area of work that is about bringing through special beings, be they human, faery or otherwise. It is not written about much as it can be misused and it is a difficult subject to broach. Whenever sex and magic are put together, doors open that can quickly lead a person down silly, dangerous, or just plain stupid roads.

To work with sex and magic, you need to be in a place of maturity, with a sense of responsibility and balance. Believing that sex magic will bring you power, a great sex life, or power over others is a sign that you really should not be doing it. The results of this type of magical work are not about the participants, but for the spirit or door that is being opened by the process. When a couple makes love in a magical way, it can open up major doorways to many worlds to allow a spirit to pass into our world. Pregnancy is not just about human babies: it can be about birthing many things. But like any pregnancy, it carries with it a great deal of responsibility.

In the ancient world, sacred sex with a priestess would make sure the bringing through of a future sacred king: that is, reaching through the worlds to find the soul that is most suitable for the job. Ancient history is littered with tales of special births: babies born that are of a deity and a human, or half faery and half human. And seeing as we already have more humans than we could possibly need on this trashed planet, I will go more into the creating and birthing of faeries rather than anything with human form.

5.5. Magic, faeries and sex

Traditionally, faeries are conceived by two people who make love in a sacred way while the woman is menstruating, and the male is mediating a faery being. It is not that a 'faery ovum' is placed in her womb: it is that the nature of the woman's body as a vessel, coupled with the power of the moonblood and the focused intention/mediation opens a door through which a faery being can step into the outer world from the inner world. It is most certainly not the only way a faery manifests itself, in fact it is probably the rarest way, but it is an interesting way. The faery being takes on some of the human 'personality' and has more of an alignment with the human world than other faery beings.

The being does not have a gestation period, as there is no physical body. But the being will clamour for contact and will ask for a physical window to be made for it to have a more open connection with the human world. This can be achieved by making a model, painting a picture, anything which gives the being eyes and ears to look out of. It uses the statue or painting as a window through which it can better commune with humanity.

This is similar in process to deities and statues/images. The image is made and the consciousness of the being steps into it to use the image as a means of connection. This is not the same as a being that has been trapped or bound into an image or statue or even a person: that is a totally different process that I think is unethical and dangerous. It is used by Tibetans, was used by the ancient Egyptians, and sometimes still happens in various religions around the world.

So the window gives a connection with the world. To break that connection the window must be destroyed. That will not destroy the being, only its tool of connection. So it bodes well to think carefully before you bring something through in this way: like sulky teenagers, they are not so easy to get rid of once birthed.

The urge to do this creation is spurred by an ancient stirring within us to reach back to a time when we were properly connected with faeries, animals, and the land. It is within our nature to be a part of the whole, to be 'in the Garden' and as such we strive both consciously and unconsciously to reconnect somehow, someway.

Particularly earth-based paths have become interested in the idea of sex with faeries, which is a whole minefield in itself. I won't go

5. Accessing and working within the Faery Realm

into it in any detail as I personally feel it can easily become seriously imbalanced and parasitical. If you get the urge to experiment in such a way, I would suggest that you think long and hard about opening your energy levels with a being that you don't know. Would you sleep with a stranger off the street?

Sex is a major opening of power portholes and can enable the person to move quickly and effectively through the worlds, and can open deep powers within ourselves: hence the use of sex with Tantra. But such opening of power can quickly go wrong if there is not a sense of focus, balance and harmony. The person that declares that they sleep with a faery lover because their husband is impotent/ignores them/screws only sheep, is saying that they are happy to sleep with random strangers. Just because the faery being has no body it does not mean that there is not an energy exchange: and under such imbalanced conditions, the chances are that such a union is heavily parasitical.

The rules of health, disease, energy parasites, power surges, and bringing through souls that apply to sex between two humans also apply to human interaction with faeries. So common sense and self-respect are important things to think about.

There are many stories of people who are half faery from mixed unions but how does that work if the faery has no body? Well...When you make love, it opens up the worlds. The purer (and I don't mean moral, I mean spiritually clean...as in no rape/parasite sex, goats or chickens...) the love making, the higher up the Abyss the porthole opens. When you make love as a woman and the man who is making love to you is mediating a faery being, there is a chance that as the porthole opens, it opens on the 'faery' frequency as opposed to the 'human' frequency. This, again, is a method within Tantra (it's not really about bizarre-looking sex positions...). So the child that fruits from such a union has spirit elements of faery as well as human.

Mixed being marriages are talked about in the Old Testament: for example, humans and Titans (ouch...) and there are many lines that flow through humanity today.

Obviously the rule about the porthole also works in reverse: the more degenerate the sex, the more likely a bottom feeder will come through. And that moves onto an important point if you do magic

5.5. Magic, faeries and sex

and you have inner ability: having a condom on or being on the pill only stops human babies coming through. The sex act can also bring through many beings that have no physical manifestation: it depends on what is going on in your head (scary thought) when making love in a magical way. The imagination is an extremely powerful tool and if your imagination is used regularly for visionary magic, then it will click into work mode under such power conditions as sex. Hence the biblical saying that if it is in your thoughts, then the deed is already done. That is how magic works.

So back to faeries...if you are used to mediating powers and beings, then that is how you could birth a faery. Just be aware that if you make it, you are responsible for it and you have to learn to live with it/them.

Chapter Six

Polarization: magical dynamics and partnerships

When working with magical beings of any description, eventually the issue of polarity will come into play: we are by nature polarized beings and as such are vulnerable to any imbalance in any direction. Our physical universe is made up of positive and negative, so you would think that as a species we would have got such power dynamics down to a fine art. Wrong! With the advent of monotheism everything else went out of the window as far as western spirituality goes (and also a large chunk of eastern spirituality). That movement, which started in the late Bronze Age, gave us the concepts of good and evil, day and night, and one true god ruling over all (a megalomaniac storm god who gets pissed off easily: yeah, good choice).

Now, such thinking is in itself polarized, right? Well, yes, apart from the all-knowing god, but because the polarization revolves around issues that we are told threaten our souls (bad, evil, Satan) we stay on the side of good, light, god, etc. So we become one end of the pole both spiritually and culturally, which is extremely unhealthy and unbalanced. Polarized 'light/good' power also, by nature of the stresses and tensions in the universe which keeps everything spinning and manifesting, attracts the opposite of the 'good,' 'light' in an attempt to balance itself.

We cannot be one end of a polarized scale as it is unhealthy, and we cannot be unpolarized and be in life: you have to be the fulcrum in the middle, a balance of both ends of the pole, and also a fulcrum between polarity and non-polarity. Is that possible? Well, magically yes it is possible, and it is one of the magical ideals that many strain towards.

6. Polarization: Magical Dynamics and Partnerships

For example: if you are looking to work with major power beings, like say, the Barakiel (and make sure you have a bloody good reason to work with these dudes...they are no lightweights), then you have to have a strong and balanced expression within your magical being of polarization, negative and positive: this will strengthen and compliment your physical polarity and in turn will protect your body from the massive impact that can happen when you work in vision with this order of being. They are totally unpolarized: they are unconditional beings of pinpoint consciousness and power i.e. angelic beings. To work safely with them for any length of time or to partake of their power, you must reach and work with their polar opposite i.e. the polarized version of the same power.

This is where the knowledge of working in the Abyss comes in handy, and the knowledge of the beings that inhabit the particular levels of the Abyss is even handier. The Barakiel are a high order of angelic beings that operate within the consciousness of the stars and the lightning: they are bright pinpoint power and must be balanced by something of similar status and quality. The Barakiel are one of the orders of beings traditionally 'one step away from God and held above all others.' So, who do we know who is of angelic consciousness, is bright, close to Divinity and a high level of power while also being of the earth and polarized? Lucifer.

Lucifer, the bright one, Venus, the brightness upon the earth, the light that goes and comes back (dark, light, dark...polarized, not constant) is traditionally about the earth, the land, solidity, sexuality, an angel close to god that is deep within the earth/Underworld.

Note: The casting down story of Lucifer comes from the story of the king of Tire and also the Babylonian king (*Isaiah* 14:12) which in turn comes from an older Canaanite story about the falling of the morning star into the Underworld. The linking of Lucifer to this older myth explained to people why there is a bright angel in the depths of the earth. This brightness is a major power that flows out from the earth, and the angelic consciousness known as Lucifer is the threshold being for it to manifest at the depths. The power itself (which is not Lucifer) is a polarized manifest Divine power that flows out of the land, the opposite of the unmanifest God. In the Near East this power was known as Shekhinah and in Britain was known as Brigh or the Bright one. Both were expressed as feminine.

So, if you work with the being Lucifer, you learn to work with that brightness in a stable polarized way, drawing it right through your body and processing it at a cellular level. This way, when you stand before the Barakiel and ask them to work with you on a task, your body, particularly your endocrine system stays in one piece and you don't end up frying all your nerve endings. (The lightning power that hits the earth is also the lightning power that carries messages around your nervous system)

The other thing to think about is the actions of the beings themselves: the Barakiel are defenders of the innocent, they help victims who are attacked with demonic or other magical power: they are the defenders just as the Irin are the judges. So the Barakiel are probably not good beings to use if you are seeking their power to do dodgy stuff.

The same rules of polarity work in reverse: if you are working a lot with powerful conditional polarized beings, then you need to balance yourself by working with unconditional unpolarized beings like angelic beings. By not doing this, you can fall into the usual trap of becoming unbalanced and you could eventually turn into either a nutter or a not nice sorcerer or both.

This is where the whole thing of demons comes from: they are not bad beings: they are powerful conditional polarized beings who like to push buttons (not unlike we humans). If you are balanced and you stretch in each direction as you work, then their conditionality and perchance for button pushing will not affect you.

But our society is a one sided society that views the world as good and evil and has a religious/cultural pattern that encourages fear whenever power is expressed: if it is from the depths of the Abyss, or a demon, then it must be evil/bad and must be destroyed, or if the person wants to rebel, then the demon is a bad being that the practitioner can use to be 'bad.'

All conditional beings have the capability to be good or bad or indifferent. What we call from them, how we react to them and what we do in conjunction with them will decide whether bad or good comes from them. And then you get into the mire of what is good anyway? Good and bad is relative to what culture you come from and what time you live in. So you have to start to tread carefully as things

6. POLARIZATION: MAGICAL DYNAMICS AND PARTNERSHIPS

are not so black and white: there are many different shades and how we behave influences how other beings will react to us.

Most beings that we would consider demons are an ancient consciousness that we can barely begin to understand. They are dangerous (not evil), seductive, powerful and some are out of place in our everyday physical world, and some have a defined role in our world. But the same can be said of angelic beings: our views are heavily coloured by our cultural programming.

So in practical terms, how to you keep the balance?

The basic simmered-down version is: if you are working with conditional polarized beings that are powerful, then do some opposite work to balance it out: connect with unconditional beings also. So if you are working with ancient gods, demonic beings, old ancestors, deeper faery beings etc., then do some angelic work or star power work to balance yourself.

If you have to work a lot with angelic beings or formless power, then balance it out with Underworld beings of the same level of power, or with elemental beings, faeries, etc. Your body will tell you what you are doing wrong: the thyroid often reacts to the surges of unbalanced power (along with the hypothalamus) and the practitioner ends up with either a dead metabolism or a sky high fast metabolism with added OCD.

It is like body building: too much bulky short muscle can look impressive but you cant really do much with it, just as someone who doesn't do anything at all has no muscle tone: the body and spirit need a little of everything to bring about balance, learning and strength.

6.1 Polarity within magical partnerships

Working magically in a partnership can be a wonderful and powerfully rewarding way to do magic. However, like all partnerships and relationships, it can be fraught with potholes, tripwires and the odd smack over the head with a 2 by 4.

When you have worked alone magically for any length of time, you begin to realize that there is a wide section of magic that really needs to be done with a member of the opposite sex. The need

6.1. Polarity within magical partnerships

for opposition is not about sexual preference, it's about the actual physicality of the human body. The way that a female body is put together ensures that it can handle certain types of power regardless of the sexual preference. The same goes for men: it is about the physical filter, the body, not the sexuality.

But one of the side issues that comes into play quickly when talking about magical partners is the use of power and how it affects the people around us. When you work with a power exchange, it creates a powerful bond between the priest and priestess: it is a conversation that becomes, by its nature, intense and intimate. That is not to say it becomes physically sexual, our bodies can interpret the energy as sexual, when in fact it is a conversation of energy.

For this reason, before any magical work is embarked upon, the actual relationship with the priest or priestess needs to be looked at carefully, and what the implications would be for people on the periphery. This is why some of the most powerful magical working relationships are between couples. If a priest and priestess are working at a deep energetic level, and they are not partnered in a relationship, a bit of a tangle can develop.

The spouse or long-term partner of the priest or priestess can sometimes pick up on the power exchange and respond subconsciously at a deep level by pulling away from the depth of intimacy as a self-preservation mechanism. And because it is not about sex, the dynamics become confusing for the non-working partner, and can create disharmony within the relationship that cannot easily be addressed. Nothing wrong is being done, but still the non-working partner feels uncomfortable at an instinctive level.

If the priest and priestess are also married, that takes away one bag of worms but opens another, much deeper bag of issues that would need to be harmonized for successful long-term work to occur. The first hurdle, particularly if both priest and priestess are strong magically and also have strong personalities, is the one of hierarchy. If they truly honor and respect the qualities of the other partner, and are prepared to make up any shortfall, then this level of problems will not occur.

Unfortunately this is the first stage of collapse that powerful magic usually initiates: when working with true magical power at any depth,

6. POLARIZATION: MAGICAL DYNAMICS AND PARTNERSHIPS

the first thing it will do is highlight weaknesses, prod issues and open cracks. Magic is like water: it will find the weakest part in the wall to come through. That is why, when working with high levels of power, you need to be clear, balanced and have your act together, otherwise it will slowly destroy or degenerate you.

What can happen is that as the power starts to build over months or years, one or both of the partners begins to become glamorized by the power (messiah syndrome) and starts to look down on the other partner. This was common in the last generation where historically, the men at the forefront of magic treated their partners like shit. They would become famous names and the wife/priestess would be pushed behind the screen.

This became more apparent with the advent of commercial workshops (the Company of Hawkwood, for example): suddenly the priest magician was exposed to many more people than the habitual little local group and they were worshipped like gods. The partners, although magical equals, were pushed into the shadows which immediately damages the harmony of the power exchange. It was not all male priests that behaved this way, it also happened publicly with female esotericists.

Such a problem can be sidestepped by equally sharing the work both privately and publicly, and if one partner is working silently in a group setting, upholding the power for example, or mediating the contacts, then such work is publicly acknowledged. In private, the problem can be sidestepped by power sharing: taking specific responsibility for certain parts of the magic, and taking the time to step back and allow the other partner to forge on with the work. At an everyday level, such dynamics can be mirrored, which truly enhances the magical dynamic.

This is something that equal rights action has actually damaged: if everyone is supposed perform the same function then everything becomes a mess and a power struggle. Some women in New Age and magical communities see attacking men and making them feel inadequate as part and parcel of the 'Goddess' movement. It isn't. It just creates resentment. The same goes for magical communities in which men treat women as subservient: it's wrong, it's unhealthy and it doesn't make for good magic.

6.1. Polarity within magical partnerships

Having specific areas in magic and life where one partner excels, and areas within magic and life where the other partner excels, creates a harmonic situation where both parties hold power, and both parties learn to also yield power to the other. The partnership, from a magical point of view, becomes an octave of the scales: both sides are equal in their inequality.

So, having survived the first hurdles, the priest and priestess then really get down to the intricacies of polarity and how it works. The early and interesting form of polarized energy exchange is the load share in the buildup to a piece of work.

When a powerful magical working is planned, from the moment the time and date is set, the inner side of the magic begins to work. The energies are beginning to stretch out and will start to affect the partners in various ways. This is where the necessity for male and female bodies comes in: the different bodies bring in and hold power in different ways.

Because of a woman's womb, she can hold and grow power within her to quite a high level. Men can bring through the catalyst that triggers the power within the woman to go from dormant to active: thus magic is born. In a practical sense this can create temporary issues (or sometimes a holocaust!) in the home while the magic is being 'cooked.'

Of course, there are always the exceptions to this scenario: men who hold and cook power and women who bring through strong sudden energy bursts.

Once the power is released within the working environment, it is woven between the partners as a power sharing activity. While ever the couple keep the understanding that they are working as a composite being, then the magic will work through them in a more or less balanced way depending on what you are doing. Should one or both parties begin to tiptoe down the road of ego, then a power struggle will ensue and the partnership will possibly begin the downhill slide toward destruction unless they realize what they are doing and pull back.

That downhill plunge is usually brought about by lack of respect for the other partner, or an inflated sense of self-importance brought about by imbalanced working practice. The other thing that a couple

6. POLARIZATION: MAGICAL DYNAMICS AND PARTNERSHIPS

should be aware of is that such disharmony can come about if they are being messed with by beings who don't want such a partnership in action. This usually happens when the couple is working in the field of parasite removal or exorcism: it's the grimiest, hardest and most dangerous side of esoteric service work, so usually couples who work in this field tend to be pretty well versed in such issues.

If a couple is striking out in that field for the first time, it is important for them to know that this is a major feature of the operational problems for that line of work. Major grounding, common sense and balancing work is needed on a regular basis to keep the energy and polarity balanced and healthy.

The interesting feature of polarity work is how the two bodies distribute the burden of power, often without conscious thought or decision. Upon the commencement of a line of work, each partner will begin to manifest some expression of the buildup of power. It is important to recognize this as soon as possible for what it is and take steps to work with the buildup rather than struggle against it. However the buildup manifests will give a clue about how to handle it. The skill is handling the buildup without dispersing it.

A version of this still lingers on in old esoteric circles where it is considered bad to have sex before a ritual: the energy is leeched off by the sex act leaving the priest drained of energy that was needed for the work.

Nature is often a good balancer and walking out in the forest, on the moors, or by the sea if it is possible is a good way to balance out when there is a power build up. Creative expression is another way, as is gardening, planting, making things with your hands: all are ways that any power buildup can be handled along with plenty of rest. It is all a matter of finding the action that will not take the power away from the magic, but will stop it blowing your head off (or killing each other) before the magic is completed.

Each partner will carry a certain load and it is not always a fair distribution: it is what is needful for the work. Sometimes one partner will be weighed down to the point of exhaustion with the burden of the power, while the other one is left relatively untouched. In this circumstance it is important that the energetic partner tends and cares for the burdened partner: the energy dynamic will switch around and the longer the couple works together the more complex and interesting it will become.

For example if one partner has a chronic illness and there is some power building, the power will go to which ever partner needs to be processing that power for work. If it happens to be the ill partner, then the other partner will often take on the burden of illness symptoms, leaving the ill partner free of symptoms and able to do the power carrying that is needed.

Such energy swapping is fascinating and really calls into question the nature of boundaries and how energy actually works; and it opens out the possibility for chronic illness to be load-shared between people.

All of these dynamics are dependent on the basic respect, honour and care that each partner gives to the other. With such a partnership, the potential for great and powerful magic is limitless: polarity when used correctly can create a whole new level of consciousness that could potentially take us as a generation onto the next step of magical development.

Chapter Seven

The physical implications of practising magic

If you spend a lot of time doing inner work or working in the inner realms, then sooner or later you are going to feel the impact of such work. When you work in realms that are close to our realm, the impact can be minimal or even positive: what is close to ourselves (i.e. ritual and outer court magic) takes little energy and has little impact upon the body and mind. The further away from your own realm you stretch, the harsher the impact on the human body.

In past times in the magical community, much more ritual/outer court work was done than visionary/inner work, and this acted as ballast to ground and root the magician. It then began to devolve into an almost exclusive use of outer court action (ritual, talismanic magic, scrying, etc. In more modern times (i.e. in the last century), more vision was used but in a lot of cases it was psychological pathworking, or visualizations that were constructed from a psychological base and which did not stretch out of the self: hence they had no impact and a therapeutic outcome.

Some magical lodges used astral travel with a limited core of the group: the Golden Dawn Sphere group was a classic example. The only problem with this is that the inner connections are channeled through a small number of people who then wield the power and it creates an imbalance in general within the initiates. (It is only balanced when all do outer and inner work.) This dynamic alone can blast apart a magical lodge regardless of the other issues or problems that are so common in magical groups.

But some magicians realized the potential of using inner visions more often and at greater depth: they had major results and magic leapt forward another notch on the evolutionary scale. Instead of

7. The physical implications of practising magic

a long preparation, complex seals/ritual and incantations to finally bring the consciousness of an angelic or demonic being to them in the physical realm, magicians realized they could go through a variety of stages in vision to come face-to-face with an angelic being and have a conversation with it. This development unknowingly brought with it an impact both on the magician and the environment around them.

One modernish magician who worked ceaselessly to develop this method and used it at length during the Second World War was Dion Fortune. She worked tirelessly in ritual and vision to keep back the magical inroads the Germans were trying to make into Britain, blocking their powers and invoking the ancient warriors of the sacred land of Britain to defend the realm. She paid for such work with her life.

Intense inner work is processed through the endocrine system and through the immune system. Too much deep work too often, without the right protections, rests, or supports, will eventually collapse the system, leaving the magician burned out and chronically exhausted. The other major problem that can affect magicians is the impact and infestation of unhealthy beings if the magician is working at any great depth in the Abyss: the infestation becomes physical and mental if precautions are not taken in the work.

7.1 Treating impacts

Sometimes working at depth either deep in the past, deep in the Abyss or far out with or within Archangelic beings is necessary, and if this is done frequently the impact will show by exhaustion, depression, brain fog, and muscle aches. Such work, particularly if it is frequent, will drain the body's vital energy leaving little left for the proper running of everyday functions.

Homeopathy is one effective way of coping with magical impact and if used correctly can usually divert most impact to the outer organs like the skin, and drive the body to refuel in a healthy way (food and sleep).

Now before you go rushing off to the shops to buy a homeopathy book, one thing to think about is that when you do a lot of magic, it changes how your body responds to deep and subtle

7.1. Treating impacts

powers. Homeopathy, cranial osteopathy and similar treatments are processed differently by a body that has become accustomed to power so the usual remedy pictures and indications have no meaning and cannot be used. The substance choice has to be more poetically and magically approached. (Which is why magicians of times past would study alchemy.)

Some research is often necessary to look into various substances from a magical point of view: the magician is led down the path of the alchemist. It becomes handy to learn about transformation through substance catalysts, the 'personality' of substance, and also about the magical history of substances.

For example, when inner impact or an inner porthole is staying open and affecting the body, homeopathic potencies of nitric acid can often close the contact down. Where violence or demonic power is coming through and cannot be closed off, homeopathic stramonium can sometimes help the body to calm down. When a serious blast of inner power hits, usually during attack, the homeopathic sarcodes of Pineal and Pituitary at 30c or 1M will buffer the impact.

But in a longer term scenario, it is important to know how to look after the body while it is under magical stress, and how to monitor the body so that you are alerted quickly if something is going wrong. Often magical impact will mirror illness to the point of serious physical symptoms, but when it has become so entrenched in the body, the chances are that long-term damage has already been done.

The endocrine system is the first threshold of impact, so there you would watch closely to monitor any changes that are going to escalate. In women, one of the first changes to occur is disturbance in the menstrual cycle: the cycle of bleeding starts to time in with the powerful workings rather than with the natural rhythms of the body. In both men and women, variation in sex drive is a common thing to appear. Then the appetite becomes disturbed along with the regularity of digestion and a change in sleep patterns.

The use of herbs can also be useful in supporting a hardworking magician, especially ones grown and harvested by yourself: you gain a working relationship with the plants and by communicating with them, you can begin to understand the deeper qualities of the plant,

7. The physical implications of practising magic

and what it can offer you. Shamanic magicians have used plants for centuries not only to protect and heal them, but to assist in visions if it is needed: not everyone has instant or easily accessible inner sight.

Magic can do many strange things to the body, it can also manifest certain powers that impact your body in the same way a toxic substance would. For instance, if you are working a lot with a power like Mithraism, or Apollo, or any major solar male deity, then eventually the body will begin to manifest the symptoms of gold toxicity. Such details can be easily passed by these days as most people are not aware of the pictures of metal toxicity: our everyday environment does not usually expose us to such things. And again, it becomes apparent that a form of alchemy is needed for a serious magician: you need to know the properties of gold, mercury, lead, silver, the various acids, and the numerous poisonous power plants.

In the case of gold toxicity from overworking with the solar powers, you would first look at homeopathic gold: Aurum Met is a interesting remedy from a magical point of view.

When looking at these substances for magical treatment, it is important to look at the mental and emotional pictures of the remedies as this is where the damage is usually most obvious when the imbalance comes from magic. Similarly with herbs and flower essences, the mental/emotive picture tells the largest tale of where the power is doing damage. It is common when a person begins to connect to certain streams of power, for the imbalanced form of that power to begin to express itself through their mental/emotional imbalance: this is where the gurus, messiahs, and 'senior most high magi' are born.

7.2 Working with balance

Avoiding such imbalances is usually the best way forward, and that can be achieved by pacing the work and spreading out the power across a variety of working methods. Ritual, vision, seeing, recitation, meditation and hands-on power transfer are all methods that can be used to achieve a certain goal. Using any one of these methods a lot can cause an imbalance and if one single method is used in excess it can cause illness, and sometimes severe illness.

7.2. Working with balance

Another dynamic that is interesting which can help to redress the balance of power is the use of completely exteriorized magic: a physical action with intent, when done by a magician who is heavily versed in visionary magic, can become powerful without much energetic impact. For years I could not figure out how this actually worked, I just knew that it did.

Eventually it became apparent that a magical worker who had connected in depth throughout the inner realms for a good length of time became 'connected' to an extensive collective of power and consciousness. When a magician did a simple physical action with magical intent, all the power of the collective flowed through the action.

If the connection to the inner collective is not there or established strongly enough, then the physical action does nothing. This then explained to me why all the writings from the sixteenth and seventeenth centuries on ritual, sigil and talismanic magic didn't work well in most instances: it didn't fail because the magic doesn't work, it would fail the magician didn't have the inner connections and power. By not publishing that fact it kept the practical application of power in the hands of those ready for it. Without inner power, it became a meaningless jumble of shapes and words.

If you have a lot of work that must be done, share it out with a partner (or group) if that is possible. Change your working methods frequently and balance out the methods you use so that intense inner work is balanced by externalized ritual. Take frequent salt baths and keep your working area and rest area clean, clear and balanced so that you do not have to deal with any little nasties anywhere.

If you work a lot on vision, vary the realms that you work in and the beings that you work with: don't become a stuck record or it will carve a groove in you that could damage you. It is also more fun to work with a variety of beings and it keeps the work fresh. It also makes it harder for other people to tap into your work or to interfere with it: being predictable is never good!

If you have to spend a lot of time swimming around in the depths of the Abyss, make sure you also do some lighter work like faery work to balance the load: it's all about spreading out in a harmonious way. If you do a lot of angelic work, then do some ancestral work to

7. The physical implications of practising magic

counter it. Failing that, a six pack of Guinness, the movie Hellboy, a large bar of chocolate and some good tobacco will do the trick.

Another thing to consider if you are doing tons of inner work is to get out on the land and recharge your batteries in nature. Working with animals, growing things, walking, swimming, anything outside and not man made will refill you and start you back on the path to balance. Lying on stones or on the earth is good for grounding and the sun can work wonders in cleaning you off (unless you live in Arizona, in which case it will just crisp you).

7.3 Food

What you eat is also important and can aid or prevent you from doing your job. If you eat a lot of toxic junk then of course your body will be in no state to do any sort of deep work for too long without it beginning to show. If you are young you can get away with it for a while, but as you get older, the ability to shrug off such poison begins to diminish and the toxic waste begins to pile up. The deeper the inner work, the more your body will react to the toxins and the sooner it will show the damage.

Working for lengths of time in deeper realms is like mountain climbing: you have to be fit, healthy and look after yourself to survive it. What you eat is the starting point to your health and what work you do defines what you can eat or not. If you want deep sensitivity in most realms and a high level of sight, then you will have more success if you are vegetarian or vegan. Meat is an anchor, it lowers your frequency and ties you closer to earth: it is perfect for you is you are a healer or you work out with the public a lot. It creates a barrier that stops certain powers from seeing you and it can help to give you ballast if you work pulling out parasites.

If however you spend a lot of your time chasing demons, conversing with angelic powers or Abyss diving, then meat can sometimes become a liability. In some cases it blocks your ability to work with these beings or even to see them, or for them to see you. It can also become a problem if it is not clean meat: if it has a lot of toxicity in the muscle fiber and also a lot of fear hormones released from suffering before its death, those hormones will play havoc with your adrenals and also affect how your energy is perceived on the inner. Wild hunted meat is the cleanest for magicians if you do eat meat. If you do not have access to that type of meat, try to find a local farm that sells its own meat.

The liability comes in when you are dealing with polarized beings and you are holding within you the flesh of a being that has gone through profound suffering before you ate it: you will appear to the beings around you as a form of monster. It's not about morals, ethics or anything like that: it's about working practice, tools and common sense.

I eat meat when I am doing certain types of work. Most of the time I do not eat meat because I work at depths where such a diet is not helpful, it blocks my sight and stops me getting into certain realms. I have no problem shooting, killing, skinning and eating an animal: it is good to know your food, know where it came from and what it truly is. And when I have to live in a city or work on a lot of people, then I need meat otherwise I would get eaten alive by every parasite going.

The other thing that can be interesting as part of your health regime is your water: recitation over water before you drink it is an old and powerful concept. The water absorbs the sacred power of the word and then you take it into yourself as nourishment. Again it is a strange form of alchemy: by using recitation you change the quality and power of the water, and as you take it into yourself, it changes you also.

7.4 Practicalities while working

When you are working, first make sure your working space is balanced, clear and ready for work. Whatever element you are working with, make sure it is also 'clean': water should be drawn from a river/spring or at least filtered, a flame should come from wood: matches where possible and not directly from a lighter, etc. and the candle should be simple, not perfumed or shaped like a being/person/hippo. Be aware of your directions and what is coming from those directions. Don't have power objects in the room if you do not work with them or you do not know what they are or what they

7. The physical implications of practising magic

do. Also be aware that if you are doing deep magic and you have an object in your working space that is not compatible with your brand of magic, you can end up with an agitated energy in your room. For example if you are working in an esoteric Kabbalistic format, don't have a statue of Kali in your working space as the two don't magically mix well.

If you do bring magical objects into your working space, make sure that you fully understand what beings are in them, not just what they represent. Some tourist objects can represent one deity (like Ganesha, Kali, Shiva, etc. but can actually be holding a spirit from the local area where it was made, and the spirit will probably not have anything directly to do with the deity.

If you buy such an object, it is a good idea to magically strip it first. Or, if you want to work with that deity, strip the object and then put the deity in it yourself. The only time you do not need to do that is when the object has been properly tuned and used magically or spiritually. Some deity statues are blessed in temples and antique ones can often be enlivened with the deity form or personality. In this case just be aware that it brings that power through, and make sure that is compatible with whatever else you are working with, otherwise you might end up with a war in your workroom!

The other thing to watch out for, if you are working at any depth in the Abyss, is not to have objects that represent humans, spirits or animals in your workroom. A stray power can take up residence quietly if you are not observant with your sealing work, and you could end up with more than you bargained for in the cute fluffy teddy that is on your shelf. If the object has eyes, ears etc., the being can use that representation to move through and cause havoc. (Sometimes these powers get bored and think it's funny to move into a statue, doll or soft toy and annoy you.) I'm sure that anyone who has done any length of time as an exorcist will have come across a mask, statue or doll that has a little 'something' in it that is causing problems for someone.

Prepare your working space by the use of sound if you are going to be doing heavy work. Certain types of music and voice are superb at flattening spaces and preparing them for deep work. Chants, drums etc. are all sounds that affect the space and can create an energy that can make the work easier.

After you have finished working, close your work properly and then go have a bath and something to eat. Taking a bath with salt in it removes any stray energy that is around you, and food grounds you.

Above all, learn to listen to your body and respond to what it is trying to tell you. There is too much machismo in our society these days: people are expected to shrug everything off and are considered sissies if they look after themselves. That is a ignorant way of working: you last a lot longer and look good for a much longer time if you listen to and care of your body.

7.5 The effects of inner contact on the endocrine system

For a while I spent a great deal of time working in small experienced groups, pushing the boundaries of visionary magic from its then limited scope in the magical field. During the 80s and early 90s, visionary work was either approached from a psychological point of view, or was approached magically through long, drawn-out, prewritten scripts that were designed to guide the initiate through inner ritual paths and bore the shit out of them. Having said this, I have since learned that to take someone deeply into a place, or to approach a deep level of consciousness, a long, drawn-out path can sometimes stretch the consciousness of a practitioner and can facilitate a deeper contact.

I wanted to approach the work in a different way. I wanted the visionary work to reflect the reality and immediacy of stretching the consciousness from one world to another without allowing the imagination to 'play' in the psychological realm. This meant that I had to work only with practitioners that had enough internal discipline and experience to know the difference between real and imaginary contacts, and to work in uncharted territory.

One of the things that we all immediately noticed was that our bodies were preparing for the work a few days before. People began to get hungry and tired about 3 days before the work (the magical

7. THE PHYSICAL IMPLICATIONS OF PRACTISING MAGIC

tide going out). The day before the workings, women were beginning to bleed regardless of where they were on their cycle. This was of particular interest to me as it signaled that the female hormone cycle was directly involved in the distribution of power in a magical working.

This in turn raised questions about why the menstrual cycle was considered to be 'unclean' by the monotheistic religions (whereas the pre-Christian Celtic culture used the menstrual cycle as a power base for battle and magic). Did the 'unclean' status deflect attention from the power available to women at certain times of their cycle? In such cases, the power would be suppressed which in turn would force an unhealthy outlet for that power: pre-menstrual strain, tension, and rage. Anyhow, that is another topic altogether.

The morning of the first working day, everyone felt a massive inrush of energy ready for working. After the two-day working sessions, everyone would independently experience a serious slump to the point where most practitioners were unable to go to work at their day jobs the following day. The body was reacting as though it had worked physically hard for two days, even though the majority of the time people spent the day sat in a chair.

The first thing I noticed with myself and my fellow coworkers was that we had begun to react to certain substances and foods. Our bodies were becoming intolerant of minor depressants and stimulants. The deeper we worked, the more sensitive we became. Mediating a consciousness was also creating a 'burnout' situation throughout the endocrine system. The higher the level of being that was contacted or mediated, the harder the impact was upon the hypothalamus, thyroid and adrenals. The effect was a massive slowing of the metabolism, increase of appetite, increased need for sleep: the body acted as if it had severe prolonged fatigue. When the work was continued over months, muscle fatigue set in with a pattern that mimicked chronic fatigue. If the work undertaken was new, or was visions that had not been worked with for generations, then the physical impact was at a maximum. If the work was current or recent (last two thousand years) then the impact was minimal.

One of the interesting asides is that if the work included high-powered angelic/Tree of Life work, some people experienced burning

7.5. The effects of inner contact on the endocrine system

sensations and reddened skin. I did find, after about a year of this, that coffee, which is a power substance, would lessen the contact a lot and relieve the pressure on the body. The more coffee was drunk, the less the power impacted the body.

I started to track the effects of substances on the body using tarot. My reasoning was that if tarot (which I had been using since my early teens) showed the patterns of possible future paths, then it could show patterns of present paths within the body and where those present paths could lead. I devised a layout that was specific to the human body so that I could pinpoint the source of effects and the likely future pattern that the body would take from that substance.

To make sure that the system worked, I teamed up with a medical doctor[1] who was also familiar with magic. I tested the deck layout by looking at patients. She gave her patients a number and I had to read the body picture of that 'number.' The body picture was compared to the medical notes to see how accurate the deck reading was.

Over a period of time, what became clear from the readings and the actual bodily reactions of the magical workers is that the immune system via the thymus was being affected, as was the hypothalamus.

The immune system was kicking in and reacting to certain types of inner contacts as if they were bacteria or viruses. The primary immune system was not kicking in, therefore there was no sneezing or coughing. But the deeper immune reaction was surfacing in the form of fevers and inflammation. This was causing the weaker members of the groups to drop out.

It was noted that the body changed how it reacted to things. Most people became much more sensitive to allergens and medicines, and much more reactive to homeopathy. It was also noted by most members of the groups that the work seemed somehow to blur the boundaries of the body. This was a most bizarre situation in which a magical worker was inheriting or acquiring another person's physical symptoms: in their families, if someone was ill, the symptoms would move from the sick person to the magical worker if they were in close

---

[1] She was a DO, a doctor of osteopathy. In the USA, DOs do the usual medical training of a doctor plus extra osteopathic training. She had also completed an extra two years of cranial training.

7. THE PHYSICAL IMPLICATIONS OF PRACTISING MAGIC

proximity. The sick person would have a temporary reprieve. This was not done intentionally and in fact started to become a problem.

Using the deck, we worked out ways that this process could be blocked, but these didn't always work. We also found that you could work on one person to cause an effect in the other person, raising intriguing questions about the nature of illness and symptoms.

The initial impact upon the body seemed to be slowing of the metabolism. The body seemed to literally 'chunk up' in preparation for work, a cycle of work, or an impact.

Then an inrush of energy would accompany the work to the point where the thyroid seemed to go into overdrive. People working would experience a high level of energy, a lowered appetite, needed less sleep, would urinate more, and would be able to operate, think and process quickly. People would also have a sense of being 'hot' and/or burning, but this was not reflected in actual body temperature which stayed pretty stable.

Twenty-four hours after the working, the body's system would appear to crash. Temperature and blood pressure would drop, the person would need lots of sleep, and they would feel bruised and disorientated. They would feel cold, hungry and tired. Their hair would go dull and the person would seem to age. The reaction was as if the thyroid had slowed right down. It would take a week for the system to right itself.

Longer-term effects seemed to occur mainly in women and manifested as menstrual abnormalities, mood swings and thyroid dysfunction. The effects in people who were doing major work only two or three times a year seemed minimal, and in the longer term seemed to be beneficial. So there is also an issue of timing: space your workings out and basically do not do too much.

It was interesting to watch people over the span of fifteen years and see the long-term effects of the work and how it shifted their consciousness in a beneficial way.

Doing heavier work too many times did seem to have a chronic inflammatory effect upon the body. And people who had minor physical problems did experience a major flare-up of their conditions (asthma, IBS, etc.) if they did not approach the work correctly.

7.5. The effects of inner contact on the endocrine system

Longer-term patterns seemed to be more pronounced in women than in men. Men had a much lower reaction to the work than women did.

What I found interesting, though I have no idea how something like this could be looked at scientifically, was that people who had mental issues (depression, mental illness, OCD, etc.) did not last beyond a couple of hours into the work. They would feel physically (not mentally) sick and would often begin coughing terribly or would become nauseous.

What also became obvious, and this happened a lot, mainly to men, was that when the level of power went right up, a small number of people became emotional. Some became weepy or passive-aggressive (mainly women) and some became hostile or difficult (mainly men). Although interestingly in people with Celtic descent, the pattern seemed to reverse, which was weird and may have just been a hiccup...but that would make a fascinating study all on its own...the DNA determination about how a body reacts to power.

All of this was really interesting to observe because, after watching this a few times, I realized that they were reverting to childhood, mainly teenage patterns of behaviour, which took me back to the deck to look at the hypothalamus. Up to that point I have been looking at the thyroid, the adrenals and the thymus. When I realized that the endocrine system was freaking out in all directions I tracked it back to the hypothalamus.

The repeated picture was that as power flowed through the inner landscape and reached the body at a tissue level, it seemed to flow first through the hypothalamus which in turn affected every other gland in the body.

I treated people with a hypothalamus sarcode at 50M (when the symptoms were triggered by inner power, it needed a dose comparable with the inner power levels) level which gave a relief of symptoms temporarily but it didn't last more than a week. I also learned that the effects on the body were increased tremendously if they were thin. It would seem to put their system into freefall, with the blood pressure dropping dramatically and the thyroid then swinging from fast to slow.

If the person put on some weight, i.e. ballast, they seemed to stabilize better. The conclusion I came to was that high levels of

7. THE PHYSICAL IMPLICATIONS OF PRACTISING MAGIC

work need only be approached sparingly, like a catalyst, and then subsequent work to follow up is done at a much lower level over a longer period of a time. That way, the body gets a healthy balance and in the longer term truly benefits from the work.

7.6   The future

Magical practice is speeding up along with our culture, consciousness and cars. If we wish to really push the boundaries of the Inner Worlds beyond what has been done in the last few hundred years, then we need to make sure that our bodies are suitably prepared and up to speed for such a burden.

Magical practice and knowing when not to do magic, diet, living conditions, body types, relationships and location all play their part and I feel that we are on a threshold of some extremely interesting times (unless all the dippy New Agers have their way in which case we all go poof in 2012). If we and the next few generations get it right, we could truly push the inner boundaries in a massive leap of magical evolution. It is up to us.

It is time to move away from the psychological structure of magic that was so beloved of those who working in the early twentieth century, and revisit some of the much older (Renaissance) approaches to magic, operating in a much more holistic way that includes practical alchemy, medicine, herbalism, astronomy, theology, anatomy, science, art and music.

Some new commercial magical books/systems do touch upon such things, but often under the veil of 'hidden wisdoms and secrets,' or misinterpreted or badly paraphrased text. Getting your range of knowledge on such subjects is best achieved by studying in-depth texts written by people who are well-versed or specialized in their particular subject matter.

A magical library should have, besides all the usual magical writings, a good selection of anatomy and physiology books, homeopathic *matera medica*, extensive herbal reference books, lots of ancient history, a good bible (Douay Rheims) and apocrypha, a concordance, elemental tables, basic geology, physics and geometry reference books, archaeology, historical and classical mythology, chemical tables, music theory and a good history of art book.

This way you are able to reference and source a lot of what is written about in magic. It brings a deeper understanding about what you are actually experiencing and where that experience is coming from. Some modern commercial magical books have 'facts' within them about history, mythology, medicine, etc. that are either misunderstood or taken out of context to fit an uneducated pet theory of the writer. As a classical education becomes less and less common, it is easier for such writers to get away with that type of behaviour.

The other sin that seems to happen a lot these days is plagiarism in the form of one generation of magical writers 'lifting' work from a couple of generations ago when such writing was a little more obscure. If you are well read, there is much less chance of you being taken in by such charlatans. With modern magical writers, always check their sources and do not be afraid to respectfully challenge them on their work and expect a coherent response. If they get hostile or defensive, that should be a really good sign that something is wrong. If they say they cannot discuss it because its secret, then they are highly likely to be full of shit.

Some magical writers feel that they have to give a history or source for their work when it actually comes from an inner source that they cannot identify. This is a difficult situation for them, as most people these days want to know about lineage, masters, etc. They are tempted to make up a source and end up getting themselves in a mess. My opinion in this matter is, if it works and it is balanced, then it doesn't matter if Mickey Mouse taught it to them. It always goes back to commercialism versus free work: if it is work that is done because it is right to do it and money is not part of the equation, then the work will be done and people who want a famous line of magicians can go look in the commercial glamour department. That leaves the serious workers to get on with magic that needs doing as opposed to magic that sells.

Chapter Eight

Inner landscapes of the people and the land

When you get into the depths of a person's spirit, you trip across what is known as the 'inner landscape.' This appears in the deep consciousness of the person as a landscape which reflects their physical and spiritual health. It is not imagined by the person and often people are not aware of them, but a person's mental, spiritual and physical health can be assessed and approached using this interface with the inner person.

Similarly, when you go into an inner landscape of the land, you can often see deeper issues that are affecting the land that are not obvious on the surface. Here you begin to see parallels between the human body and the land itself: they are octaves of each other and are constantly interacting.

Why is a human landscape a 'landscape' and not a body? I have absolutely no idea. All that I know is that when you go in, it is a landscape that you come across, not an inner body. I once got into cautious discussion with an osteopathic doctor about seeing this 'landscape' in a young person I had been working on.

In the USA, osteopaths are fully qualified doctors trained in hospitals/universities. I nearly fell over when she said that she had also seen such a thing and worked with it regularly in the course of her practice as a cranial osteopath.

When I first discovered the inner landscape, it was totally by accident, and happened while I was working on someone using vision. I saw a door in the brain and had to go in to see what was there. I found myself in a room full of boxes and filing cabinets, with piles of papers, bags and general mess. I started to clean it up and let some

8. Inner landscapes of the people and the land

light in through the window. The chaos in this place reflected the character of the person I was working on.

A month later, I was working on them again and when I went back into this room that I had found, I saw grass trying to grow through the concrete floor and trees trying to get in the window. I figured that nature was probably better for a body, so I tore down the building and let nature in. A few weeks later when I went in, I found sparse, harsh moorland and a cold wind. The person I was working on was someone with heavy mental problems who was a sociopath. The work was having a curious effect, and the person began to get urges to spend more time out in nature, which I took to be a good thing.

So I became a landscape junkie and had to look at everyone's and anyone's. The next foray into a landscape was on a young girl with growth issues. When I got into her landscape I found a beautiful meadow, a river and lots of pretty flowers. But in the corner was a dark place where nothing grew, and there was a little girl huddled into the corner weeping. I was horrified by the pain this child carried.

I gently picked her up and laid her in the meadow with all the flowers, and then I went back to the dark place to try and lighten it. I could not trigger any change, so I bricked it up and planted roses around the wall so that the darkness could not come back. While I was doing this vision, the young girl whom I was treating, who was partially asleep, began to cry. I didn't wake her, but let her weep while I worked.

The effect was amazing: her growth issue suddenly wasn't an issue and she made major leaps both physically and mentally in the following months. I realized that what I was working with was powerful, it worked, and I needed to know more about it. I discovered that the weather in the landscape often reflected the short-term health of the immune system: if it was storming, then chances are they were about to come down with a virus.

If there were emotional problems, it would often show by overgrowth or lack of foliage, and if there were mental (i.e. chemical) problems, it would show by the appearance of man-made structures. Magical and psychic attacks showed by beings wandering around the landscape, or the appearance of shapes like Platonic solids. I was fascinated and worked hard taking things out, gardening, weather watching, etc. on anyone I worked on.

But after a couple of years of doing this work I began to notice something about the people I had worked on. When I got close to them, I got a feeling that I had intruded on something that was not supposed to be intruded upon.

I began to look deeper at these people from a magical sense and I began to realize that by dealing with major issues in their landscape, I had trodden their learning path for them: I had preempted the fate lessons they needed to tackle for themselves. Remember the sociopath with the filing cabinets? I now know, years later, that those files and boxes were blocking and containing unhealthy power so that the person could not access them. Reawakening the harsh landscape gave them access to a dark power, which they went onto wield mercilessly and aggressively. Their inner landscape had cluttered up and isolated that power until that person was ready to face it themselves. I had stupidly and arrogantly sidestepped a natural process.

There were only a few instances where I got a strong sense that I had stepped in and worked where someone was just too exhausted to deal with something: this was usually where they had been magically attacked by someone and were not able to cope with it.

In those instances I learned a great deal about magical attacks and what they looked like from an inner point of view. I was looking at them from an inner angle that I hadn't perceived before. It looked different from the 'inner' sight of the attack I was used to looking at. I then realized I was seeing the attack in its 'backroom' sense: I was seeing the actual construction behind the frontage, the nuts and bolts of the creation. This in turn gave me far more information that I needed to dismantle such attacks.

I learned eventually that if the landscape was not being affected by magic, but by illness, fate or a natural process, not to plough in and change it, but to stand, observe, and learn what I could from what I saw. It seemed okay to occasionally talk to the person in their landscape, to offer advice but not to take action. It gave me a much deeper insight to the person's issues, illnesses and mental states. It

8. INNER LANDSCAPES OF THE PEOPLE AND THE LAND

also told me a great deal about their spirituality: their soul was often reflected in the flowers.

Many things appeared in the landscape before they appeared in the body or mind, so it became a good indicator of what was coming and what needed to be addressed by the person. When the person tackled their issues themselves, the landscape changed and matured in a grounded, permanent way which was much healthier than having it changed by someone else. When an outside influence changed the landscape, it often obviated certain processes that were important for the person and therefore the change effected was temporary or incomplete.

Things that were wrapped over with vines were viruses, issues or parasites that the body had put into storage until it was ready to work on them and eject them. When I saw this I realized that the inner and outer immune system had to mature properly themselves so that they could strengthen. If I dragged off the viruses/parasites etc., the inner immune system was not dealing with them and therefore was not gaining experience and strength. It was like watching the effects of unnecessary vaccination.

One of the few occasions that can justify an intervention in the landscape is a full blown possession, which is almost impossible for the person themselves to deal with. Once the being has been removed, then the victim can keep an eye on their own landscape. What can make it so difficult for someone to get rid of a possession themselves is that the being will often begin integrating into the landscape itself and will no longer appear as a being at all. Everything you look at is probably a part of the being: that is a major job and as such is best left to an experienced exorcist.

The land also has an inner landscape, and the true health of the land, its power places, its illnesses and its issues can be identified by looking at its inner self. I really didn't think about this until I got back to the land of Britain after living abroad for eleven years. The land where I was born reacted the minute I landed and I felt its strengths, weaknesses and illnesses through my feet.

I felt really bad for having left the land for so long and made my mind up then and there to do what I could for the land as an apology. I began to look at the land in a deeper sense which showed the many areas of work that were needed. It also showed me the areas and realms where other people were already working or had been working for a long time. I looked closely at what was being done to see what I could learn and I watched how the land reacted to such work.

What I found truly fascinating was something I fell across just recently. I was walking across the Desert away from the Abyss in a magical vision when I saw cocoons on either side of me. Angelic beings and other strange creatures were bound up upon the land and looked strange indeed.

I asked the being I was walking with what these cocoons were and they replied that they were beings that had no place in the land at present because they were so destructive. When I came out of the vision, I later went to look at the land of Britain to see if those cocoons were simply in the inner realms, or if they were mirrored upon the land itself.

Sure enough there were beings trapped in rocks, in the roots of ancient trees, in bogs etc., and they were the same beings that I had seen near the Abyss. Then it occurred to me that the land worked upon the same mechanism as the human body: when invaded by a destructive consciousness, the immune system isolated and then bound that consciousness until it could be safely dealt with. It was fascinating!

I then started to look at the inner structure of the land in areas where there were buildings. To my amazement, some of the buildings appeared and some didn't. The ones that appeared had been there for hundreds and hundreds of years, but more recent buildings did not appear at all.

So then I looked at the land where my house is and some of the local houses appeared (some date back to the twelfth century) but mine didn't. Certain things began to make sense. I live on the side of a wild hill with ancient forest up above me and springs all around me. Living in the house sometimes is busy: many beings saunter through our house as if we didn't exist.

When I looked at the house from an inner point of view, it didn't appear: we were not in the inner landscape as the house was too modern so beings just didn't see us. They could probably feel us as

8. Inner Landscapes of the People and the Land

they passed through the ancient forest, but they would not be able to figure out what they were feeling. So we were/are a main thoroughfare for all and sundry. The answer to this is to work in vision to build the house on the inner landscape so that we appear to all the beings tripping back and forth through the woods. First though, I have to figure out what effect that will have on the land in general before I make any more booboos.

But it does make for interesting thinking about what effect the houses have on the inner landscape when they do appear. Does it make it easier for the land to cope with such intrusion if it has incorporated it into its own pattern? Or does it ultimately lead to an imbalance that will express itself though the way the land lives and breathes?

What I think is important is to be at least aware of the overlays, imprints and changes that buildings, magical patterns and religious structures have on the living, breathing land and what we can do as a part of that intrusion to lessen the impact and restore what we can to a more natural state.

It also begins to raise questions regarding magical work that has been done over the years to affect the land in Britain in one way or another: the British Israelites are renowned for the amount of work they have done over the years to affect the land of Britain to suit their religious and political agenda. Similarly going back through time the Freemasons, the Golden Dawn, and way before that, the Normans and the Romans have all done their dirty work to affect the land in one way or another.

Similarly it also begins to raise questions about our own landscapes: how much does our magical and spiritual work affect the inner landscape, and is it really for the better?

8.1 Energetic load-sharing: a short look

The idea that we as beings are separate from each other is a misconception that feeds, among other things, a sense of helplessness and spiritual emptiness. Energetically, power is constantly flowing back and forth between people, the creatures around us and the land.

8.1. Energetic load-sharing: a short look

It is part of the communal soul and is the strength that drives the 'power in numbers.'

But our modern day culture has no place for such a 'truth': We have no words for it and we are discouraged from talking about it in general. And yet it is something that affects every sensitive person on a daily basis. If you are a magical worker, then the effect is massively amplified and can cause all sorts of problems.

Rather than talk about human energy boundaries in general, which is another subject all of its own, I want to focus in on the act of energetic 'load-sharing,' both conscious and unconscious.

Historically, this was one of the many uses of the storyteller or bard. The bard would go from place to place and recount tales of great acts of courage, battles with humans and non-humans, terrible tragedies, great joys and wondrous happenings. People would listen to these tales and be entranced, they would cry at the sad bits, be angry at the unfair or cruel bits, and be silent and still at the tragedies.

On an inner level, when people shed tears for the sorrow of others, the suffering of the original victim was shared by those who wept: the load became spread out. This way, the suffering of the individual was never more than they could bear. The more the story was told, the less was the burden on the victim's soul. And if the story was told repeatedly down the ages, then any terrible suffering became watered right down and the soul of the original victim could flow into and beyond death without the burden of pain.

This ensured that suffering was never allowed to impact an individual to the point that it would damage them permanently, and that the suffering would not become ingrained in the generations of their family: it kept the generations clear. Suffering was a group affair and was dealt with without the risk of lingering genetic damage. None of this was thought about consciously by the people, it was just the way things were done.

This method of load-sharing still survives today in various tribal cultures and in some of the Roma tribes around Europe. It is one of the reasons why people from these cultures will ask about the truth of a story or the root of a story. If a story makes a person cry, they want to know that their tears are going to the right place. If you cry

8. INNER LANDSCAPES OF THE PEOPLE AND THE LAND

at a story or film that is total fiction, where is the energy of those tears going?

Fragments of this instinctive behaviour survive in today's modern culture by the unconscious act of holding the hand of a dying person: it is not only about the reassurance of touch. Dying takes a great deal of energy and sometimes, in a slow and difficult death, the sufferer might not have enough energy to die. So the family sits around and takes turns to touch or hold the hand of the person dying: their energy is feeding the journey.

Babies, toddlers, old people, sick people, unbalanced people, all of these groups have a greater need for energy, and in the normal world they would be living in a multigenerational extended family/community where the load of energy that they need would be available to them, and the impact from providing that energy would not be too great for any one family member.

These days, such structures of family are almost gone and the burden of providing energy can fall upon one person.

Another and greater example of this load-sharing, at the other extreme, is the marriage between sovereign and the land: this is the basis for sacred kingship/queenship. Upon being consecrated as sovereign of the land, the energy of the land and the human become intertwined. The health of the land is echoed in the health of the king/queen and *vice versa*. If the sovereign becomes unbalanced, so will the land. The reverse also applies: if the land is imbalanced, so would be the sovereign. The job of the sovereign, in such a case, was to bring their body back into balance to rebalance the land. If they could not do that, then they would be sacrificed.

This was one of the reasons why the sovereign was held to such vows of marital honour, self-sacrifice, etc.: they had to be cleaner than clean. That way, they stayed in balance and so did the land. Whoever thought that one up obviously wasn't that in touch with humanity.

In today's world, sensitive people still engage in load-sharing, often without realizing. When a powerful event is about to happen that will have a lasting impact on society or the land, people often become tired and sleepy: they are giving up their energy for it to be used in the pattern that is being woven by fate.

8.1. Energetic load-sharing: a short look

Magically, this innate human ability to load-share is often taken advantage of by unscrupulous magicians, teachers, and leaders who literally feed off of their followers or students to fuel themselves or their magical agendas. This has become more common in the last few decades with the rise in 'guru' culture. It is also an energetic system used by churches and other religious organizations. Once you become a part of that organization, your energy becomes fair game to feed whatever being, egregore or structure is behind it all.

There is a positive side to such magical load-sharing, though. Some groups commit their energy through service to the land and the sacred places. Druid groups in particular who tend the sacred sites often become deeply connected to the land and their energies become entwined with the sacred places. To the sensitive person, it often means that they become deeply connected to a, and they can often feel if it is being abused or misused in any way: they become a communal part of the land itself.

I think that just having an awareness of such energy dynamics helps our bodies to field unhealthy or imbalanced situations, and that awareness also allows us to make informed commitments with our energy to the land, family, and community that we serve.

Chapter Nine

Magical protection: working methods

When people get seriously involved in a magical group, one of the first things they learn is how to protect themselves magically. After a while it becomes tempting for the magical student to cover themselves in protection at all times. They conduct the lesser banishing ritual of the pentagram and festoon themselves with protective talismans. This is of no help whatsoever if you truly want to progress into the depths of magic and experience what is truly out there. It is like sex with twenty thick condoms on.

The lesser banishing ritual of the pentagram is the most commonly used protection ritual in ritual magic. Its popularity dates back to the original Golden Dawn and is a good example of their clunky and overstructured approach to ritual magic. It was and is overused and ends up defeating the purpose of the work the magician is trying to embark upon. To do this ritual before a major working is essentially wiping out all the inner preparations that are going on in the Inner Worlds to meet and connect with your work.

So why and when do we need protection?

If your work is clear, your working space is properly maintained and you have good working practice methods, then there is no need for protection. Modern magicians in general are heavily overprotected and then they wonder why they cannot connect easily to beings in the Inner Worlds.

In the hospitals of days past, we used to wash our hands all the time, cover our mouths when we sneezed or coughed, burn infected waste and keep the area clean and tidy. Since the cutbacks in training and overuse of antibiotics, we don't bother with any of that so much. As a result, we have lots of resistant hospital infections. The same goes for magic: too much protection and too little practical experience ends up with vulnerable people who are likely at some

9. MAGICAL PROTECTION: WORKING METHODS

point in their work to come up against a real nasty and not be able to deal with it. It will brush your banishing ritual to one side like dust and then do as it will with you.

If you are constantly protected when you work, you are not learning to deal with minor nasties as they come along and you are not building skills, strengths and understanding of the more unsavoury side of the Inner Worlds. With these skills, strengths and understanding, you would be able to deal with most nasties that are put in your path. You will also begin to understand which banishings work easily and quickly, and which ones take time and too many tools.

Magical work should be approached in a clear way, with clear intent, good knowledge of what you are doing and in tandem with the right powers for the job. In such a setting you do not need protections: it is built automatically into the work you are doing.

Everyday magical rituals really do not need sealed spaces, banishments, etc. Far from it: the magician should be trained to work anywhere, at any time, with no tools or dressing. The natural protection comes from knowing what you are doing, where you are going and having good reasons for doing what you are doing. That way, all the natural structures, patterns and beings are there for you to work with and are not blocked by talismans or banishments. How could you possibly expect an inner contact to come and work in your space if you have sealed it, done a banishment and react immediately if some being does turn up?

I am not saying that you will never need these skills: you most likely will, quite a few times, but they should not be a daily part of your magical practice. And the regular wearing of a magical talisman for protection will create a weakness in you that will make it hard for you to function without one on.

9.1 So when do you use banishing and talismans?

Banishings are only to be used when something comes into your space and you have tried all other ways to get it to go. The first thing to do is not to react when a being moves into your space. Initially you need to find out what it is. Is it a parasite? Is it a dead person?

9.1. So when do you use banishing and talismans?

Is it an inner contact trying to work with you? Is it a nature being drawn to you by the magic it can see? Is it a lesser demonic type of being that you have inadvertently allowed into your space by playing around with portholes that you don't understand?

Once you have found out what it is, then you can ask it to leave, show it the way out, and give it a chance to go of its own accord. You can tell it (nicely) what will happen to it if it doesn't. If it chooses not to go, then you tell it to piss off. If it still doesn't go, then it is time to get rid of it. There are a few ways of doing this. The lesser banishing ritual of the pentagram does work, but it is clunky, time-consuming and needs tools. The other important thing to think about with a straightforward banishing is where are you banishing it to? It needs to simply go back where it belongs. It may have been called into this realm by other magicians and not know how to get back.

Some old Christianized versions of ritual space banishment and cleansings can be adjusted to work (Dion Fortune used a variant of this) using salt and water. Then there are visionary ways of taking the buggers out. I prefer this method, as it is more fun. I go in vision, give it one more chance and open a porthole for it. If it doesn't go I get a good hold of it by the scruff of the neck and take it to the Abyss where it is unceremoniously dumped back to where it came from. If it is a largish or powerful being, I call in angelic help, or dragon-based help.

Before I do any of this, I tune into a state that I meditate on regularly which is an expansion of the soul beyond the body: I regularly work on stretching out in all directions, becoming the boundary-less being that we are in our full glory: it makes it bloody hard to get a hold of someone if they have no ends.

If it is a really powerful nasty or a demonic being, then it is a good idea to work with angelic beings: they are really into putting these dudes back in the Abyss and they uphold your body to stop it getting impacted or intruded upon. But always make sure first that you fully understand why those beings are in your space and what drew them there. Just because a power is demonic does not mean it is 'bad': it might be doing a necessary job, in which case you ask it to go do it somewhere else because you are busy (and demons always make a mess on the carpet). These sorts of powers are incredibly

9. Magical protection: working methods

clever and intelligent, and are good at manipulating you around to their way of thinking: this is where you learn to be unemotional and unresponsive to bargaining.

Talismans are usually needed if you are not experienced at dealing with heavy beings and are going to a place that might be infested with them. By place I mean in the physical realm. If you are inexperienced in inner work, then you should not be going into dangerous inner places. Dangerous outer places are bad enough.

Talismans are good for kids, pregnant women, old people and sick people once they have been stripped of inner goo (talismans not only seal things from coming in, they also stop things getting out). Using talismans if you are a magician tends to weaken you and overprotect you. It is best to use them if you are doing nasty dangerous work and you are slightly ill.

Talismans are best homemade: ones that are sold in magic shops are a fancy waste of time. It doesn't need to look like anything: you can use virtually anything to make a talisman, but stone and metal hold the magic the best: it is what you put into it that is powerful. The ritualized sigil talismans are okay, but they are limited for today's world of magic: they were designed for a world that no longer exists and they are also created in a generic outer way with no inner content. The only way something like this will protect you from 'a heavy' is if it is interesting and the demon stops chewing on your head to have a closer look at the shiny pretty talisman.

To make a talisman is simple but takes focus and energy. There are many different ways to make them and many different powers that you can use to fuel them, but think carefully about what power you use. If you use a deity, then you might be in for more than you bargained for: if you wear the protection of a deity, it will expect you at some point to dedicate yourself to them, or at least do something major for them which might not be in keeping with your lifestyle.

If you use faery powers then you are truly nuts: they are conditional beings and they have a wicked sense of humor which is often at your expense. I wouldn't trust them to protect anything: its not that they will not do a good job, it's the other mischief they get up to in the meantime.

You can use angelic powers but be clear about what you are using: know your angels and don't overdo it as most are extremely powerful and are likely to blow you up. You need to work with one that specializes in protection and guardianship.

The other option is to work with inner contacts that you have and that are used to working with you. You can work around the directions, asking a contact in each direction to put something into the talisman to give you whatever protection you need. It is better for them to decide what protection you need, because if you specify things for them, then there is a chance that you will have missed something.

Before you work on your talisman, put it in salt to strip it. Work with the beings/contact to put the power in by letting them work through your hands: place your hand over the talisman as you work in vision or ritual with the contacts.

Afterwards put the talisman on and leave it on, don't take it off to shower, etc. They tend to run off of your body power so if you do not have it on, then it will power down. When it has done its job it will fall off, break or explode (which can be quite spectacular and impressive). In general though, it is better to build up your own inner immune system and get strong.

9.2 House protection

The issue of house protection can get interesting. The usual form for a magician is to have the house sealed so tight that a cat's fart cannot get through the protection. Living in such a protected environment is often not too healthy and can end up counterproductive.

My house is usually like grand central station: beings are coming and going all the time, dropping in to connect with me, coming for help, for sanctuary or to just rest a while. It is interesting to note that in Buddhist culture, the temples have wind chimes on their porches to attract ghosts at night: they draw the spirits to a friendly place of rest at night. So I scratch my head when I see people with wind chimes outside their homes...

When a magical home is kept clean and balanced, and you work as a priest/ess to all beings, then there really is no need to seal your

9. Magical protection: working methods

home. If they all get too much for me I just tell them all to piss off for a while and leave me alone. It is also interesting that if an inner intruder with bad intent comes near, the other beings will tell me so that I can watch the intruders, find out where they have come from and why, and then dispatch them promptly.

It doesn't hurt to have a spirit guardian outside the home, but just make sure that they allow in any being that is coming to you for help or sanctuary. We have some great ancient guardian beings that are native to Dartmoor so I just drop them a nod every so often and they keep an eye on the house.

This approach also gets you used to not reacting so much to intrusions, attacks, etc. If you are used to beings coming and going from your home and then one with a nasty intention comes along, instead of being repelled it is allowed to wander around a little so that you can study it and figure out what it is about and why. That way you get to know an awful lot more about people's intentions towards you and what their strengths and weaknesses are. If the baddie sent to you is not a construct (thought form) but a being, then you can often ask it (with bribery) who sent it and why.

If it is a thought form or golem, by observing it closely it will tell you a great deal about the person who constructed it, and what their weaknesses, strengths, etc. are: it is a part of their mind so you can use it to look closely at them. Golems as inner constructs only work on the victim when they do not understand how the sacred lettering of Hebrew works in magic.

The best way to avoid the regular use of protection is to have healthy, powerful and knowledgeable ways of working: even at a beginner phase, clarity works much better than protection. It is also important to have a healthy body. Like the outer immune system, the inner immune system needs to be strong and healthy: look after yourself inwardly and outwardly. Eat well, use herbs and resins burning around the house to keep it clean, use salt after doing readings to clean your hands, and put a bowl of salt in a room after a lot of magical work: it soaks up any magical residue.

Most of all, use your common sense. Don't invite weird beings into your home, don't wander into unhealthy inner or outer places, and don't indulge in parasite-infested pastimes: don't swim in cesspits

9.2. House protection

and then wonder why you are a mess. A cesspit is any unbalanced magical system: books, teachings, biographies, etc. of unhealthy, parasitical or downright silly or nasty magical things.

The other main caution is: if you do magic at home, don't sit down and watch any exorcist movies that are based upon the real records, diaries, etc. of someone. There is a good chance that the original being, if portrayed well enough, can come through the movie and hook into you. The recreation of a real event can sometimes act like a doorway for the original being to pass through: it's like a passive form of invocation (as I found out...ouch!). No amount of protection would have stopped that. And it is bloody hard to pull a rabid demon out of yourself with no help. (Don't want to go through *that* again...)

The best protection of all is to use your common sense and some really awful perfume.

Chapter Ten

Sigils and seals

What they are, how they work and what to do with them

When you begin the study of magic, the first thing that smacks you between the eyes is the massive array of bizarre signs, weird shapes and alien texts.

When people first begin to work with signs and sigils, they often misunderstand what these signs are and how they work: they assume, in our fine modern world of psychology, that the signs/sigils stand for something or represent something. Wrong. That is not what they do and that is a bad way to start to try and work with them (can you see the wagging finger?): if you assume it stands for something because of its shape etc., then it will not work for you.

Sigils and seals once formed, become their own consciousness: they are beings within their own right. They are fragments of the power that they come from and they can work as a part of the hive being. So for example, if you work with an order of being that is powerful, and then later you want to work again with that same quality of power, but without the full-on nuclear power hit, then you would work with the sigil of that being in vision or in ritual: a fragment of it. The other way of working with these fragments is to string a few of them together so that they work in harmony and join their powers to create a specific form of magic, usually protective. Just make sure that the powers that you weave together get on: war raging will not a powerful pentacle make!

10.1 Angelic and demonic sigils

The sigil of an angel or a demon is like a fragment of their power, and also a key to their power when used correctly. When you want

10. SIGILS AND SEALS

to work with an angelic or demonic being, first you need its name or its sigil to bridge to this being. There are three basic ways to do this type of work: either you bring them to you, or you go to them, or you bridge them into something through the sigil or name.

The thing to remember, regardless of which way you go, is that these powers are not a joke: they will kill without thought and they will bring destruction down upon you if you prompt them to: you have to choose your words clearly. Doing a rite in a strange language like Hebrew or Latin might summon Metatron, but you might also order a pizza or a hit on your neighbour by mispronouncing what you are saying!

If you use the sigils to ritually bring the angel/demon to you, then be prepared to use a lot of energy, mess your room up and have fleeting contact. It's not an efficient way to work as you never get enough time to actually do anything, and the energy it takes to bridge that being into your world is not eco-conscious! And if you are successful and they decide they like it here and you did not attend your sigils correctly, they may decide not to go. Hmm, that could be a problem.

The second method is to go to them using the sigil. To do this you work in vision and use the sigil as a guide: you descend or ascend the Abyss or pass through the Void using the sigil as a key and a guide. When you are at the right area, the sigil will appear on the walls, or the one you are holding will glow. It is safer to commune with these beings and ask them to help you in their own realm and in their own form: they are not being squeezed into a human realm, which is not comfortable for them, so they are less likely to be pissy if you go to them.

This works well, the work does manifest out into the outer world and they operate at their own power level because they are on home turf. The problem is your ability to hold it together in the depths or heights of the Abyss. It takes a lot of energy (all angelic and demonic work will whack you one way or another: just find the least exhausting method) and it is more dangerous. You will have to know how to protect yourself without blocking your ability to work, usually by working with other beings, and will need to navigate yourself around without being distracted or glamoured. Once you find the area with

10.1. Angelic and demonic sigils

the corresponding sigil, you make your connection with the being, sort out the task that drew you there in the first place, and then get out.

The third method, which doesn't work for everything, but does work well in some circumstances, is the pure use of the sigil. This is where you need to know the power levels of these beings, and be clear about what you need from them. If you are simply looking for their protection or their power to seal something, for example, then you would just use the sigil. The sigil itself holds the power of that being and allows you to draw a little upon it: it is like a mini-me. So if you are after sealing or protection, simply use the sigil on whatever needs protecting or sealing.

There is no fancy drama, ritual or anything else involved: just draw the sigil and it works. All the dressing is usually there either to look good, or because someone doesn't know that it is dressing. Most magic that we use today goes back to the sixteenth century and they were massive drama queens in those days: the more Mysterious it looked the more awe people held the magician in. I'm from Yorkshire, so I'm not into all that shit.

To work with demons or angels their sigils or names are important as part of the working tools, and they must be used correctly for it all to work. Just make sure you have a good reason to work with such beings and that you are fully aware of what they are and what they do. Luckily if you don't know what you are doing, it tends not to work, so stupidity can be a saving grace sometimes. If you are attracted as I am to red buttons, then I can tell you from burned experience: if you want to work directly with one of these beings, do your homework, do your inner workouts, and move thoughtfully and carefully.

Angels are just as dangerous as demons and demons can be just as helpful as angels: just make sure you know their job description! If you are still at the baby phase of wanting to use magic to get a big car or a big willy, or to smite the neighbours/ex-wife/boss, I would suggest you do not use these beings: you may be in for a major learning curve if you do.

Most common reasons to work with such beings is either in a war situation, i.e. world war: a good example of such work was Dion

10. SIGILS AND SEALS

Fortune and her Battle of Britain. It burned her body out and killed her, but she stopped the German magical elite from repeating the success of Claudius when he used Etruscan Apulu magic to conquer Britain (which he did successfully).

Other sensible reasons for working with such beings would be for major exorcism, working on a seriously magically bound or pinned land, to build or destroy a temple, etc. Big jobs, they are big job dudes: they will most certainly not tend your garden for you: that's a faery job.

10.2 Deity sigils

Divine sigils work in a similar way to angelic/demonic sigils: they are fragments of the original power: they are not representations of anything. They can be the source of endless hours of entertainment: watching someone trying to 'unlock' the key and discover what the sign really means can be good fun: maybe humans are just becoming too cerebral.

So you would use the sigil to mark things for example that need the protection of that deity, or belong to that deity. They can also be used as inner keys to get into places, a little like a VIP pass. They only work this way if you are given the sigil by the deity as opposed to looking it up in a book or off a statue. When you work with deities in vision they begin to interact strongly with you, and may offer you a sigil key that opens many inner doors for you so that you can go about your work. If the sigil is used in service for that deity, then it often develops into a priesthood mark that people who are priest/esses of that deity will have upon them. These marks appear upon the inner body of the person so that anyone with sight can see it. Other people who also bear that sigil will see it and recognize you.

Sometimes the sigil will have a shape correspondence to the deity, but most often it doesn't. The most famous magical sigil that corresponds to deity is the pentagram: the five pointed star. It has had many uses down the ages and is now an image used by a wide variety of pagans. It has an old and deep connection to the Underworld through its Sumerian usage: it was used as a pictogram to represent the Sumerian word Ub which meant cavity or hole. This is remarkably similar to the British Goddess Sul: Sul is an old Celtic word for hole, eye or gap and Sul is a goddess of the Underworld, of cursing and curse lifting.

So in that context, the pentagram could be used to access ancient Underworld deities along with all the other usage it has had over the years. It has been known to occasionally open the minds of sullen Nintendo teens who suddenly discover a world of rebellion, symbology and the hope of wild sex.

Deity sigils can be used in conjunction together to create a harmonic in physical manifestation. Using deity sigils from deities that are in harmony with each other is an age-old method, for example a pattern of the world by using deities from the directions and seasons. Once the pattern is created and the sigils in place, then the whole thing can be used to weave land magic by weaving the powers of the various deities together and keeping them in harmony.

Deity sigils can also be used to enliven a piece of land and infuse it with the power of that deity. A remnant of this is the use of corn dollies at planting. Drawing or etching out the sigil over a piece of land will bring the power of that deity right out into the land, which is maybe the source reasoning of the Cerne man and the white horses.

If you work with one deity and you use their sigil a lot, just make sure that you are doing it for the right reasons, i.e. because you have dedicated yourself to that deity for a span of time or for life. If you blindly mess about with deity symbols because it looks cool, then there will come a time when you become bored or the fashion changes. You will want to move on but deities are not that keen at being tossed aside so easily and can become pissed off or even vengeful. So if you decide to deck yourself with a certain deity sigil, make sure it is for a finite length of time and be aware of what you are wearing and why.

10.3 Magical seals

Magical seals, like the impressive ones used by eighteenth and nineteenth-century magical groups, are and were used for a wide variety of good and bad intentions. The use of magical seals stretches back far in to antiquity, to the world of ancient Sumer, Egypt and

10. SIGILS AND SEALS

Mesopotamia. Magically they were mainly used for protection, to seal something into a container, or to keep beings out of a building or area. They were used upon thresholds to affect the person who crossed them, and they were used around the neck to protect the body from invasion and impact.

Today's usage is more or less the same. The magical seals are made up of a 'sentence' of angelic/demonic sigils combined with sacred text and sometimes a deity sigil. The 'sentence' would sometimes be encased in an overall sign to contain it and pressurize it (i.e. make it more powerful and stop it being messed with). An ancient and impressive version of the use of magical seals is the Babylonian demon bowls which are vessels covered in script and glued together with pitch. Inside is often eggshell, human skull or bone with sigils and script upon it. This is a demon 'prison,' a trap in which a demonic entity has been trapped and sealed. The sigils and script around the bowl would encase the demon and stop it escaping.

The use of early sacred script or alphabet was deliberate: for example the letters of the Hebrew alphabet are considered by some to be expressions of G-D, they are sacred sigils which have the potential to bring through power themselves. That is to say that the letter itself has its own power. It is not dependent on anyone using it in a certain way to make it magical: it is magical itself. It is a part of an ancient movement of the magical power of air, of utterance, and remnants of that ancient Mystery still survive to this day in the form of the religions of the book and the word. So when you start to string these sacred letters together to form words combined with sigils, you are getting into some ancient and powerful working methods.

When you recite the letters as sounds, or write them as shapes, you are mediating a power of Divinity: a potent form of magic. If you use such magic without the deeper understanding, it will work if pronounced exactly right, but its true expression will evade you and the mediating of such power without understanding will eventually take its toll upon the body (ever noticed that non-Jewish Kabbalists who do heavy ritual nearly always end up fat?)

Such magical sealing is still in use today, although personally I find it easier to take demons back home and deposit them where they belong rather than end up with a house full of containers that some idiot could open one day.

In modern magic, seals are most often used as protection. The wisdom of the constant use of protection is debatable but the seals do work when done properly using the right powers. It is best to use them when you have to do heavy magic and you are under the weather or under a major attack. The seals can be used as a wearable amulet: it can be drawn upon an object or marked out over an area.

Large magical seals are used in certain branches of magic to keep out spirits while the magician works. The seal would be marked out upon the floor or on the altar and it would keep out any beings other than the one being summoned.

One of the oldest magical seals seen around the British Isles is the swirls that cover some of the Neolithic tombs, stones and chambers. The swirl or series of interlocking swirls are extremely effective at sealing in power and trapping solar (sun temple) power. If the swirls are on the inside of the container, they will trap whatever is in there: the whole surface needs to be covered in interlocking swirls. If the swirls are on the outside and are shiny, then they will draw the being or power to them and the being gets trapped in the endless patterns as though mesmerized.

One of the dangers of magical seals is that life can become too comfortable and safe with them if they are used too many times for everything that you do. It is best to keep them for sealing in things that need to not see the light of day ever: it will guard something for you so that you can get on with your work.

An important factor in the decision to use seals that must be considered is the human energy cost. When you draw a seal or sigil for magical use with a specific intention, the seal draws upon your energy stores to 'power' itself. If you use lots of seals and sigils for trapping, drawing, whatever, then you are going to get drained after a while.

The other danger that can happen from the overuse of magical symbols is that you never get to learn to deal with all the various beings that are in the Inner Worlds. If you are so heavily protected that nothing can ever get near you, then you will end up never knowing any Inner World beings. This is a sad byproduct of the

10. Sigils and seals

middle ages: people were and still are controlled by fear, and that paranoia of vulnerability seeped into magic as well as everything else in people's lives.

Our culture and the insidious effect of the church upon our consciousness breeds a fear of the unknown, of the Inner Worlds and all the beings therein. Most young magicians start from a standpoint of fear, and the magic develops out of that standpoint, hence the proliferation of amulets, protective pentacles and magical seals.

Like all magic, used sensibly in context magical protection is powerful, but it must be used from a place of knowledge and calm, not curiosity and fear. That way, you don't spend all your energy casting circles and summoning demons, only to freak out and banish them as soon as they appear: demons get confused if you do this and it gives the rest of us a bad name.

10.4 Platonic solids and geometric shapes

Magic is like a science: it is about learning how the universe works, what particles, powers and energies do, and it is about the realization that magic works like a mathematical poem. It is logical, it makes sense and it is a natural part of the universe. Physics and magic are basically the same thing with different names: they both work with and are aware of the powers that flow through space, and they are both littered with workers who are maladjusted. Some of the most interesting magical conversations I have ever had have been with particle physicists: but then, some of the most unintelligent dogmatic and down right stupid discussions I have ever had have also been with physicists: so I guess science and magic really are two sides of the same coin.

Platonic solids and geometric shapes often appear in magic simply because they are a natural part of our world. They are the purest form of a power expression in harmony with itself and when a being appears to you as a Platonic solid you know you have reached one of its deepest and most powerful forms. When the angel of death and destruction appears before you as a cube, you know you are in for a bit of a bumpy ride.

10.4. Platonic solids and geometric shapes

The forms that beings take to appear to us, i.e. wings, eyes, swords, teeth, fire, etc. is their way of talking slowly to us: they play down their size, cool their power and dress up from images in our cultural imagination so that we can interact with them and understand what they are about. If an angelic being appeared before you as a cube, you would blink and scratch your head before finding yourself fried to a crisp. If an angelic being appeared before you with a flaming sword, fancy armour, nice hairdo, big wings and a cheesy grin, then you know that the angel is really downplaying it for the ants (or it is a parasite dressing up for you).

The more you work the Abyss, the thresholds and the Void, the more you will begin to see that the Inner Worlds are like a conversation of pure form, of harmony, shapes, sounds and energy. The beings with faces, wings, horns, etc. are just our feeble way of trying to understand the enormity of that which is all around us.

So back to Platonic solids: if you see one in vision then chances are you are hitting an angel full on, or something connected with angels: Platonic solids or geometric shapes are often used as angelic sigils. If the angel appears to you in that form, then chances are it is safe for you if you can communicate at a level which uses no imagination or emotion: angels are really like Asperger's physicists. You will have to communicate in mathematics, physics and logic.

If you cannot communicate in that form, then it is best not to call them in that form: having a premenstrual emotional artist in the flows of power outputting, standing before a confused cube, is rather entertaining.

But those forms can be used to bring in that power to use at a impersonal level, so if you work that way it is usually in temple construction or a similar practical job. An ancient example of this is the Ka'ba: a perfect cube temple that stands at the centre of an ancient power site. Today it is the spiritual centre of the Islamic faith but before that time it was already an ancient structure that housed many deities.

Its legend is that it was built by Adam to the heavenly specifications of the Angels. It works in a specific way to do with utterance and the magical power of breath/sound, and the myth states that it was built to house paradise on earth. It is a balanced harmonic form that mediates a pure power of air into the consciousness of humanity for us to work with: how much closer to paradise can we get?

When you think of geometric shapes in this context, and then you go back to the seals of Solomon and look closely, you can begin to see what people were reaching for. Just like all other sigils, they are powerful when used a certain way, but every shape must be exact and in the right combination, and used with the knowledge to unlock them.

10.5 Mandalas

Mandalas can become interesting tools simply from a learning point of view and although they don't really have much to do with western magic, I have come across a couple of things that are worth mentioning just because they can be converted for use. (I'm all into inner recycling: it saves time and mess to learn from others.)

A few years ago I was living in California and teaching in an art centre. In the rooms opposite me a small group of Tibetan monks were working away at building a mandala to cleanse the area over a series of days. I was fascinated and wanted to know what it was all about. I was fobbed off by the only English-speaking one who told me about creating pretty patterns to bring peace and then destroying them because nothing was permanent. I wasn't buying it: I could feel all sorts of powerful things going on in my backyard and I wanted to know what these people were doing.

So at the end of my class each day, I would go and sit in meditation where they were working and watch on the inner what they were doing. Only one of them, the eldest, picked up on me and would come and sit by me and probe to find out what I was about (the spy being spied upon...cool, huh?).

The land that the centre was built on was ground that had been devastated by gold mining and was hostile. I was interested to see what they could do, as the land there was quite badly out of balance and many nasties were wandering about on the inner planes there.

Over the days I watched as they created an amazing picture pattern. I was more amazed to see that the nasties were becoming obsessed at seeing what was going on and were getting trapped in the picture. As they were trapped, the form of the picture seemed to change their ability to express themselves: they were being forced into an image form that they were unfamiliar with.

I had no illusions about the power of this culture and its ancient magic: I was fully aware of the depth of shamanic knowledge under the veneer of gentle monkishness and the 'harm no being' did not stretch to inner world beings at all (nor, it would seem, to dissenters, but that's a different matter).

I observed over the days many beings, good and bad, natural and demonic getting trapped in a beautiful, complex pattern that had them changing and shifting in an unfamiliar world of colour and form. I was expecting at the end, a ritual that would separate out the natural faery and land beings from the unhealthy beings, and free them back into the land, before putting the more demonic unhealthy beings, who had been raised by blasting, back to where they came from.

I was horrified when I watched the ritual breaking of the sand pattern and saw all of those beings, good and bad, have their inner patterns trashed and magically torn apart. They were cast into the river and I was furious: so much for Buddhist compassion. Their methods were grafted onto a foreign land that had already suffered much at the hands of men: they just added to it in their own way. In retrospect, I do not think for one minute that the monks were aware of what their actions were doing, nor do I think any of the destruction as a result of the ritual action was intentional: they were working on impermanence in a dogmatic ritualized way.

But, to get away from the personal story and emotion, it is interesting to see what a pattern can be used for and how it works. And once you have understood that, then you start to look at the ancient artwork in temples in a different light. If you study in more depth what sort of patterns where used where, what powers were used there, and what their opposing powers were, then you will start to understand what pattern does what to whom, and how you can use those patterns in your magical service.

The use of sigils in magic is a whole branch of magic on its own once you start to look closely at it, and it can take years for pennies

10. SIGILS AND SEALS

to drop about certain texts, images and patterns. But the more you learn about sigils, the more you approach them like the rest of magic: to be used sparingly and with intelligent understanding.

Chapter Eleven

Inner world parasites

Just as the outer world is full of various parasites, so are the inner realms. Most are pretty harmless, some are needed for our survival and health, some are just annoying and some are just plain nasty and dangerous.

Our bodies are full of bacteria, viruses, fungi, and microbes that 'parasite' off of our energy but they also serve a purpose for us: a symbiotic relationship that helps the world go around. Problems arise when some of these beings get out of balance and overrun the body. The same rule more or less applies in the Inner Worlds and the two worlds are inextricably linked: don't make the mistake of trying to approach the Inner Worlds as something removed from our everyday outer existence: they are one and the same.

Bacteria have an inner consciousness, viruses can be seen and affected on the 'inner': whatever has an outer form also has an inner form. The rule doesn't always apply the other way around, which can make life a little complicated. Inner parasites sometimes have an outer manifestation, but a lot of the time they do not. They do however often leave a trail of outer effects that can be identified, and the trained eye can spot the telltale symptoms in a person, animal, or object pretty swiftly. (Unless you are like me and can stand looking straight at the salt while asking where the salt is: I was born as a woman with man vision).

Wherever there is energy, there is a parasite either feeding or trying to feed. That energy can take a variety of forms and some forms are yummier than others to a hungry parasite. Some parasites are intelligent, some are sort of intelligent, and some are morons. The sort of energy that attracts them can be anything from sex, violence, death, birth, hormone rises (young teens are particularly vulnerable) pleasure, pain, emotion (love, hate, anger, etc.) drugs, and so forth.

11. Inner World Parasites

Some people are more vulnerable than others, some are pretty much immune, and some people get terribly overwhelmed by these beings.

As far as inner work goes, parasites are usually pushed out by good working practices and a healthy magical operational method. They tend mostly to appear in the fluffy New Age parlours, attaching themselves to frail egos and masquerading as an 'ascended master' or an 'angel,' spurring their hapless victims to channel banal advice and feeding off the power rush the speaker gets when people give them attention or status.

The more dangerous parasites in the magical world tend to attach to egos in the magical world, feeding a loop of messiah ego, greed, and power lust. The fundamental magical and religious world is full of people who feel they are saviours, messiahs, adepts, and magi who deserve great things like power/money/status, and the parasite feeds off the feelings of power and ego. It also manipulates the victim to set up a feeding chain.

It is important to note at this point that if a person is on certain types of medications or drugs, it can allow the parasite to dig in deeper and feed freely. It talks to the host through the host's thoughts and feelings, spurring on their actions, paranoia, and greed. The more people join in the magical/spiritual group actions, the more food the parasite has. Hence cults, which have a high tendency to be parasited, tend to have secretive, paranoid, egotistical, and glamorous leaders.

Parasites can also inhabit a land area, feeding off of what happens there: hence the need to work in a clean, clear space. Some areas can be so badly infested that it is not worth trying to clean them up. Mental institutions that have been around for a long time are a really good example of a parasitic area, as are meditation/spiritual centres that allow anything and everything in.

Just building an awareness of these beings, what they 'feel' like and what an infested place feels like can be a useful tool in inner work, as at some point you will undoubtedly come head to head with one. It's like Kindergarten: the head lice are just ready and waiting! It is important to note that there is a major difference between a parasite, which is usually just annoying and draining, and a demon.

A demon is a totally different kettle of fish and most people, even in the magical worlds, will not encounter one in their lifetime.

11.1 Dealing with and removing parasites

Parasite removal has traditionally been the forte of Shamanism and similar tribal magic: magicians tend to ignore them at their peril and priests try to bless or banish them. But what are they?

Well, if you are a magical worker and you want to deal with and be familiar with all types of beings, then you need to become familiar with parasites along with all the other choice and yucky beings that live in our universe. A trip down the Abyss will teach you a lot about these beings, how they operate and why: If you are going to deal with a being, you need to know everything about it. Why? So that you do not shoot the innocent is the shortest answer. Knee jerk action is not a part of higher magic: intelligent communion is: beings are just beings, they only become 'bad' to us if they are in the wrong place in relation to our wants and needs.

Just because something looks nasty to us doesn't mean it's bad. If it's dark, it doesn't mean it's bad. If it is munching away on your energy, it doesn't mean it's bad: it just means they are probably in the wrong realm. Every being becomes parasitical in a way if it is out of balance or out of its proper environment. The job of a magical worker is to discern what it is, why it is doing something and what to do with it.

Most parasites find their way to our realm through a variety of portholes that we as humanity open up by our actions. Once they are in our realm, they can have all sorts of effects upon our lives, most of which are negative. But what they feed on tells us a great deal about what they are and where they belong.

In modern shamanism, the parasite is taken off, and is taken away by a helper being. There is no discernment about what that being is, why it is there, where it belongs, etc. Although these questions do not matter to the victim that really just wants the bloody thing off, it should matter a great deal to the magical worker.

Back to parasites. First what needs to be identified is its food source: what does it eat? Most parasites tend to feed off the energy

11. INNER WORLD PARASITES

generated by emotions, be they fear, anger, etc. Any strong emotion will provide a meal so the parasite quickly learns to manipulate the host into generating such yummy emotions. This can be achieved either through manipulating the host's imagination or through the manipulation of the host's endocrine system.

The endocrine system is the gateway of the body to the Inner Worlds: this is where magic is processed as it passes from inner impact to outer physical impact. Heavy magic tends to affect the thyroid, the pineal, hypothalamus and pituitary: the control centres of the body. This is why too much of a burden of heavy magic will 'burn out' the hypothalamus, thus rendering the magician vulnerable to all sorts of constitutional illnesses.

Parasites operating through the endocrine system will usually go for the adrenals (generating fight or flight mode) creating fear and stress, or through the reproductive organs, creating hormonal imbalances and feeding off the subsequent emotional rollercoasters. To dig into the endocrine system in such a way they need to be there for quite a long time and can be separated out from ordinary endocrine illness by a carefully approached list of questions regarding the emotional state of the host for a few years before the endocrine problems.

In general the body's immune system will evict the parasite before it manages to dig in so deep. But weakened hosts can have this sort of long term problem and it must be looked at carefully.

Most infestations present themselves through emotional, sexual, magical or violent outbursts, with lesser ones presenting through constant primary immune system triggering.

Let's have a closer look at the more obvious and dangerous parasite presentations. The reason I am looking at these more extreme ones is that the lesser ones tend to either be pushed out naturally, or some hapless modern shaman from Glastonbury will come along and pull it out. But the more extreme ones need not only taking out, but putting back where they belong and the pathway they used to get in must be closed up.

11.2 Emotional parasites

These parasites usually get in during an initial emotional situation like a divorce, death, failure etc., something that generated a lot of energy and made the victim visible and edible. They slip in and then begin to generate a feeding loop in which the parasite generates activity, usually through the imagination, that keeps the emotive flow going and the victim in the constant clutches of their despair. The victim feels severely depressed or angry, or in emotional pain, and the parasite settles in for nightly dinner.

Usually the first heads up that people get that something is wrong is that the victim is not getting over something: the pain continues, they spiral into the depths of dark emotions and nothing brings them out. Antidepressants at this stage will only disable the body's ability to shake this being off, so the infestation is actually made worse by the drug, often creating a suicide situation. So it is important, for both sides of the reasoning to make sure that the emotion is from a parasite as opposed to a chemical depression. The usual way to tell is if you take the parasite out, the victim gets better within hours. You can also use tarot to look if you do not have the inner sight abilities to look.

After an emotive parasite is removed, the victim will be emotionally frail for a few weeks, and will need a careful eye along with homeopathy or herbs to strengthen and rebalance their system. They will also need an input of energy as theirs will have been sucked dry, so energetically feeding them would be a good idea, along with closing up any holes that the parasite left behind. (For the actual removal method, see below.)

11.3 Sexual parasites

Sex is an act that generates a lot of visible energy and if that act is not protected, then every parasite within a hundred miles will come running for a piece of the action. Sexual parasites work primarily through the imagination though with time and practice they can begin to affect the sex organs directly. The emotive energy that is released with desire is a particularly potent energy and the parasite will do anything it can to keep that level of the first 'high' going. This

11. INNER WORLD PARASITES

drives the victim to find more and more ways to get that initial arousal 'hit,' with it fading as the parasite becomes normalized to the energy level.

A longer-term victim of such a parasite will have sexual problems in which little excites them and there is a constant searching for new ways to get a 'hit.' Again, one has to be cautious to ascertain if it truly is a parasite and not a hormone imbalance, although a long-term parasite will eventually begin to affect the hormone levels as it attempts to manipulate the body's chemical balance to suit its appetite. This is analogous to the recent discovery that viruses will affect the imagination, emotions and endocrine system to force the host into actions that will be favourable to the virus. Sound familiar?

11.4 Magical parasites

These little buggers are just downright nasty. They are initially attracted by the power of a magical or religious act that has been conducted without proper balance of power structures/patterns and inner contacts. These horrible things are the main reason for a magician to stop and think carefully if he/she should throw the known structure out of the window when doing high magic. If you forge into new territory magically, make sure you know what you are doing and that you are properly balanced in the way that you approach your work.

If not, the magical energy generated will attract a particular type of being that can wreak havoc around humans. They do not necessarily attach to the magician: they go for the nearest 'sensitive' and dig into their thoughts. So anyone who happens to be nearby who is a sensitive or seer is in real danger of these beings. They are a slightly higher order of being than the emotive or sexual parasite: their energy needs operate on a high frequency (hence you will find them deeper in the Abyss). Because of that, they tend to be far more dangerous: they feed off threshold energy, which for us translates eventually to death.

They will talk to their victims, isolating them from their families and friends, telling them they are in constant danger or that a particular person is evil. They will slowly manoeuvre the person into a state in which they think they have to kill someone for some real reason. Most people fight this and seek help. Unfortunately medical help will immediately drug them, which allows the being to dig in deeper. But if the person is not parasited, but is mentally ill, then they need the drug initially to calm them. So it is a difficult situation which must be handled carefully.

More often than not the victim will have been convinced by the parasite that anyone trying to help them is the enemy: these are intelligent beings who do not give up their hosts easily, and most be approached carefully. If they see you coming they will try to urge the victim to self-destruct so that they can have a gorge feed before bolting. My personal approach to someone who is infested with this type of being is to consecrate a scarf as a sacred stole, come up behind them and carefully, in a friendly manner, put it around their necks. This gives you a short time to talk to the human and explain what is going on and what you need to do.

With this sort of infestation, it is advisable to have a mental health professional assess the victim after the parasite has been lifted, just to be on the safe side. The victim will need a great deal of aftercare in the form of clean energy, good food, sacred baths and lots of sleep that is protected by a sacred flame. It is probable that the victim will have flashbacks, and will have echoes of the infestation at the same time each year for a few years. It is a good idea for the victim to preempt this by actively doing something like a spiritual cleanse at that time of the year.

Once you have cleaned the victim up, taken the parasite home and sealed up the porthole it used, try and find out what magical act or which magical person attracted the being in the first place. If it is an adult who should know better, try to resist the urge to beat the shit out of them: just let them know what their actions are doing.

The reason why those types of parasite should never be left in the host is that they are the order of being that will generate a lot of violence and emotion in people. They get into teens and mentally ill men: for some reason, it is rare for them to dig so deeply into mature women. When the being is lifted the difference is astounding and almost instant (within a couple of hours). One teen that I worked on who was suicidal, self-mutilating, hearing voices and planning death, looked terrible. I stripped the being out with a doctor present and the kid was totally different within two hours. They ate and slept for the first time in days, and awoke with little memory of what had been happening: the previous two weeks were a near total blank.

If you do not get such a dramatic reversal of symptoms, then the chances are it is not a parasite and the victim needs medical help.

11.5 Parasites of the dying

These parasites tend to move into old people and people in comas. They live off the life force of the dying, and off the sensations that they get to feel through the victim's senses. In return they block the natural mechanism that would allow the person to die: in effect they keep their host alive so that they can live through the body of the host. When a person is old or severely injured, the natural defence system against such parasites collapses and they can move in unchecked.

Sometimes they can get so ingrained in the person, that a natural psychic who is not used to such beings would assume that the original person had gone and another being had taken its place (which does sometimes happen). But more often than not, if you reach deep in, you find the original person squashed into a corner, unable to use their body and unable to die: it is a terrible situation for them and for everyone else concerned. If you take the parasite out, the victim will die. If you leave it in, the victim is stuck in no man's land.

In such situations, it is most compassionate to take them out. It is also the most ethical: you are restoring the human to their original fate pattern of death. Keeping someone alive at all costs is not a good thing to do. The family might want the person to stay alive regardless of the parasite, but it must be explained to them that their loved one is not really there much anymore, what they are holding the hand of is mainly a parasite. If there is enough of the human left, then they will survive the extraction. If not, they will die shortly after.

Under such circumstances, it is advisable wherever possible to include the family in the extraction process so that they have a sense of control and inclusion in such a difficult emotive situation. It would also be wise to protect the family from parasites at this highly emotional time.

11.6 Minor parasites

There are tons of minor orders of parasites that live off emotions, pain, sex, magic, drugs, drink, certain rhythms, and hormonal imbalances. The list is endless and the effects in general tend to be minor. Usually the body can eventually shrug them off naturally, or the host slowly realizes that their actions are creating a bad situation, and they change their lives accordingly. Some parasites come in useful and symbiotic relationships can develop, just as the bowel needs bacteria, so our emotive selves sometimes need help. In teen years kids become vulnerable to parasites, but unless they are particularly sensitive or open, it is best to help them deal with it naturally so that they build up a basic immunity to these beings. That translates to helping them identify what is them and what is the being: identify the 'food' source that is attracting it, and help the teen to decide how to change their environment and actions to make them less visible and less yummy.

11.7 Removing parasites: practical application

Obviously the first thing is that the person you are working on has to agree to be worked on: forcing an extraction is not such a good idea, unless it is a severe attack in which the victim is unable to ask for help: that is when you use a stole to give them time to think.

Never, under any circumstances, physically assault, handle or hit the victim in an attempt to drive out the being. Not only is this the Neanderthal method of extraction so beloved by Christian fundamentalists, it is also plain and simple assault.

The other thing when working in this way as a worker rather than a healer is that you will need to work in a partnership. There will be times within the session that two people will be needed.

Make sure that you are both clean, working in a clean space and that you both have a clear mind that cannot be messed with. It is a good idea to go into the Void or a similar thing within your own tradition to strip away your surface life and step into a deeper level of your consciousness before working: this ensures that there is nothing that the parasite can latch onto in you. Reach out within the Void for

11. Inner World Parasites

the tools that you need for the job—just keep your intentions clear within your thoughts and the necessary tools will emerge.

The parasite worker will need to reach deeper into the Void and connect with angelic consciousness, usually an Angel of Air (see article working with angels) and have that being come out to work with you.

Within the partnership, one person should focus upon the human and the other upon the parasite. The worker who is tending the human never leaves the human's side, vision or otherwise, while the other worker takes the parasite and deals with the Void side of things. For example:

Human worker

Work in vision, starting at the top of the body and work your way down, looking deep into the body, around the adrenals, the heart, the thymus and the head. Once you have found the being, bind it: if it is one of the more intelligent magical beings, pass it to the parasite worker. Once you have cleared them of all parasites, pull out any umbilical cords or connections, seal them at all the access points and rebalance them by ensuring that the inner body is equal on both sides of the body's midline. (An imaginary line of balance that runs down the centre of the body)

Finally fill them with grounded earth energy and put them in a salt bath.

Parasite worker

When the being is handed to you, disable the being by using angelic binding with the Angel of Air. Immediately take the being to the Abyss by passing through the Void (or through your own version of such a place). You will need to descend into the Abyss to make sure that it goes where it is supposed to go. You can work with the angelic consciousness that resides within the Abyss to take you down and bring you back up again.

Once down at the level where the being belongs, release it and look around for a porthole or crack. You will recognize the light/scent/energy leaking into the Abyss from the human world that attracted the being in the first place. Seal up the crack, again using the angelic worker that is with you and take another look around just in case you can see something that caused the crack in the first place. If you identify the cause, and can deal with it simply, then deal with it at this point of the work. If it looks more complicated, or you cannot immediately identify the reason for the crack, then you must come back at another time and focus properly upon the problem. Just bear in mind, if you come back at a later date, you will need to reconnect with the being to get the sense of where the crack was.

Once all is finished, make sure that you both clean yourselves up properly and that the victim is closely watched and helped for a while by family and friends. Go back a few times to check up on them until you are sure they are strong and able to fend off another attack. At that point it might be wise to talk at length to them to find out how it got access in the first place and what could be done to avoid such a situation in the future.

11.8 Summary

I haven't gone into too much detail about working methods so that if you haven't a clue, then you will not be able to bumble your way through something and do damage. If you have knowledge or are a natural, then hopefully this section will help with ideas and working methods: either way, the idea is to stop people and make them think a little more about how these beings operate and why. They are not evil nasties: they are hungry out of place beings just looking for a home and a meal. I'm sure cows and pigs find human omnivores evil: it's all a matter of perspective.

I am also hoping that this section will encourage people to pause for thought before undergoing powerful magic, just to make sure that any hapless youngsters nearby don't get sucked in and end up with nasties inside them.

Chapter Twelve

Removing ghosts and other unwelcome guests

Sometimes unwelcome guests come into our homes and workplaces, creating anything from mild discomfort to outright chaos. Sometimes they were there all the time and we move into their 'patch' triggering a hostile response, and sometimes we move to an area or property that is sat on unhealthy, unbalanced or just plain dangerous land. To us that equals sleepless nights and many strange happenings.

Most of the time when people think they are being haunted, in actual reality, they are not. It is much rarer than people think unless you are unlucky enough to live in a place that is a magnet for such energy. In the British Isles for example, the relative number of powerful 'possessions' of houses is much less than the USA, even when you take into account the vast territory of the USA in relation to the small isle of Britain.

The reasons for this could be many: length of time of population and cities upon the land, amount of wild territory, reuse of sacred burial land as building land, etc. Whatever the reason, the USA is a far more haunted land than Britain, and its hauntings can be spectacular.

The different types of hauntings must be dealt with differently according to what type of being you are dealing with and why they are there. Do not automatically assume a presence is hostile just because it is there and rattling your windows: it might be trapped there, terrified of you and desperately trying to get out.

We react to hauntings in a hostile way because they can be frightening, and they are frightening only because of the lack of understanding of what is happening. Unless of course you happen to be sat upon one of the really nasty unbalanced sites that attract

12. Removing ghosts and other unwelcome guests

every parasite and lesser demon around for miles and they all end up in your kitchen: that's scary!

When dealing with beings in this situation, it is useful to have no emotion whatsoever when you are working. When dealing with unsavoury beings, no emotion is safe: there is nothing they can poke or play upon. Do not fall into the trap of feeling sorry for them, or being fearful of them, or even friendly with them: they do not belong in that space, so they have to go.

12.1 Types of hauntings

The first one to cover—and actually the least common of all hauntings—is the presence of a dead human. When someone dies, they tend to normally go through the death process and they might try to hang around the house of a little while before slowly fading off. Those that do hang around at home after a while should not be encouraged by loved ones left behind, no matter how tempting that may be. It prolongs an unhealthy situation for them and for the living. There are times however, particularly if it is part of the culture of that family, when dead people to stay connected to a family line as a guardian for a while. In these circumstances all is well and it isn't a problem.

Some humans die in a state of anger, greed, or with a need for revenge. These people in life tend to be types who find it hard to let go of anything and will hang on for grim death to anything that will allow them access to the living world. Their enormous output of emotional energy attracts parasites that begin to feed on the situation and may even try to impersonate the dead person to carry the haunting on even when the dead person has moved on.

The way to deal with a dead human is to go into death and deal with them face-to-face at that level (rather than an aggressive banishing ritual). It is much better to ask 'uncle Harry' to go and take him by the hand as you walk him into death to make sure he goes, than to ritually impact his soul by magical banishments. The method of working in death teaches them to stop and think about what is happening and what they are doing. If they go with you voluntarily, then they have learned and are moving on.

12.1. Types of hauntings

If you get an unhealthy dead person hanging around doing damage, then you get them by the scruff of the neck and frogmarch them through death. Again this is better than a ritual banishment, and it tends to work better anyhow. Sometimes a mass conducted by a Catholic priest will move a dead person on if the transubstantiation ceremony is used, but this depends on the skill of the priest and the dead person's reaction to the ceremony. If they are in tune with that faith, they can use the ceremony as an impetus to move on.

Many years ago I was contacted about a haunting in Manhattan USA. A woman could feel her dead husband standing over her in a rage night after night: she was sleep-deprived and stressed out. I went to have a look, as sometimes when people think they are under attack, they are not.

He was indeed there and angry. Before he died, he controlled a large businesses empire of which he was the cutthroat owner. They had begun the process of separating and had not approached it legally, but were about to. He was killed in an accident and was fuming that his wife was the sole beneficiary of all his estate: he had not got around to changing his will.

I went into the death vision to speak to him. When I found him, he presented himself as a man sitting inside a heavily armoured tank: this was his projection of himself as a dangerous man. I tried to talk to him while he sat in his tank but he would not come out and would not see sense. So I reached in and pulled him out by his collar. He refused to move, to stop attacking her or to listen to any sort of reason. I dragged him to the 'river,' made him drink lots, and then marched him over the 'bridge' into death. (To read about the death vision, see notes on death and birth.)

The haunting stopped immediately and never returned. I showed the woman how to cleanse her apartment from an inner point of view and how to tune it. She never had problems again.

Most hauntings by dead people stem from their frustration at not being able to finish something up, not being able to let go of family or belongings, or the need to pass information on. Once that has been achieved, most do move on, but some do stay as they want to stay connected to their old life. These ones really do have to be moved on.

12. REMOVING GHOSTS AND OTHER UNWELCOME GUESTS

Be aware though that sometimes the being that presents as a haunting is actually a parasite that is 'wearing' the persona of the dead person. The dead human was probably there for a while, but a parasite moved in and eventually took over the haunting so that it could feed off the emotions its presence generated in the living.

If you go into the death vision and you find that it is a parasite that is doing the haunting, you will need to separate it from the dead person's persona (a little like wrestling its coat off) and then take a firm hold of the parasite and take it into the Void to send it back to where it belongs. The persona that was stripped off like a coat will also need to go into the Void.

Once a home has been stripped of the presence, it will need cleaning from an outer and inner point of view, and then it will need tuning. This can be a simple affair using a simple flame, consecrated salt and water, and then bringing the power of the Void into the house. Music can be powerful in affecting a space, and calm sacred music can be used afterwards to just still the space and restore a sense of calm.

12.2 Land-based entities

These hauntings tend to be more dangerous and dramatic than actual dead people, and must be approached with caution and intelligence. If they appear suddenly after a span of normality in the house, the chances are it has either come in or been triggered by something brought into the house, or something happening at the house.

Sometimes these beings have been there for generations and are a part of the land. In that case there is nothing you can do about it and the best option is to leave. I lived in a house in north California for two years that sat upon a site that was terribly unbalanced and dark. All sorts of parasitical beings ran around the house messing with the family, and one bedroom was unusable because it was so badly haunted. No amount of cleansing, banishments, bribes and threats got rid of it. It came into people's dreams and fed them hatred, paranoia and general mental instability.

In the end we threw in the towel and moved. I later heard that on that street, people regularly went mad and one tenant had gone on a killing spree after spending time there. Yum! The being was part of that land, and was known to local Indians as the 'black snake.' It had been disturbed by the aggressive gold mining years before, which had brought it up to surface in a hostile manner. Later, a yellow fever camp sat upon that spot where people were forced to stay when they got ill. Many people died there in terrible circumstances which fed the whole unhealthy land pattern. There was nothing that could be done: that land needed to not have humans on it any longer: it needed to be left in peace to slowly compost and regenerate.

Most land beings that come into houses are attracted by a particular energy and the first step is to identify what attracted them in the first place. Sometimes rituals or magical work can attract them, which means you are not clearing your space or opening it without properly tuning it.

Sometimes the energy a teen puts out can attract them, or your house could be sat on an energy vortex (which sucks) or you could be unlucky enough to live upon a patch of land that is of death: that means it has a large area that is considered access to the Underworld. In those areas, the veils between the worlds are thin and it will be like living in Grand Central Station. In those types of cases you need to keep your house fully tuned at all times, have a sacred flame going at all times and do regular 'let's clear out the dead, confused and hungry beings' sessions.

In the USA, the native Indians knew about these areas and did not live upon them but instead they chose to bury their dead there. Nashville (in fact North TN in general) is a good example of this, as are Milwaukee and Chicago. These areas have lots of hauntings, lots of strange parasitical beings floating around, and consequentially have a much higher incidence of violent killers and mentally unstable people. The areas often stretch for hundreds of miles and affect anyone sensitive who lives in that area.

In Britain, stone circles, churches and Roman temples tend to adorn such places in an attempt to harness the power and use these Underworld entrances. These land areas are not 'bad' or 'evil,' they are just powerful: they mediate power that connects with death, the Underworld and the destroying element of Divinity within the land. So if you work with them in context, they are balanced and powerful.

12. REMOVING GHOSTS AND OTHER UNWELCOME GUESTS

If you try to live on top of them and raise kids, then you are in for a shock.

If it is not rooted totally in the land and you have something trying to eat your cat, giving lurid dreams to your teen and bothering you night after night by rattling things etc., the best thing you can do is send it back to the realm where it belongs. Praying at it will do nothing: it is probably not aware of human religions and it will wonder what on earth you are doing. Such beings often appear scarier than they actually are and some take great delight in dressing up in 'scary suits' taken from your imagination. These beings work through the mind and affect the mind the most, so you work with the mind to get rid of it.

First rule: no emotions. Second rule: total focus on what you are doing. Third rule: know where you are going to put it before you grab it. The best way is always to take them into the Void and release them there with the order for them to go back where they came from. Taking a being like that into the Void takes great focus as you are working with stillness, which is bloody hard if you have a wriggling screaming 'being' in your grasp.

Alternatively you can take it down into the depths of the Underworld and leave it there, hoping that it will not find its way back again. If it is particularly nasty, then if you have access to a fireplace or a fire pit, build a fire before you start. If you cannot get it into the Void, cast it into the fire to send it back to its own line.

Should you ever be silly enough to grasp hold of a being that turns out to be much more powerful and nastier than you thought (and this is something where I talk from personal stupid experience) go straight into the Void within you and expand your consciousness to the eternal soul that is you. It will not be able to keep a hold on you and will fizzle off you. If you know where in the Abyss it belongs, call upon the Sandalphon while in the Void and step out at the Abyss to put it back where it came from.

This underlines the importance of having the regular practice of meditating upon the Void or a similar concept. You need to do such a discipline every day if you are doing this type of work: only then will you be tuned enough to silence your emotions and mind, and expand your soul while in danger. It has to be a second nature act: it is not something that works if you have to think about it and struggle with it.

A good thing to do if you live on a power site is to go into the inner landscape and take a close look. You might have to 'build' your house into the inner landscape: sometimes these beings wander into the house because they do not know that the house is there. If it hasn't been there for long (and I am talking hundreds of years) then chances are the inner landscape is still forest or whatever is local. So beings wander around the inner landscape and find that a 'patch' has interesting and sometimes yummy energies to feed on. This is your house and your energy. Just as you cannot see them, they often cannot see you: you just feel each other. If the house is built in the inner landscape, then they can see you and will avoid you unless some bright energy attracts them.

12.3 Possession of a house by demonic forces

This is a rare occurrence, much rarer than people think: what most people think of as 'dark demons' usually turns out to be a land-based consciousnesses. If such an occurrence does happen, the approach needs to take on a series of defined steps. First you have to identify what drew them in. Beings of this power do not just wander blindly into a house: something summons them or they come in with something. Identifying the source will tell you a lot about what type of being it is and what to do with it. If it is aligned to a particular tradition or religion, then you must deal with it in that context.

Demons are not beings to mess with (no shit!) and must be dealt with angelically using the Abyss. If you don't know how to work with angels (or another culture's equivalent being) then don't try and do this level of clearing: you will get hurt. Only attempt this type of clearing if you know it is a weak form of demonic consciousness: anything bigger needs a fully experienced exorcist.

If you do know how to work with angels (and I don't mean the fluffy bunny New Age image of angels, more the bloody great big things with loads of eyes/heads/whatnot) but are not sure how to approach this sort of situation then follow these stages:

1. Identify the source.

12. Removing Ghosts and Other Unwelcome Guests

2. Identify what element it is most aligned to.

3. If it has come in on a religious artefact, then work within the frame work (not the method, just the framework) of that religion if you can.

4. Use the archangelic beings most aligned to the being's elements, usually fire and air.

5. Be in the Void at all times and do not be teased out for anything.

6. Seal the room where you are working and open up the four directions.

7. Work through the archangelic fragments, so they are within you as you work, bind the being using recitation and take it to the Abyss.

8. Work with the archangel in the Abyss to take you and demon down to where it belongs. Do not harm it and do not have any emotion at any time. Do not listen to anything said to you, hold total focus on what you are doing at all times. Once you have found where it belongs, unbind it, seal up the crack into the human realm that allowed it out in the first place.

9. Clean yourself (sacred or ritual bath) and the space thoroughly afterwards and then consecrate the space.

10. Go into the Void and be still: allow anything to fall from you that doesn't belong with you.

11. Don't do anything for a good 10 days after. You need to be dense and to rest. This type of work takes an extreme amount of energy and can kill you if you do not approach it properly. The Inner Worlds must not exist for you for a while until your body has recovered. You will be tired, bruised, and will need lots of food and sleep for quite a few days after. Dealing with this type of being changes you forever and you have to be aware of that. You become battle scarred and more visible to that order of being in the future.

In real terms, it is best to leave this sort of work to an experienced exorcist. If this is an area of magical work that you truly want to learn, then you need to find an exorcist and apprentice yourself to them. I have written a handbook for exorcists, but it is a book to be used in tandem with actual training, or as a reference book for current practitioners.

12.4 Possession from an object

Occasionally people bring strange objects home that they found on holiday or in a junk store and do not realize that they have just brought home a statue or object that has a being living within or attached to it. It will wreak havoc in your home and the longer it is left to run around, the stronger it will get.

If you suddenly start to have strange things happening in your home, the first thing you ask is, "did anyone buy something or get something recently and bring it home?" If they cannot think, go into vision and look around the house on the inner. It will usually show up there. I have had a Hawaiian Ku marching around my house attacking my kids, along with various other strange and wonderful beings that caused chaos through curious acquisitions.

If you identify the source by looking at the 'inner' house, then that source has to go in the fire. Do not think for one minute that you can strip it out of the object because you want to keep the object: learning to let go is important! It probably cannot be fully stripped out and will need to be sent back to its own realm by going into the fire. So build a fire and burn it. Doesn't matter what it is worth: it is potentially dangerous.

It is a simple but effective way of handling these beings and it works instantly. The other way you can deal with it is to physically send it back where it came from. So if it is a religious/cultural piece, send it to a priest/ess of that religion with an explanation. They will give it a home and that will probably be where it belongs.

Having spiritual or cultural artefacts that are not tourist pieces and not of your own religion/tradition in your home is generally a bad idea. They can clash with what you do magically and that can have disastrous results. I have personally witnessed tragic events brought

12. REMOVING GHOSTS AND OTHER UNWELCOME GUESTS

on by someone conducting magic in a house full of religious magical statues from another culture where the two forms of magic clashed badly. The result was a freak house fire that had fatalities.

The golden rule with any of these situations is not to get emotional in any way, to stay focused and calm, and to know what you are doing. If you are out of your depth, then hand over the job to someone else. If you are ill, tired or hormonal, then don't do this work.

Chapter Thirteen

How to deal with simple magical/psychic attacks

If you are a magical worker i.e. a teacher, priest/ess, healer, seer etc. in service to your community, then you are one of the unfortunate ones who lives life on the firing line. I use the term worker as opposed to practitioner, because if you are working in service, then it is a job and you are a 'worker.'

The magical worker, when acting as an interface with the Inner Worlds for the outer world, needs access at all times to inner contacts, the inner energies and to have extreme sensitivity to what is around them. You cannot do that and have protection on, as the protection will interfere to some degree with your ability to filter and mediate: it will lessen your sensitivity.

And yet if you spend your time taking off parasites, lifting curses, dragging groups of people around the Inner Worlds or peering into the future, then you will have regular natural splats and the odd directed attack from some unsavoury immature person. Usually the splats and attacks are fairly minor and do not take much to deal with, but if you are working a lot and are getting hit a lot, then the short term solution isn't really practical.

Natural splats (parasites, psychic sludge and grime) are dealt with by daily magical hygiene: use lots of salt when washing and take a blessed bath using salt after working. Don't put the same clothes back on, throw them in the washer and put clean clothes on.

Attacks are slightly different as they are so varied, usually emotively driven and can just be bloody annoying. Mostly they are badly done and have a short shelf life, but a few of them in succession can end up like a squeaky wheel or door: this doesn't really do any harm, but it drives you nuts.

13. How to deal with simple magical/psychic attacks

But attacks like that, simple and not dangerous ones, are a bit like the common cold: the body and soul can use them to process things, to strengthen your inner immune system and to give you an elephant hide. The common cold is often used by the body to process and dump all sorts of stored toxins and viruses, and an attack has a similar use for the inner you.

Not reacting or defending from an attack or attacks can put you into a very interesting space if it is done properly. When you first sign up to be a magical worker in service, there is a certain road you can take that has its own inherent protections, backups and knowledge bases. That road is the road of the inner servant/worker. It is not religious, not connected to any system and can be used within any magical or spiritual system that has similar ethics.

It is a simple case of opting out of day-to-day fate and putting your life in the hands of the Universe. There are a variety of ways to do this and the one I know best is the edge of the Abyss, communing with the angelic being within the Abyss, handing over your fate in service, and submitting to the power and knowledge of the Universe.

What this means is that past actions which have tipped the scales and need rebalancing are not processed by the usual means: this generally entails having to face, be confronted by or having a taste of your past misdeeds and acts of total stupidity. The submitting to the power of the Universe triggers the automatic basic protection, access to knowledge and ability to bridge massive amounts of power, but only when truly needed.

The protection is only from that which you cannot handle alone, or from anything which stops you from doing your job properly. The 'knowledge access' is the ability to tap into whatever information or knowledge you need to achieve your service, and it only comes to you when you need it: you often forget it afterwards (which is really, really annoying). The bridging of massive amounts of power is truly awesome and blows your socks off: but again, you have no control over it: it comes when needed and at no other time.

Instead, you work off your karma (for want of a better description) by being of service to anyone or anything that is put in your path. This also means not making money from it: it must be free from all energetic rules, ties, and balances, and also from any temptations.

In practice, this method allows the Universal power to get on with its job and you to get on with yours. I have found that not taking action against an attack becomes a powerful thing: the attacker gets to learn the hard way why not to attack by being allowed free rein to 'hang themselves.' This means that unstopped, they burn out and eventually have to face their own actions: you are allowing their true fate to continue by not interfering.

It also, with that thin veil of protection to stop too much accumulation, strengthens the worker by regular 'exercise.' If you are truly committed to a life of service, then you will be given lots of work to do and the tougher you get, the harder the tasks become. You strengthen by adversity, which enables you to deal with the real and serious nasty things that can happen in the many worlds around us.

It's strange: the deeper you go in magic, the more it becomes apparent that in ninety percent of cases, it should not be used.

One thing that is important to consider before you go tripping off heartily to the Abyss to declare your life of service is that the deeper the magic and power you have access to under service conditions, the faster and harder your 'karma' becomes. The act of stepping into the shoes of a worker is a profound one: you are held above all others in terms of the need for wisdom, maturity and integrity. If you knowingly do something that is harmful, vindictive or just plain selfishly wrong, then you will have the large hand in the sky swinging down to slap you bloody hard on the bum: your scale balancing is instant.

This has nothing to do with right and wrong, moral codes or anything like that: it is about cause and effect. With having such access to power, you move up the ladder of power evolution. With that move up the stakes get higher, the effects get stronger and the balancing gets faster. This is just about how power works. You need to have balanced scales, so to speak, to work deeply in service. That way, if you have to deal with serious demonic entities, there is nothing they can blackmail you with, threaten you with or jerk your chain with.

13. How to Deal with Simple Magical/Psychic Attacks

And that is important for the safety of your life and the lives of those close to you.

Anything that you do towards another person or place creates an energetic pattern, so living a simple life free of complex illicit affairs, weird sex with goats, curse compulsions or Marks & Spencer's shoplifting sprees, tends to keep you fairly pattern free. And that in itself makes for a simpler life. So if you screw up, you will get the balancing action almost immediately and with bells on, just to make sure that you have got the message.

If you don't want to go down that route for the sake of protection, then the other option, which is simpler, but is less of a magical move up the ladder so to speak, is to go into the Void whenever you work and whenever you are attacked. This really should become a daily meditation in which you still yourself to such a point that any magic/being that is on or around you will immediately become apparent.

In that stillness, you learn to pause before reaction and take time to look at what it is that is on you. And I mean really look. Once you learn to look at magic in a clinical fashion without emotion, you will begin to see its construction, its signatures, its emotive content, etc. This tells you a lot about where it has come from and why. With that knowledge, you then slowly peel it off and let it vanish into the Void. Take no action towards the sender: don't even have emotion or thought regarding them: as a worker, the task of educating the sender will be taken care of by fate, not by you.

And that is also a point to remember: someone who has the immaturity to curse or attack will not truly learn anything from retaliation or punishment. They will only stop doing it when they learn why not to do it, and that wisdom is usually brought about by deep personal suffering. That suffering in turn brings compassion and maturity. You are not responsible for the development of someone's soul: you do not have access to their deepest self to see where the learning is truly needed. Therefore you turn that action over to the structure of fate and get on with your job.

The other option is to get a shotgun and every time someone magically attacks you, you blow their kneecaps out. But that can get messy.

Chapter Fourteen

Dismantling Hermetic or Kabbalistic curses

If someone should ever curse you, just hope that they are an idiot and do not know what they are doing: that way you don't wake up dead...

Ritual curses that emanate out of the 'Western Mystery Tradition' have many forms that do many things, but what they all have in common is their source of structure. To dismantle a curse you have to work within the language that was used to build it, using the same tools and types of beings that the 'curser' used.

For this section I am focusing purely on curses launched from people who operate within the Hermetic, Western Kabbalistic magical forms. The methods discussed within this chapter will most probably not work if you were attacked by a true Jewish Kabbalist or Chassid, but then, what would such a religious person in Israel want with a hermetic magician in Bromley?

Also, if you are cursed by someone from one of the many old tribal traditions (not a New Age reconstruction)...dude...you're on your own...

One would think that someone who has reached the level of Major Adept in a magical tradition would have a little maturity about them and would not take to blindly attacking on the magical plane anyone who upsets their applecart. But unfortunately it does happen and we do have to learn to deal with it. Magical practitioners who have not reached such a stage of training can also probably pull together some sort of attack, but they are usually fairly minor and can be dealt with using common sense, an inner clearing and a lot of salt.

The types of curses that are outlined in this chapter are curses that are powerful and serious. A serious attack or curse needs careful

14. Dismantling Hermetic or Kabbalistic curses

thought and consideration. Make a wrong move and a carefully crafted curse could kill you. It's not a joke and it has nothing to do with belief: it is the construction and moulding of powers that uphold the universe and they will take you out if they are pointing at you.

14.1 What is a Hermetic/Kabbalistic curse?

A curse is a construction using patterns, beings, energies and shapes that are brought together to achieve a goal. That goal could be anything from stopping someone speaking, writing, walking or going to a certain area, to the extreme of killing someone or making them seriously ill. It can be used against a person, place or thing. The structure of the construct holds the intent, the being gives it life and action, and the energy runs it. Usually curses don't 'run out,' they will continue for as long as the energy source is going and until it completes its task. Sometimes they can run for generations.

Then there is the basic law of power mediation: to bring something from the inner to the outer it must pass through you first: the mediator or doorway for power is affected by what they bring through. It is a simple and basic law and everyone seems to forget it.

This universal law is not about morals, it's about the nuts and bolts of the universe and how the balance of power works. Every time you put something out, a pattern is created which has life of its own. It has to run to completion and cannot be stopped. If it has come through or from you, then you are inextricably linked to it (even if you attach a scapegoat to it to avoid the backlash) and it will affect your fate one way or another until it has run its course. This is the basis of karma, and this is why 'sorry' doesn't work: it's not about how you feel, what you think or what your morals are. If you jump on one side of the seesaw, the other side will pop up, it's called physics.

Another interesting side of this law is that once the pattern of the curse is released, that pattern is connected to the curser as a part of their being or 'fate.' If that curser should then go onto consecrate a person, that consecrated person also becomes a part of the pattern. Why? Because a true consecration flattens your own soul fate and you take on the mantle of the line into which you have been consecrated.[1] There is only ever one consecrated human in a particular line just as there is only ever one consecrated sword, cup, etc. So by the act of being consecrated, you become one with the consecrator which means everything that consecrator 'is' magically becomes a part of you—hence the need to be slightly picky when choosing which magical line to be consecrated into. A truly outstanding example of this is the consecrated line that runs through W. G. Grey.

Although that pattern cannot be stopped it can be redeemed: just because you inherit the line habit of cursing doesn't mean you too have to curse. You can choose to rebalance the seesaw by offering in service to dismantle the damage wrought by your fellow priests. This is somewhat of the redemptive basis for Christianity. You cannot be indifferent or opt out: if you are in the line where the consecrator cursed people, you will either curse or will lift curses.

The sensible choice is to lift them...But if you are in that inherited line, the stronger your inner abilities, the stronger the urge to attack will be. The rebalancing comes from having the strength to overcome the urges, and to not try and justify attacks to yourself. This resistance in turn pulls away energy from the parasitical beings that are often wrapped up in such unhealthy lines. The beings, like the line, are passed from generation to generation and they build their working knowledge of the human psyche as they go along: this enables them to find newer and juicer ways to lean on the urge to attack.

14.2 How do curses affect the victim?

So, you are unfortunate enough to have been cursed? That truly sucks! Curses affect their victims on many levels depending on what the curse was aimed at. If it was a simple curse to stop you communicating, or to isolate you or to stop you doing some activity, then no matter how hard you work or how good you are at something, unbelievable blocks will fill your path. The body will react to the curse, particularly if you are sensitive. Usually most curses are at this level as few people are truly nasty enough to curse to the death.

---

[1] N.B. Consecration is not the same as initiation or ordination.

14. DISMANTLING HERMETIC OR KABBALISTIC CURSES

If you have been cursed to the death then your body will definitely react to it and you will also find yourself in the most bizarre accidents and close shaves. If the curser is good at what he/she does and you have no real protection, then you will probably die of a strange illness or you will be killed in an accident. (Don't you just love my positive outlook on life?)

If you have been cursed to the death and you have some real protection, then you will become ill and you will survive a series of close shave freak accidents. If you happen to be unfortunate enough to have a close family who are all magical or who are sensitive/physic/empaths, then it will spill over onto them too. They will suffer the same illnesses and accidents, most of the time not quite so strongly, but enough to cause concern.

By illnesses and accidents, I do not mean that if you stub your toe a lot and get lots of colds then you are cursed, I mean that if you suddenly begin to suffer from life-threatening illnesses for which there is no visible cause, and you are suddenly in near-fatal accidents, nearly get shot or do get shot, are attacked by muggers, rapists, wild animals and this is happening on a weekly basis, chances are there may be something wrong.

If you survive the initial attacks, then after a few months the body and the energies around you begin to shift and adjust around the curse: you begin to learn to live with it. It will mean that your life will be a string of bizarre accidents and strange illnesses, and people will react to you in negative ways. Your life will probably fall apart and nothing that you do in your outer life to improve your lot will work. So the curse goes from acute to chronic. If the curse is never lifted, then chances are you will die before the time you were fated to die and the life you live before that death will be full of suffering. Don't you just love positive thinking?

If it is eventually lifted, then chances are you will be left with physical and emotional scars or disabilities, and your lifespan will still probably be a bit shorter, just not as short as it would have been if the curse had not been lifted. The blocks in your life will fall away and any energy that has been blocked from you will now rush in like water escaping from a dam.

14.3 So what about protection?

Well, there are two major ways of protecting yourself: covering yourself with magical protections, or turning over your trust to the inner worlds. The festooning with magical protections works to an extent and only to the level of your own magical skills. If you are in for the long haul, then magical protections will take up a vast amount of your time and energy which in itself is dangerous. In the long term, it is not a good or wise option.

The best protection comes from beings that uphold the structure of the universe. If you call upon specific beings to protect you, then your level of protection will depend on what level of power you can use to interface with these beings: chances are the beings have far more power in their pockets if you just let them get on and do their job rather than giving them a set job description which is what a summoning basically is.

The way to do this is simple and yet complex: if you are doing inner/magical work, then make sure it is for the true service of the Universe: this in itself will bring a certain level of protection with it. Don't do the service just to save your own ass, though: do it because it is the right thing to do.

Call upon the power of Divine Being to guide you and to protect you from that which you cannot handle yourself: the curse will not be lifted from you, nor will your life get easier, but it will stop you being killed and it will put you within a loop of cause and effect. If you learn compassion, patience and generosity out of the suffering, then lifelines of compassion, patience and generosity will be thrown out to you to give you what you need and no more. It will not stop the learning or strengthening process that happens with chronic curses, but it will give you the chance not to be destroyed.

It all sounds spiritual, and that is because it is. Heavy death curses peel away all the pap from one's life and from one's magical experiences, and what you are left with is a view of the Universe. You learn that taking action in the inner and outer worlds, regardless of what that action is for, shortens and limits power. Witnessing and upholding the natural flow of action in the Universe however, exposes you to the true extent of power that flows through all the worlds: it is breathtaking.

14. Dismantling Hermetic or Kabbalistic curses

This is the magical basis for the religious saying, "let God deal with it." It does work, but only if approached the right way. You cannot turn over your responsibilities, nor can you dump your learning path. What will happen is anything that is truly beyond your ability to cope with will be dealt with, and the rest is up to you. It will teach you a lot, it will strengthen you and it will test you to the extreme of life, but it will not destroy you unless you let it.

Basic practicalities: don't do protection rituals, and don't summon beings to protect you. Go into the Void and learn to be still, call out for Divine Being to send you beings to help you in any way that you truly need help, and make these meditations and calls a daily practice. And in return, be truly of service/help to those around you who are placed in your path, and to the Inner Worlds. Learn to trust and communicate properly with the beings that work with you, let them do their job: don't try and direct them.

Don't do anything that triggers the various levels of the curse : i.e. going to places that you were bound from, seeing people you were blocked from, doing activities that were part of the curse (ie. writing, teaching, magical practice, etc. Go to ground for a while and be patient. Your body needs time to adjust so that you can survive in the long term.

Do not, under *any* circumstances get into the silly New Age Wiccan fantasy of 'sending it back.' A curse is not a poison pen letter: it is a heavily crafted piece of magical structure with a bloody great being attached to it. Not only will it blow your boat out of the water with tripwires, but you are also getting into a 'conversation' energetically with the sender. This will cause a deeper digging in of the relationship between curser and cursed, and the dance will continue for much, much longer. It will also obviate immediately any deep inner protection that you might be getting from the Inner Worlds.

To care for your body is important...and the following advice will sound like the exact opposite of what is healthy! You will need power substances that block certain energies and make you denser. So if you are a vegetarian, start eating meat. Coffee, tobacco and chocolate are all power substances that work in various ways to filter inner powers, which is why they were used by the priests and kings in the Central

14.3. So what about protection?

American cultures. Coffee is a wonderful blocking tool as it affects the serotonin levels, which is one of the things that inner attacks work through: the endocrine system is vulnerable during an attack and will probably burn out along with the immune system if it is a chronic curse.

Stay away from gambling, lotto cards, bingo, anything that involves you possibly gaining from chance: this obviates inner protection and inner providing. You can only be on one fate wheel at a time and by going onto the luck/chance fate wheel, you climb off the wheel where you have handed over your fate to a higher and more sensible power.

Stay away from alcohol, as it will open you wider to the effects of the attack, as will most drugs. Also anti-inflammatory drugs can be counterproductive as they seem to mess with the body's ability to cope with a full-on attack. When first attacked, the body can have an immune reaction as it will see the attack as an invading being, which it is, and will respond accordingly.

More usually, the victim quickly becomes sick with all the symptoms of a major acute infection (high fever, breathing difficulties, rashes, severe headache, etc.) but the blood tests will reveal nothing. Once the acute phase is over, the body will settle into a chronic illness mode and will slowly degenerate. The illness usually takes on the pattern of autoimmune disease without the usual blood markers. The illness can and often does become severe over a few years and even when the curse is lifted, the damage can take years to mend.

Don't do heavy inner work, don't frequent power sites, try to stay as invisible as possible until you can find someone to lift it. And that moves onto the next important point: do not try and deal with the curse yourself. No matter how powerful you think you are, most structured curses have booby traps that will trigger if the cursed person goes anywhere near them. Think of the curse as a nuclear bomb strapped to your abdomen: it is best to let someone else deal with it as they can look from a different angle to you and will see tripwires that you cannot see from your perspective.

This in itself is a bummer as people who have the true ability to lift such curses are not particularly thick on the ground, particularly in the higher echelons of the Western Magical World. Most of

14. Dismantling Hermetic or Kabbalistic curses

them these days have weakened themselves by selling out to the workshop and commercial publishing merry-go-round which by its greedy nature disempowers and disconnects people from deeper levels of power.

The other problem is that technical knowledge is not enough: the person needs to have access to true real power, needs to have an experience of working with many different types of beings and needs to have a strong sense of adventure so that they will not be easily scared off. In fact, technical knowledge is the least important thing in that someone with the correct qualities, connections and inner contacts can be given a technical crash course. But they have to be connected to a priesthood to draw upon: when a priest or priestess is consecrated into a tradition, they carry the power of the collective within them, which practically means collective contacts and collective power.

And if you eventually find someone with all those qualities, then they have to be willing to delve into danger: curse removal, like bomb disposal, is dangerous. It is also a lengthy, drawn-out process that can take weeks or months depending on its construction. Once the first layer is off, then the cursed person can work with the lifter if they are skilled enough, and then the dismantling will take less time and have less of an impact on the lifter. This is the other thing that tends to make it difficult to get someone to work on lifting a curse: it takes a lot of energy and has a massive impact on their body. It is hard graft work and like all hard work, it makes the body tired and sore.

14.4 Dismantling the curse: working methods

Note: there are parts of this section where I will deliberately avoid too much detail: for those who are too dumb to figure out why, putting out too much information about how curses are constructed would be a little silly, to say the least. Hopefully the middle ground will get the info to those who need it without giving it to those who want it.

"A curse is a construction using patterns, beings, energies and shapes that are brought together to achieve a goal." Hmm, so what does this mean in real terms? The use of Western Kabbalistic Magic usually moves into the realms of angelic beings and these beings are

14.4. Dismantling the curse: working methods

the most commonly used being for cursing. They are like point and click beings: you get their 'frequency,' use ritual to bind the being to the curse and off it will go. Demons on the other hand are a little trickier to use: they are closer down the pole to density (see section on the Abyss) so they have desires that can be used for bargaining. That makes them potentially unstable: they will seriously think about it if the cursed person offers them a better payoff. The same can be applied to faery beings: they like to haggle. So if the attacker is Hermetic and the curse is skilfully put together, chances are that the being involved is angelic.

The two most common elements of the angelic beings are fire and air. You can spend half a lifetime learning the names, attributes and family trees of various angelic beings, but to strip a curse off, what you really need to know is what element or attribute is it: is it an angel of fire? an angel of destruction? This knowledge is the key to the first stage of stripping off the curse.

And the more powerful the angelic being is, the less human its representation will be. The closer to humanity an angelic being is, the more sympathy it can have with humanity and the less likely it will be to allow the curser to bind it into service. The further up the Abyss the angel is and the further away from humanity it is, the less chance there is of it being even remotely interested in humanity. The point is, the further away and more powerful these beings are, the less of a humanoid shape they will have. Closer to humanity they tend to have eyes, wings, etc. The further away they are, the more they take on the appearance of Platonic solids, multifaceted complex shapes, or even mathematical structures. The truly devastating and powerful archangelic beings further up the Abyss tend to appear as their element or source construct: a tornado for air, a wall of flames for fire, etc.

It is prudent to note at this point that if someone has constructed a curse using this level of being, chances are they have a lot of ritual help (i.e. a group) and a lot of people to draw from energetically. The people might not be aware that their energies are being used in such a way, and that innocence has no effect on the curse: it will work anyway as they are just a battery to draw from.

14. Dismantling Hermetic or Kabbalistic curses

It is often a group gathering where the people are all focused on one thing for a period of time, like a workshop, teaching session or prayer session. It is irrelevant what they are doing, just that they are all together at one time, an element is present (a flame usually) and that there is a central point of focus (an action, ritual, meditation or prayer). Alternatively a large gathering of people who are on drugs can be used, but this is less focused and less reliable. This need for a large, focused group immediately cuts down the number of people who would attempt to construct such a curse as most people do not have access to such resources.

What that battery of energy does is launch the attack: working with such beings takes a great deal of energy and creates massive impact, therefore sharing the load is important.

The ritual itself can take many different forms, although there are some pretty old ones kicking about that are not too difficult to get a hold of, like the Pulsa D'Nora, but as I said before, the technical details are not that important: it's the contacts, inner ability and focus coupled with a power source that is needed.

The other ingredient for such an action is connection to an inner priesthood through a consecration. This is not a mandatory ingredient, but it will put a massive amount of power behind the attack.

With these ingredients, you can see that it is not simple and easy to curse someone, but such complexity makes it a lot easier to narrow down the search for the perpetrator. More often than not there are at least two people involved for a death curse, though singular attacks are not unknown.

14.5 What do they look like on the inner?

First you have to decide what is the safest way to look at them? Some heavy curses are tripwired to attack anyone who approaches them on the inner. You can use a tarot reading using the Tree of Life layout to look and find out what element of angelic being you are looking at. To get a clear answer you will first have to push aside any inner veils that hang around the situation and give false readings. A good way to do this is to ask the cards to tell you the truth, not what someone wants you to see: sometimes the simplest and most obvious method is the most powerful.

Once you know what type of angelic being upholds the curse, then you have to go into the angelic structure of that being and operate from within it: a fragment of that being will work through you and the being upholding the curse will see an angelic fragment, not a hyperventilating curse lifter! It is probably wise, when you do this, to have a partner working with you to hold the gates open and support you energetically. If you are terrified (which is a healthy state to be in when stepping through angels) the partner will carry the physical reaction to such fear so that you are not distracted by not being able to breathe.

When you look at someone one the inner who has been cursed, they look odd to say the least. Apart from the state that their inner energies are in, the curse itself can often look bizarre which can be off-putting and confusing to someone looking at them for the first time. The person is often surrounded by strange sigils or script: this is the binding that is spoken aloud, usually in Hebrew as it is a sacred language and holds power.

Then you will see either a being attached, around or even within them if a lesser being is used, or you will see a strange three-dimensional shape over their heads, which is the angelic being itself. Sometimes you will see the victim impaled by a magical implement and/or surrounded by wind/fire/rocks. Sometimes they are bound with concrete or tentacles if lesser elements/beings have been used, and sometimes, if they have really pissed someone off, they will have everything but the kitchen sink on and around them.

The area around them will often look like a war zone or a vacuum, as the curse will be affecting everything around them.

14.6 How are curses taken off?

The whole curse will not be taken off in one go: they are usually multifaceted, complex and may have been reiterated many times to strengthen them (some people are just so anal about their work: they keep going in and making improvements...sheesh!).

14. Dismantling Hermetic or Kabbalistic curses

The first thing you have to do is to strip off the angelic being. Once that is off, then the rest is just time and detail, as the angelic being hangs everything together. Next you have to cut off the power source without harming those people involved, and dispense with any parasitical beings that have come along for the ride. If the groups of people powering the curse are still ongoing, then you have to either keep cutting off the source of power, or you have to divert it to less dangerous uses. After that, it is a long road of stripping off layers of script using the angelic working contact you have, pulling out the magical implements and returning them carefully to the original inner implement, and then pulling off all the blocks, bindings, etc. that you find.

If you know who the attacker is, and they have something that belongs to the victim, chances are that object or bit of DNA (hair, etc.) is being used to direct the action. You will need to go in vision, find the object and take the inner form of the object into the Void where the inner imprint can no longer be used to launch a new attack.

Also, if the attacker is clever and devious, they will have constructed or trapped a scapegoat being to take any backlash, fate impact or energy kickback from the attack. This will appear to the lifter as a vastly inflated being that is not bright and is bound in slavery to the attacker. It will probably be attached to the site of the temple/working space that the attack is constructed in. It would be compassionate to unbind such a tormented creature and cut the cord that binds it to its master. It would also be wise to take it into the Void.

This whole process can take weeks or months. It is time consuming, exhausting and has to be done carefully and methodically. During this process you also have to be careful to make sure that if the attacker becomes aware that the curse is being lifted, that you take proper precautions to make sure that a new attack cannot be launched—and if it is launched, that it doesn't find its target. Usually the first time someone is attacked they are blissfully unaware of what is coming. The second time they tend to be a little wiser and are ready.

Another useful procedure that can be used if the angelic being attached is of a high frequency is to work in the realm of the Tree of Life. When the soul manifests in the position of Daath, it takes on a complex structure which is made up of angelic consciousness through which the soul manifests into life. Tracking up the tree of someone's soul will bring you to this structure and it is here where damage will show itself if high-level angelic beings have been used. The complex pattern looks a bit like a Metatron Cube and if an angel is still attached, it will show here. The trick is to take the shape of the angelic being off and repair the complex pattern back to its original form. The danger is not recognizing what is the threshold pattern for the soul and taking that off instead of the angel. If you are not used to working with angels and thresholds as geometric patterns, then this is a technique that would best not be used.

Seeing magical cursing at this depth is intriguing and educating. Most of the time, when someone has sent something of this depth, they are not fully aware of its power and complexity. They call up specific angelic beings that are bound and wind them into the curse. The rest happens automatically from much earlier constructions, which often the sender is not aware of. Magical names, patterns and invocations if used in the right way will do the job if there is inner energy behind them: it's a bit like ready-constructed software. The real danger is when you have a Kabbalist who really knows what they are doing, has a sense of justification and a bad simmering temper. The deeper their knowledge, the more dangerous they become.

14.7 What is the cleanup procedure?

The cursed person will be sludged, chronically sick and low on inner energy. They will need ritual salt baths, connection with nature, good food and time to rest and recover. The lifter must make sure that they clean themselves and the room well after each session. (Also make sure that before you start, the room and the house/apartment/temple that you are due to work in is clean, balanced and tidy: you must leave no corner for nasties to hide in or attach to.)

Just as curse removal takes time, so does the recovery and it can take months or even a couple of years, depending on how long the cursed victim was under attack, for them to recover and regain their full strength. What is important, however, is that they begin a regular

14. Dismantling Hermetic or Kabbalistic curses

meditation practice to bring their consciousness back into action. The lifter must also be aware that what they have undertaken was a massive physical strain and must rest/recoup adequately for a few weeks before taking on another such task. Thankfully, these situations do not happen often, not at this level anyhow.

Chapter Fifteen

Short tour of the Tree of Life without Kabbalah

The Tree of Life structure was put together to map out the externalization of Divine Being into substance. It was also a working tool: by putting together a coherent structure that people could see, it allowed people to actively interact with and observe the power of that Divine Being. Because the structure reflects such power, it is complex and intricate: the more you look at a powerful pattern, the more you will see.

One of the problems with presenting such a pattern to humanity is that they will focus on the intricate patterns and take great delight in finding new and more complex patterns: they lose sight of the real power and what it is trying to express. Therefore you end up with lots of people who all know the spheres, the pathways, the names and interconnections etc., but they do not look at the passage of Divinity through the Tree or within themselves.

Today in modern magic, people are expected to learn the paths and patterns of the Tree of Life by learning words in a sacred language that they do not understand. That in itself disables a lot of the power that can be accessed. The sacred names do hold power within themselves but the spheres are not dependent upon that power: it is a filter that can be approached with a different sacred utterance or breath.

But the reason to move away from that Kabbalistic pattern is deeper and more important: any pattern, though it creates a safety net, also limits and shapes power, dictating how that power can be connected with. The patterns and networks create paths of thought that discipline the mind, giving focus and strength. But eventually, for the mystical mind, it limits the expansion of understanding and

15. Short Tour of the Tree of Life without Kabbalah

heavily filters the ability of humans to interact with Divinity and angelic beings.

Once that pattern has been fully learned, it becomes inherent within that human so that even if they walk away from that pattern, it still lives within them and still limits them to some extent. I do think that this was intentional as a protective measure, but I also feel that such a protective action is counterproductive for humanity. We always think we know better than the universe, rather than trusting such power.

The pattern can be loosely worked with, stripping it down to almost nothing and looking at the natural flow of power and how the natural inner pattern works. If such a thing is dangerous for someone, then the chances are that that they will not get it. This is the whole point of not limiting each other as humans: you can never really tell what a fellow human is truly capable of: it is not for us to judge, filter and exclude. Nature will do that naturally.

Using the structure as sparsely as possible enables the human consciousness to comprehend something so vast without cluttering it with dead ends, endless mazes and important sounding titles (which we all love so much...). If it is inappropriate for that person, they will not understand it, they will be blocked from it or they will lose interest. This is the most common trip-up for humanity. Real power is not glamorous: it doesn't twinkle and give us importance and it doesn't give status or titles. It is simple, hard work, and requires a lot of focus and perseverance.

15.1 So what actually is the Tree of Life?

It is a map that shows the power of formation from formless Divine Power to the world and everything in it. It is the progression from formlessness to substance: it maps the creation of the Universe. It shows the focused eternal soul descending into physical form and acquiring emotion, intellect and imagination. It shows where we came from and where we return to. The outer pattern of the Tree of Life in Kabbalistic terms is a reflection of a pattern that exists on the inner planes: humanity has just made it a little more complicated.

15.1. So what actually is the Tree of Life?

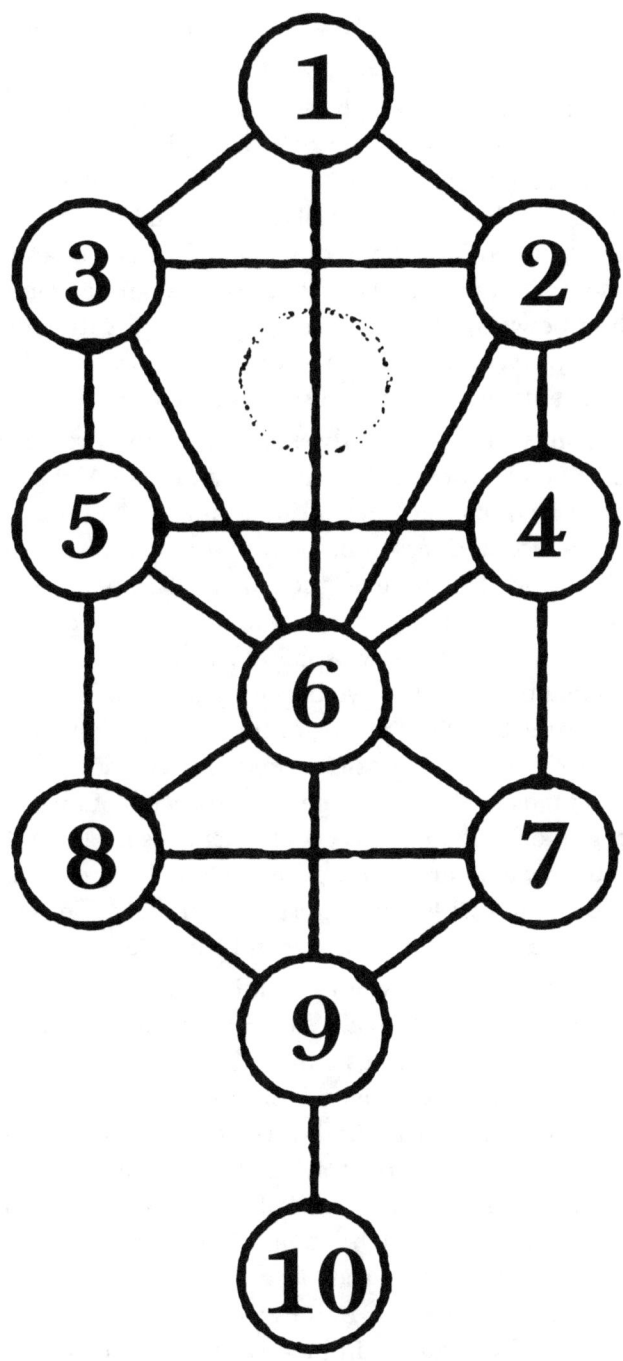

Figure 15.1: Diagram of the Tree of Life

15. Short Tour of the Tree of Life without Kabbalah

The first sphere is the first breath/act of consciousness out of the Void: it is Divinity unpolarized, poised on the brink of expression.

The second and third sphere are the separation of Divine consciousness into negative and positive. Without that split, life and the universe cannot happen as everything that takes on physical manifestation is polarized. This polarized Divinity stands (from our perspective) on the other side of the Abyss. The Abyss appears to us in vision as a vast crack in a Desert landscape, and essentially it is a dividing line between Divinity and the rest of creation/destruction (the Universe). It is also a place/state of storage and profound learning, hence its official Kabbalistic name is Daat.

Once Divinity crosses the Abyss, it begins the process of taking on form. The polarization that occurred before the Abyss is repeated and mirrored: Divinity becomes positive (forth sphere) and negative (fifth sphere) action and inaction, forward momentum and movement withheld. The fourth sphere is the 'forward into creation' power, and the fifth sphere is the 'brakes on the power of creation' or 'destruction.' Between those two spheres sits the sixth sphere which is the fulcrum that balances the two opposing powers. The three central sefirot provide the building blocks for the inner soul of the soon-to-be created living being/world: positive, negative and stasis between the two powers in tension. At this stage in the process of formation, for a vessel to begin forming to allow a soul to express itself in the physical realm, it must have inner dynamics that will link together the deeper powers of formation with time, substance and fate. Those dynamics are also part and parcel of the powers of the three central sefirot.

When you get to the seventh, eighth and ninth sefirot, you are now in to the 'production' area of mirror dynamics that are evident in all living things, and for us as humans, they are dynamics that flow through every aspect of our lives from how we act, how our bodies work, to how we operate within our fate paths. These three sefirot are very much about *how we live* and are dynamics that the magician can actively engage in their life and work. Sefirot seven and eight are our 'two feet' that carry us through fate and life, and they are powers of discipline/endurance and release/loosening. These dynamics in their deepest true sense is how our bodies work, and the same dynamics can be intentionally engaged in how we do our magic and how we live our lives.

15.1. So what actually is the Tree of Life?

The ninth sefirot is about fate patterns, genetic patterns, blood, ancestral lines, and also about our imagination, our emotions and our dreams: how we dream and imagine our lives to be. To exist, we are a thought first. The inner idea and pattern of the body is formed, then the ancestral/fate patterns begin to form.

The final sefirot is our living body, our world, our universe: it is everything around us. It is Divine Power manifest into human or physical form—the Divine Universal consciousness that, breathed out, takes on physical form and becomes a human body, a tree, a planet. This is the root of the teaching that 'God is in everyone' and we are all Divine Being. The tenth sphere is also the world, creation manifest, the vessel for life itself.

Now you have to keep in mind that the Tree of Life with its spheres and paths is simply a map of a creation process. It is not really a natural pattern, but it was created by a man as a way to formalize the pattern that is the expression of Divinity within humanity.

That map has now become complex to the point of ridiculousness and has almost come to a point of uselessness. The above description is an attempt to take it back to a simpler form. As humans we love to list things, organize things, pattern things and form groups, tribes and hierarchies. That immediately powers down our ability to truly experience the natural magical world around us, and to truly partake of that world without conditions. It is the stepping out of the Garden: by having to have knowledge and control, we obviate our ability to truly *know*.

Some of this harks back to former discussions regarding working with angels and the Kabbalistic filters. Kabbalah teaches certain patterns to open up a filtered threshold through which we can work with angels. But it limits how we 'see' that angelic being and how we work with it. That angel can only respond within the parameters that we set, which also limits the angelic being in its ability to interact and work with us. Now I am not saying that the Kabbalistic way of working with angels is not powerful: it most certainly is. What I am saying is that it limits us from the true scope of that being, both in our experience and how we work with it.

Working with angelic beings without the rigidity of that structure opens the door for that angel in all its true power. The angelic being

15. Short Tour of the Tree of Life without Kabbalah

itself determines how much of that power you will have access to through that door. It will give you access to what you need and no more. It will not stop your access based upon your intentions as there is no moral filter with these beings: if you can handle the power, then you will get access to it. If you cannot, then you will not.

And working with the progression of Divinity into humanity is much the same: if you can take the pressure of riding with Divinity as it falls out of the Void and into life, then you will go along with the ride and observe what truly happens. If you are not able to hold that level of power, nothing will happen.

Working through the Tree of Life pattern enables us to take apart what we see in a deeper experience and break it down into manageable parts for understanding. It also allows an observer or researcher to look closely at one aspect of the progression and zoom in on it. For example, from the Tree structure we can see that the pattern for mind and emotions are formed just before the body is formed. It has an inner as well as outer quality to it, but it is not part of the eternal soul, it is only an inner part of this life expression.

Chapter Sixteen

The Structure of the Abyss without Kabbalah

The Abyss, like angelic beings, has been the territory of mystical Kabbalah almost to the point of exclusivity. The complexity of real Kabbalistic training has so many tangles, filters and dead ends that it can encourage the practitioner to become focused upon patterns to the extent of truly missing what they are attempting to work with.

Some of that structure was originally woven into the training methods as a safety valve, not only to discourage idiots and casual glances, but also to create a 'firewall' from an inner point of view. When you work with an Angelic being, you are potentially playing with a 'nuclear' type of power. The names, attributes, patterns, shapes and rituals filter and form the power that you work with, and dictate what method of interaction is used with such a being.

So you get a focused, filtered, power controlled contact that does specific things and does not move out of its structure. Although that is still powerful and dangerous, it is much safer to work with as a magical practitioner.

If you do not use these filters, shapes and patterns, then you are faced with the true power of the Angelic being in all its glory and you have to be extremely focused, unconditional and balanced. You also have to be willing to die if it is necessary.

This rule is also true for working in and with the Abyss. If it is approached with its magical filters then it can be worked with safely but in a limited and filtered way. The more patterns, attributes and rules we apply, the less of the Abyss we are able to access.

And yet accessing the Abyss without such filters is asking for trouble unless you know what you are doing. Many a hapless magician has been burned to a crisp by reaching down or up the

16. THE STRUCTURE OF THE ABYSS WITHOUT KABBALAH

realms of the Abyss in pursuit of power. If you reach into the Abyss for power, it will destroy you in one way or another eventually.

When you reach beyond the surface world in magical practice, you reach into worlds of beings and power. If you reach beyond that level, you begin to touch upon the workings of the universe and the structures/beings that make sure the universe continues to exist and function (the universal boiler room). If you are stupid enough to think that you can reach into the boiler room to tap into that power for personal gain, then you are an idiot.

If you want to reach into the boiler room to be of service, then you are still probably an idiot (it is extremely dangerous) but at least you are a worthy idiot and with such selfless intent, you will probably be protected to an extent. If humanity does not create its own filters, then the Inner Worlds will do it for you, and theirs tend to be far more workable.

The inner filters work to protect you from complete destruction, but they will allow enough power though to do the job and teach you something: bear in mind that humanity always learns the hard way. It can be a difficult lesson, though usually a important one.

What is the Abyss? If you strip all the formal padding away that has been attributed to it, you are left with a multidimensional freeway for power and consciousness. The way that we see it when we look at it from an inner point of view is just the way our brains perceive it: it has no real form as such.

The Abyss is a highway from the highest form of consciousness to the lowest: the two extremes meet one another and are of one another. It is mirrored in the Tree of Life with Divine Being at the top and Humanity at the bottom, so the Abyss is Divine consciousness without form at the 'top' and the densest of beings at the 'bottom.' If I try to describe the shaping too much I will really get my knickers in a twist, because the dimensions of this structure are many and are beyond our ability to grasp.

Divine Being is at the top, then archangelic and angelic beings, at the point of Humanity is the Desert/abyss, which is the area that is our fulcrum for the whole thing. Below our fulcrum are demons, bigger demons and then Divine Being in its densest form. (Which is also primal and newly-birthed humanity.) In between those levels are lots of interconnections, levels of consciousness and a wide variety of beings. The structure also bends in on itself, so that the top and bottom are the flip sides of one another. Humanity in the middle is our balanced state between good and bad, no form and density: we are the fulcrum of the Tree.

At this point it is worth noting that when magicians figure this out (that humanity is the fulcrum) many tend to trip out on being the master species. Those tend to be the stupid ones. At the fulcrum is also the rest of our physical world: the animals, plants, etc. Everything that is physically manifest is in our realm of the fulcrum. The other levels are different worlds/states of consciousness: hence shedding your humanity is one of the keys to exploring and working with the Abyss.

In reality humanity tends to veer from that centre line in both directions: so the Satanists dive down and the Messiahs reach up (they tend to get nailed to bits of wood if they go too high up...). The goal of Humanity is to stay at that midline: to keep the balance of substance and non-substance, good and bad, in perfect harmony, and to stay in their own realm.

That is why it is so important when you work deeply in the Inner Worlds that first you go through the Void and shed your everyday world. Then you approach the Abyss unconditionally, without selfish intent and with proper focus: that way you cannot be dragged to one extreme or the other. This is also the reason why, when you first begin working at the Abyss, you are often asked if you are willing to give up your life. You have to be willing to let go of everything, therefore nothing can be used to seduce you and nothing can hold you back. If you can shed life within life, then you are a step further on in the Mysteries (this is the root of the death within life initiation).

Another point to look at with this pattern is what happens at conception: the act of making love reaches through the worlds in search of a consciousness to bring into form. If you imagine that the couple is making love at the bottom of the structure (which is also at the fulcrum) they open an inner vortex that stretches up through the Abyss until it reaches as far as it can go. Then a soul tumbles in from that level and falls into conception.

16. The Structure of the Abyss without Kabbalah

This is the basis for the sacred union: the sex between priest and priestess, Queen and King, etc. Their lovemaking would be focused and with spiritual intent for bringing through a sacred child. They would go through a variety of physical and mental preparations, and the act itself would be held in a sacred space. The method used is also mirrored in the Mysteries of Tantra.

The flip side of the sacred union is debauched, unhealthy forced or unconnected sex where the vortex does not reach far up and brings through unhealthy beings. Faery children are born when the vortex reaches to the Faery Realm: one or both partners mediate a faery being while making love so the Vortex reaches up to that frequency.

It is like tuning a radio: whatever frequency/wavelength you are on, that is what you will bring into your body. And it does not have to be a physical child: this can also bring through inner beings when done with intent.

So, back to the Abyss. Not only is Divine Being 'up,' it is also 'across.' When you cross the Abyss, you are into the realm of Divinity polarized, and then unformed but preparing for form. To understand this better, look at the Tree of Life: you cross the Abyss and you hit Divinity split into Male and Female (Chokmah and Binah) beyond that is God without Form but in preparation (Kether).

This split into Male and Female is purely for the fulcrum/human realm: we are by nature polarized beings (male/female, positive/negative) as is the world around us. Divinity filters through that polarization so that Divinity and humanity can be aware of each other. The further away a being is from the Fulcrum, the less aware of humanity it is.

The dimensions and twists of the Abyss can be mind-bending: God is up and also across. And Divinity is also down in its most dense twisted form, as is the human form—which brings about the reflection of the ability within humanity for great good or great evil. It depends which part of the pole you are sliding down (or up). The best way is to get blindingly drunk, then it all makes sense.

In practical terms you would work in the boiler room (remember the boiler room?) for specific reasons rather than sightseeing or personal gain. If you are in the business of creating a sacred or faery child, if you are working with Angelic consciousness, if you are working within the realm of death, if you are an exorcist, a worker in Universal service, or if you are stupid enough to want to stand at the foot of God, or connect with a demon, then the Abyss is for you.

The closer to the fulcrum a being is, the more aware it is of humanity and it will be either 'friendly' towards humanity or 'unfriendly.' The further a being is away from the fulcrum the less aware of humanity it is and it will therefore neither be 'for' nor 'against.' Also, the further away from the fulcrum a being is the more powerful and less physically formed it is and the less able it is to manifest in the physical realm. It has to pass down the Abyss towards humanity to appear in our world: hence the angels and demons taking human/animal form.

To work with true angelic form without a human filter, you have to go up the Abyss to its own realm and meet it as an inner being. The same is also true for what we call demons. The two sides of the Abyss beyond the fulcrum reflect for us the two sides of power: threshold mediation power becomes angels and demons, the extremes become Divinity in dense form or formlessness, etc.

All the levels between have their own 'fulcrums' that appear as tunnels and as the beings of those levels come to the edge of the Abyss, they have their own 'up' and 'down.' Our spiritual evolution is about being cast 'down' and finding our way back 'up' to formlessness.

If you are an exorcist, this boiler room can be especially useful as it enables one to commune with beings at their own level in their own realm as opposed to how they express themselves when they are in our polarized worlds. It is also safer to approach some of these beings this way. However the rule of the Abyss, as always, is to be focused, be in service, and have no wants or needs. True clarity and the Void within keeps a worker safe in the deepest realms and keeps the inner filters in place.

That is not to say you won't get the shit hammered out of you: you probably will. But that is just the side effect of working at such depth: it is not from any being attacking you. The deeper or higher you go away from your own realm or the fulcrum, the more of an impact it is going to have on your body. Even though you are working through your mind, the power filters through the physical body and you will

16. THE STRUCTURE OF THE ABYSS WITHOUT KABBALAH

feel like you have just built a house singlehandedly while being beaten with a cricket bat.

What can go wrong? Oh, lots! If you are a skinny, spotty, black-clothed, chain-festooned Luciferian intent on communing with demons to expand your power over women, men, groups, and to get a bigger willy, then one of three things will happen:

1. You will not manage it but will end up connecting with bottom-feeder, parasite-type beings. This will take you down a path of feeling terribly important and possibly depressed at the same time. You will become paranoid, depressed, withdrawn and even spottier (the power flows through your body and will enhance any imbalance, therefore if you were spotty to begin with, it will get worse).

2. If you should happen to have natural abilities and are able to connect with beings, then you may in fact connect with a lesser (nearer to our realm) demon who may offer you just what you want and have a really amusing time at your expense, and your willy will not get bigger.

3. If you are truly naturally able to connect with beings you may reach a deep 'demonic' or Titan consciousness that will look at you in complete fascination, being unable to work out exactly what you are and what the hell you want. These beings can be disastrous for humanity not because they are 'bad' but because of the sheer power they mediate.

The same is true of going 'up.' Angelic beings closer to our realm tend to be worked with in the Kabbalistic patterns (among others). You can also work with them outside of those patterns, but you do need to be focused with your intent and concentration (otherwise all that will be left of you is a pair of slightly burned shoes).

If you have natural talent for connecting with beings, you might also reach up quite far and come face-to-face with an archangelic being (well, not quite face-to-face: as with the deeper demons, they are rather large...) which, like the deeper demon or Titan, will look at you with total astonishment before trying to communicate with you. If it does, not even your shoes will be left.

There are methods for working and communicating in both directions with these beings, and the methods are simple, direct and hard to maintain. If you chose to toss aside the magical structures/patterns and don't do it via drugs (which is the worst possible way, just because of the lack of control: the drug is in the driving seat) then working through the Void or carrying the Void within is your best option.

If you are working from an intention of universal service, then you will have the natural inner filters in place, and working through the Void will bring you to a fraction of the being you need to work with. Note the use of the work 'need.' When you go through the Void, you are connected to what you need for the job, not necessarily what you want.

If you work through the pattern of the Abyss, take the Void within you and the same filters will be in place. You have to try to maintain a balance, though: if you are working in the Abyss, work in both directions. This not only ensures that you gain a working knowledge of beings on both sides of the 'fence,' which is handy in any deep work, but it also maintains a sense of inner balance, which is also important if you are engaging in deep useful magic.

Those workers who constantly reach up and work only with angelic beings, climbing higher and higher up the ladder of angels, eventually stretch too far away from the fulcrum and 'cease to be' (or in Yorkshire terms, they fry themselves). The prophet Enoch 'who walked with God and was not' is one example. The angels are the beings that bring pattern into being, and also dismantle patterns—including humans.

And what happens if you only reach down the Abyss, going deeper and deeper? Well, I guess you become a conservative politician. The beings of the lower Abyss are ancient beings that manipulate and hold patterns in being. So you implode physically and mentally.

But for sensible, balanced and powerful work, work on both sides, and up and down. Work for true intent and with focus: and by true intent I don't mean 'good' or 'bad': I mean true intent, for a job, something that is not selfish. Good and bad is relative to your culture/religion, it depends on which end of the action you are on. But

16. THE STRUCTURE OF THE ABYSS WITHOUT KABBALAH

the difference between selfish and unselfish acts is a big difference in the inner worlds. Selfish acts will work, but they only work to a point. Unselfish acts that are a part of service to the Universe have almost limitless access to power: it is all down to what you are capable of holding.

Chapter Seventeen

The eighteenth-century pattern of initiation in Britain

In the eighteenth century in Britain, ritualized gardens started to appear on the properties of wealthy landowners. The best example of these can be found at Stourhead, a 2,650 acre country estate at the source of the river Stour in the southwest of England. The estate is about 4 km northwest of the town of Mere and includes a Palladian mansion, the village of Stourton, ritual gardens, the Spread Eagle Inn, farmland and woodland. Stourhead has been owned by the National Trust since 1946.

The house and ritual gardens were built and developed by the Hoare family in conjunction with Capability Brown, namely by Henry Hoare II (1705–1785) an English banker, and subsequently his grandson Sir Richard Colt Hoare (1758–1838). Sir Richard Colt Hoare was an English antiquarian, archaeologist, artist, and traveller of the eighteenth and nineteenth centuries. He was also the first major figure to conduct a detailed study of the archaeological history of his home county of Wiltshire, and is considered the 'grandfather' of British archaeology.

These ritual gardens developed during the Enlightenment era, where most landowners and intellectuals were involved in the new developing concept of ancient rite and Freemasonry, and of the esoteric Mysteries in general.

The gardens at Stourhead allude to the Aeneid and the story of the descent of Aeneas into the Underworld. The Aeneid was written by Virgil around 20 B.C. as a foundation myth for the birth and greatness of Rome. Within the texts are many different tales that are littered with mythic and magical themes, and book VI of the Aeneid features a tale of struggle, victory, ascent and destiny of the mythical hero Aeneas the Trojan who became an ancestor of Rome.

The layout and buildings of the garden are loosely styled along the steps taken by Aeneas and are woven in with esoteric themes and allegories. It presents a ritual pattern of discarding the mundane in search of the gods, with the theme of initiation running strongly through the pattern.

The following is an account of what I found in and upon the land of Stourhead in Wiltshire: I was manoeuvred by a series of odd circumstances that ended up with me staying in Mere for a couple of days and being invited to spend that time wandering the gardens at Stourhead to see what I thought about it, and what I could pick up magically from the site.

I spent two days walking the garden and the ritual path: I went in vision and talked to the land, to the contacts and to the ritual inner contacts that are still operating through the magical pattern that is there. This is an account of what I found.

17.1 The Walk of Initiation at Stourhead, Wiltshire

In the mid-1700s, Sir Richard Colt Hoare, archaeologist and owner of Stourhead house, expanded upon his grandfather's and uncle's work in the creation of a Landscape of Enlightenment. Sir Richard, like his uncle before him, was a freemason and was instrumental in the founding and developing of an Apollo Lodge at Stourton (initially held at the Spread Eagle Arms Inn, Stourton).

Sir Richard was fascinated by ancient history and the land itself. He opened over three hundred ancient barrows in the area around Stourhead and wrote down what he found. He unearthed what later became known as burials of the Beaker People: ancient Britons buried in mounds, often in couples, near a spring with a richly ornamented cup and a copper dagger placed between them. Stourhead gardens and lake was created by damming six natural springs. It is obvious from the location of the burials and the type of burials that the springs were sacred.

The landscape that was laid down at Stourhead was a ritual initiation of death-in-life, and was approached from an angle of myth, vision and the practical walking of one's own inner landscape. The path through the landscape mirrors the life challenges that a spiritual/magical seeker follows in his quest for initiation into the temple of Apollo.

There are other ritual gardens that date from the Enlightenment, but none of them have as much depth, or as many layers of ritual significance, as Stourhead. For example, at Studley Royal in Yorkshire, another Enlightenment garden, the path to the temple of Apollo/sun and the descent into the passage of birth are masterfully laid out, but the other points along the way are for visual appreciation, not ritual initiation. It is obvious from the Studley Royal layout, and that of Stowe (in Bucks) that such early Masonic patterning was fashionable, but often a parody of the true path of inner enlightenment.

The concept was that inner initiation can be reached by walking the outer landscape of a magical life: every life has an inner landscape that can be manipulated. The initiation was approached by externalizing that inner landscape, so the aspirant walked the outer path that mapped the inner path. They were walked together under the canopy of ancient Greek and Roman allegory.

These eighteenth century gardens were laid out according to patterns drawn from Virgil's Aeneid, following the descent of Aeneas into the Underworld. But the deeper layers of the death vision and the interrelations between the deities are laid one upon the other. Some are meaningful, and some defy reason. Some are just humorous and sometimes very magical, for example: the tunnel of birth is laid east southeast in the garden, E.S.E.: could this be a passing glance to *esse*, the Latin verb "to be"? (The place of birth/becoming.)

17.2 The Stourhead initiation

If you are working and walking the garden with magical intent, the powers that flow through the patterns within the garden will flow through your body. *Your body will understand the initiation, even if your mind doesn't.*

17. The Eighteenth-Century Pattern of Initiation in Britain

Beginning

The walk begins at the Stourton village: people, life, ordinary things from which we all originate. The aspirant visits the church to pray and devote himself to Divinity and the service to mankind.

The path then leads the aspirant first on a garden walk to the Temple of Flora. Originally when it was first built it was named the Temple of Ceres: she who brought agriculture and therefore civilization to humanity.

Temple of Flora/Ceres

Above the door is a warning to all: "Procul, O procul este, profani." Translated this reads "begone you who are unclean/uninitiated/unworthy!"

This sets the scene for the beginnings of the initiation. First the fruits of one's harvest must be sacrificed to the Goddess, which is all part of the usual initiation. The aspirant turns over his fate to the Goddess as he prepares to step into the unknown.

Then the deeper, more magical actions come to the surface. Below the temple, near the water's edge, is a stone mouth opening from which flows a spring into the lake. (Originally this had steps leading down to the water's edge where the springs gushed out.)

In the deeper part of the Mystery, both in an actual ritual action, and an inner visionary action, the aspirant initiate places his sword in the mouth of the spring and leaves it there.

Back in the temple a flame which sits within the water is doused, reflecting the release of the soul of the initiate as it begins the journey towards death within life.

He is cast from the temple to wander among the trees in search of the entrance to the Underworld and the golden bough. He walks among the giant trees and searches for the oak tree that holds the golden bough which will give him access to the Underworld. Once he finds it, he can approach the goddess for safe passage to the Underworld

17.2. The Stourhead initiation

Moon Pool of Diana

When he reaches the Moon Pool of Diana he is 'stripped of his humanity': in death, we must learn to let go of our old lives and move on. An attendant takes from him 'that which makes him human' (his clothing) and sends him into the Underworld with the golden bough, which gives him safe passage, to seek out the advice of a Goddess who sits in an Underworld Cave by a pool of dark water...He leaves naked.

Grotto of Ariadne

The journey through the trees and through the 'gate of horn' takes the initiate to the grotto in which Ariadne rests (originally Colt Hoare named the female statue Ariadne, which makes the most sense, as you will come to see; but many years later she was renamed 'a nymph.' The grotto is laid out so that Ariadne lies in the northwest, opposite Apollo, who is visible through the grotto window. The grotto holds four seats for four officers in the four cardinal directions, and the doorways are northeast and southwest.

The Goddess demands silence: "Drink in silence, or in silence lave." The initiate hands over the golden bough as a gift to her and then he drinks, or washes in, the sacred waters. This reflects the wisdom of the death vision: those who wish to remember all simply wash their face in the river/water of death. Those who are foolish or wish to forget will drink.

In the cave is the Goddess of the Underworld, reflected by Ariadne, she who weaves and gives a sword to Theseus. Bear in mind this area is part of Avalon, a place steeped in Mystery regarding cups and swords. Remember the cup/dagger burials in the barrows? The story of Excalibur/Caliburn and the Grail are just distant remnants of ancient magical wisdoms of this land: somehow Colt Hoare tapped into this and worked with it.

The Initiate offers the Goddess whatever appears in vision in his hand, usually his testicles (metaphorically, not literally) an act which is connected to his rejection of the mundane/death of his mundane life in the temple of Ceres. In return she reaches into the springs and

17. The Eighteenth-Century Pattern of Initiation in Britain

pulls out his sword (that was left in the spring of Ceres), which she returns to him transformed.

Upon leaving this Grotto he meets Neptune, who points to the obelisk in the distance (Phallus).

The Cottage/Vesta

The initiate climbs a simple path that ends at a pretty little gothic cottage with a bench outside. Inside, the cottage is dominated by a hearth that holds a hearty fire. It is a place of familial comfort and cooking. Here the Initiate can rest, relax, and if not careful, be drawn into domestic bliss. If the Initiate sits upon the bench and admires the view, he will notice that the church lies directly opposite the cottage: the church is in the east (God) and the cottage (humanity) is in the west. It is a direct reference to sacred architecture.

Once the Initiate is rested he must forge onward, leaving family and security behind, willingly letting them go and stepping forward into an unknown future.

The Pantheon

The Initiate then encounters the Pantheon. In the temple are gathered Goddesses, priestesses and one man (an Argonaut) who championed women's rights to be hunters. The Goddesses are Hera, Diana, Flora, Isis and the priestesses Susanna (wife of Sir Henry Hoare II) and Livia Drusilla Augusta: *Mater Patriae* of Rome (priestess of Ceres, the goddess of agriculture and therefore civilization). The temple is guarded or flanked by Baccus: intoxicating visions, and Venus: sexual passion.

In this temple, the Initiate confronts the many faces of woman or the Goddess.

Bridge over the River

The Initiate is cast from the temple when the women are satisfied with his answers and he walks down a path. At the bottom of the path, the Initiate encounters a bridge over the river Styx. As the initiate crosses the bridge, he realizes that as he looks back, he can see nothing of

17.2. The Stourhead initiation

his life that he leaves behind: as in death itself, he has to let go of everything that was before him.

As the initiate walks, the path opens to a walk beside the lake, and across the lake is the path that he has just walked. But instead of seeing it as it looked when he walked it (a series of high and low paths, dips, bends and turns, it now appears as a mundane path with not too much happening: pretty, but boring.

Then the initiate reaches the parting of the paths. He can choose the easy path back to the life he knew before, or he can choose the path of Hercules: the ultimate test of strength.

The Path of Hercules

The Path of Hercules is steep, like climbing the side of a mountain. In the death vision, the dead person is expected to scale a mountain and as he walks, he can hear the voices of sacred and profane utterances. The mountain is what we have put in our own path in terms of spiritual structures: the hurdles we create between us and God. Religion, which is man-made, becomes a difficult obstacle to the natural flow of communion between man and Divine Being. As we climb that path, we begin to think about the difficulties and dogmas we have created for ourselves, and then we let them go. At the base of the path are some steep steps which have a series of small cave-like structures on either side that probably housed officers who were the 'voices of the dead.'

The temple of Apollo

Once at the top the Initiate reaches the temple of Apollo and pounds upon the door for entrance.

At that point, sacred utterances of the Sun are whispered into his ear. His sword is enlivened as a weapon of Apollo and he is given a scabbard. Then the initiate is lifted from the floor, and the 'hands on' passing on of power is conducted. He is then invested in the colours of the Sun (white and gold robes) and told to walk forth in the sunrise.

17. The Eighteenth-Century Pattern of Initiation in Britain

The passage of birth

The initiate stumbles down a steep narrow path and enters a dark tunnel. He stumbles through the darkness, hearing noises and feeling people close to him, close enough to hear their breath, but he cannot see them. The feeling of fear and helplessness of going into a dark tunnel at night reaches a peak, but a faint light in the distance beckons the initiate. (The tunnel at Stourhead is not too impressive. However the tunnel of the same initiate walk at Studley Royal in Yorkshire is truly terrifying at twilight.)

He emerges in the weak dawn light to follow a path that takes him back to the village, the church and inn.

Chapter Eighteen

Working with Sleepers

There are many different types of sleepers scattered throughout the various cultural traditions around the world. Throughout history, humanity has had a deep relationship with the land, and that has often translated into the tradition of sleepers. I approach this subject purely from an esoteric point of view. I am not an archeologist and I only have access to the sorts of information that anyone can find on the internet or in a library. I do have friends who are archaeologists/university professors and I do milk them occasionally for information, but on the whole I work with sleepers in the best way I know how: through vision. This is the form that I have a great deal of experience with, and this is the path that I grew up with: you work with instinct, stories and legends.

18.1 So what are sleepers?

Sleepers are people who die ritually in such a way as to keep the soul within the body after death. Through this action, the soul interacts with the land, the spirits of the land, and the people. Most of the sleepers gave of themselves freely in service. Later, this practice degenerated in some cultures to a form of forcible entrapment.

Where are the sleepers? Well, they are everywhere and are still being unearthed to this day. Archaeologists still haven't been able to figure out for themselves the difference between an ordinary burial and a sleeper. This has led to some sleepers being dug up, separated from the land that they serve, and their bodies put on display. This causes a rupture in the relationship between the sleeper and the people, bringing about terrible catastrophes for the tribes concerned.

The sleeper in the Ukok Altai is a good example of this problem. The Altai sleeper was a woman who had slept in the land for two

18. WORKING WITH SLEEPERS

and a half thousand years in almost perfect condition. She slept in the permafrost, her tattoos of spirit animals still visible. When she was unearthed and then handled in the most barbaric way in 1993 by a team of Russian archaeologists, things started to go wrong for the indigenous peoples of the Altai.

First the herds started to die, and then the people fell sick. Suicides rose to epidemic proportions, earthquakes rattled the land and famine starved the people. They pleaded with the archaeologists, the universities and then the government to return the sleeping lady. Here is a translated excerpt of a letter that was sent to the Authorities in Moscow:

> We, the indigenous people of the Mountainous Altai, are the pagans and nature worshippers. All the diggings that have been conducted and are conducted in the Altai cause us unrecoverable harm. The invaluable treasures, a spiritual heritage of the Altai people, are moved out of the region despite our protests. A burial mound containing a young tattooed woman of spirit descent was opened at the Ukok plateau in the Kosh Agachsk region. She's a sacred relic to the Altai people, a keeper of peace and welfare of our people. The Altai Princess is now kept in a museum in Novosibirsk. Being the pagans we're completely confident that the soul of the Altai Princess is full of anger because she hates being bothered and wants to be laid to sleep. The tragic events of the last few months spring from the situation. We, the residents of the Oroktoy village, are calling on the people of the Republic of Altai to support our demands for the return of the sacred relic.

This protest letter was signed from people of all walks of life and included the signature of Aelkhan Zhatkambaev, a governor of Kosh Agachsk, an area most severely hit by a recent earthquake.

The request was refused and the lady still lies to this day on display in a glass case at the University museum in Novosibirsk. The authorities have no intention of putting her back, and have since made it a crime to reinter bodies. It would seem there are plans to build a museum to house her but I am not aware of its proposed location.

As far the indigenous peoples are concerned, their fate has already been sealed: the Russian government now talks about the Altai tribal people in the past tense.

The reaction of the archaeologists is to say that either the people are just imagining their sudden plunge into imbalance, or that it wasn't really a ritual burial and that the people have been mistaken for generations. The most recent gem to come from the university is the claim that the sleeper had no connection to the Altai people at all. She was a red haired Caucasian. So?

The Altai is, and was, the crossroads of the top of the world. Different races have always come together there. Such a declaration shows either ignorance or a deliberate attempt to disconnect the people from their past.

I witnessed a similar thing happening in the UK during the unearthing of a ritual burial in Bath of a woman surrounded by men in a circle. The details of the burial were quickly suppressed and played down. An alternative 'truth' was released and since then, the story has been pretty much buried. The organization responsible for such suppression was the church: the burial was found in the area beneath Bath Abbey.

18.2 Are the sleepers still active?

Well yes, some are, the ones who have not been ripped out of the ground or who haven't totally rotted. While ever a sleeper's body stays intact, the they can pass between death and life, the Underworld and the surface world. That was why such pains were taken to make sure that the body was well embalmed: it was important that the sleeper sleep intact for thousands of years.

At the end of that time, the sleeper would be released, or would fade, and another sleeper would take their place. Or the sleeper would sink deeper into sleep, fading from the communion with the tribe and instead becoming part of the consciousness of the land itself. This is one of the Mysteries of the Titans.

18. Working with Sleepers

The problem today is that the sleepers are being dug up and released all over the world but no one is being put back as a sleeper. The world is running out of the sleepers.

When I was a kid, I was told that half the world was asleep while the other half was awake. I was told that it was important that half the world dreamed while the other half worked: this way the world was balanced. If people didn't dream for you, you wouldn't exist.

This is an interesting tale, and is probably an overlap from the days of the ritual ancestral burials. It also probably refers to the old stories of the people sleeping in the earth, dreaming about the world and that we are their dreams. While ever they are sleeping, we can exist.

I can remember being a kid and listening to all sorts of interesting stories referring to these themes. They were always set in a Catholic context: those who went before us and slept in the earth, dreamt of paradise to keep the memory alive. So when the end of the world came, we would all still remember what paradise was: our ancestors were dreaming it for us.

I was lucky in that for some of my childhood, I grew up in a mixed community that was poor and illiterate. From that community came a wealth of stories and legends that had been carefully passed down from generation to generation.

And that is one of the fulcrums of survival for these ancient Mysteries: let them live and breathe in a real and healthy way. Too many 'experts' pop up who are university teachers or librarians who 'discover' their Celtic roots, etc. by going to a few workshops, reading a mountain of books, doing a shamanism course, etc. They then write books from a garbled pseudointellectual slant of the subject in a way that is meant to be marketable for the New Age.

Most of them come from middle class, well-educated families, and their deep desire to escape such isolation drives them to dig deeper. That is a good thing. But it becomes destructive when they then become the 'Bible preachers' of such subjects, with no real understanding of what they are addressing. It becomes some remote romantic magic that only the 'experts' can do. Nothing could be further from the truth.

18.2. Are the sleepers still active?

True ancestral knowledge of the sleepers is found in faery tales, family stories, local legends and songs (Sleeping Beauty, for example). They are passed down from generation to generation orally: a few of the poorer remote communities until fairly recently were illiterate, so they developed great skills at recounting the spirit of ancient ways to the next generation.

I can remember when I was about ten years old, my cousin got drunk and placed a bet with another cousin that she could get into a small bedside cupboard. She ended up getting her bum stuck hard in the cupboard and was totally wedged there. One of the old grandmothers was sitting in the corner knitting. She raised one eyebrow and said in a dead pan way, "Well lass, you will have to stay in there forever and keep time for us all, just like Old Winny did." Old Winny was a local burial on Windy hill, a woman who had been there before people started writing records.

It was said that went you went on Windy hill, which also had a small cup and ring stone there, you could not keep your watch in time, because it would revert to Winny time. *She* kept time on that hill, not clocks. And sure enough, if you went for a walk on Windy Hill, your watch would go slow.

Because of the sayings, we all knew about Winny and what she did, she was the keeper of time for the area. These days, a series of houses have been built upon the hill, so I would love to know what their clocks do!

Some of the sleepers are old, going back into the far reaches of our humanity and can still be worked with, though we do have to approach them with caution: their concept of humanity and life is different from ours today and we have to take that into consideration.

A few years back, I was teaching at a residential in New York. We were working with a particular sleeper who had been recently dug up. I was talking with her spirit, which was preparing to go through the death vision, and she showed me that the land would be in terrible calamity if she was not replaced.

After we came out of a vision that worked with her, a man in the group announced that he was willing to take her place. He was serious and fully understood the implications. He went on to commit himself to her work and to the land. He handed over his fate to the

18. Working with Sleepers

Goddess so that when he died, he would be embalmed and placed near her resting place. He would prepare himself magically to sleep with the land.

I was shocked that a modern day man would be so willing to give up the rhythm of life and death to be of service to the Goddess and the land. But the warning is, if you are asked or approached in the inner worlds to take up such service, just be fully aware of what you are being asked to do. Taking a magical vow is no light thing and they will hold you to it.

18.3 Communing with sleepers

If you want to work with a sleeper, then first you must find out if the sleeper wants to work with you. The best way to do this is through dipping your toe in the water gently. First find the site where the sleeper is and see if you can find out anything about the burial there.

Then start by taking food offerings. Go each day to the mound or burial area and place an offering of bread and oil in an appointed spot. After placing the offering down, still yourself and tune yourself to the directions. Just be silent and listen for a while. The following morning, before diving out of bed, lie and think about any dreams you had. If the mound is active, then chances are the guardian of the burial will have picked up on your interest and will have appeared in your dream.

The guardian can often manifest as a person, black dog, or other being trying to get you to go away. They will try and discourage casual contact with the mound. But if you are sincere and determined, then the guardians will let you through: they will not try to stop you from working with the mound.

After a few days, you can try and enter the burial mound in vision and commune with the sleeper. If you decide to go through this phase, just make sure that you are prepared to work with respect, and are prepared to be of service to the burial.

A few years ago I moved with my family into an old house in the west of England that we were renovating. It was built into a faery hill that was also a burial mound. The mound had never been excavated and it was powerful.

18.3. Communing with sleepers

I worked with the children to clean the garden up, which was mainly overgrown grass, apple trees and hawthorn. As soon as I began to dig into the earth to plant things, I would become terribly tired and would fall asleep. The same happened to the children. It became a bit of a family joke: we would all go out to garden, and a few minutes later, mum and two girls would be crashed out sleeping in the grass.

Then came the nightmares. We began the alterations on the house, and I started to have bad dreams, warning dreams, that would try and get me to leave the house. I still didn't really understand what was happening until one foggy autumn morning.

Our washing machine was in a side section of the house that could only be entered from outside, a little like an outhouse. My daughter had gone out to get the washing, and came rushing back into the house as white as a sheet.

She had seen a man in a black coat with a black dog walk past the door of the washing hut and vanish into the garden. Now, our garden, which was on the top of the mound, was surrounded by thorn bushes and the only entrance and exit was down some steep little steps that ran down the front of the house and the front of the mound.

There was nowhere for this man to vanish to. At this point, it hadn't occurred to me that this was not a real man. I hunted around the perimeter of the garden, looking for a hole in the thorn bushes that he might have pushed through. It seemed to me at the time that he was probably a local who was taking a shortcut through our garden.

Two nights later, I was out getting the washing and the same thing happened, a man with a black dog walked past the door. But this time I got it. He was not real. I had felt him before I saw him and this was no human man. He was a guardian of the mound. They often appear at stone circles or burial mounds, accompanied by a big black dog.

It was then that I slapped my forehead. I can be immensely stupid sometimes. I was on a burial mound...that was working...that had active guardians...and it was the burial of a sleeper, hence the problems with the gardening. The falling asleep problem was coming from the burial: it is a protective spell to prevent looters and intruders from digging into the mound.

So I decided that if I was going to live there, then I must also be of service to the sleeper within the mound. It was late October, a perfect time for what I was about to do. I built a fire on the top of the mound. Living on the top of a burial mound has a lot of disadvantages. One is that everything you do in your garden can be seen for miles around. But luckily it was the time of the year for bonfires, with All Hallows' Eve a day away, and bonfire night a week away. I was trying not to draw too much attention to what I was doing, nor did I want to freak out my devout Christian neighbours.

I lit the bonfire at dusk and piled on all the dead branches I had gathered up while clearing the garden. Then I sat before the fire. Closing my eyes, I went down in vision, down through the center of the hill until I reached a chamber that had a stone bed in the center.

Upon the bed was laid a man who was asleep. He had a long beard that reached almost the ground and there were many birds asleep around him. I tiptoed up to him to look at him. But one of the birds made a warning noise and the man began to stir.

He slowly woke up and began to stretch. He didn't see me and was not aware that I was there. He began to recite a poem that I didn't understand, and the poem seemed to force me out of the chamber. I was worried that I had awoken him before his time, but that feeling was soon put to rest as the poem got louder.

The sound of the poem was driving me back to the surface to do something, and I realized I was being put to work. He had awoken and he wanted to leave, but he needed a bridge to help him release.

I opened my eyes and went to the east. I walked around each direction, pausing for a moment to feel if that was the right one. When I got to the East I felt that this was the right direction to work in. Normally, for releasing a person into death I would have chosen the North, but these burials have a mind of their own: they know what they are doing and we should just basically do as we are told.

I stood in the East and rooted myself with my back to the fire and my face to the darkness of the night. I connected down to the sleeper and I felt him rise from the mound to the surface. He emerged out

18.3. Communing with sleepers

of the mound via the fire, paused for a while before passing through me, out into the night and the stars.

It took a few minutes for his energy to make its way all the way through me and he felt old and strange as he passed through. Many things from the hill, faery beings, a later burial and many spirits passed through me by coming up through my feet, and they went into the fire. It was a strange sensation and when it was all over, I laid down on the grass beside the fire. I was exhausted.

As I looked out, I saw Orion, the star constellation right above me as he passed over the mound. It became obvious from the inner feeling I was getting that the sleeper had aligned somehow, on his interment, to Orion and that it was no coincidence that the sleeper I saw had been laid in the same position as Orion: when the stars passed over head there would have been a few minutes where the stars would have mirrored the exact position of the burial and *vice versa*.

After that night, the feeling of the hill changed considerably. It was empty and silent. We felt that we no longer belonged there and that it was time to move on. We lived there for only 12 months. We had been drawn to live there so that we could do our job in releasing that sleeper, and then we were dismissed!

The couple that we sold the house to had a great feel about them: they would really nurture that hill and bring it back to life after its long sleep.

If you find a burial that you think is a sleeper, tread carefully but with purpose. What follows is a vision that can be used in any burial area to ascertain what is in there, and if you should work with it.

But remember, not every sleeper wants to wake up, not every sleeper should be awoken. And not every sleeper wants to work with you. Respect and work with whatever you find and do be aware that the standards of service that were expected in the days of the sleeper might be different from the standards now. The sleeper might expect you to do things that are no longer appropriate in our modern age.

I have purposely kept the following vision simple with little description as each mound you visit will be different. But this method will give you an idea of how to approach such a burial and how to begin learning to work with them.

18. Working with Sleepers

Sometimes, the sleepers just want you to hang out with them, or they want you to lie beside them and sleep. When you do this, they will communicate with you through sleep and dreams, telling you about the earth and the weather. There are many different ways to work with such burials and you have to use your common sense in determining which way is appropriate for that particular sleeper.

18.4   Vision for contacting a sleeper

Go to the burial mound and sit comfortably where you won't be disturbed. Close your eyes and be aware of the wind around you. Be aware of any body of water in the distance, and be aware of the sun above you. Be aware of the wind on your face and the earth beneath you.

With your inner vision, see yourself descend down through the earth, passing through stones, rocks, roots and earth as you pass down and down into the hill. As you go deeper into the earth, you become aware of a guardian that is trying to stop you going further.

Let the guardian ask you questions about your intentions and tell them that you are willing to be of service to the sleeper. If the guardian is happy with what they are hearing, then they will let you pass.

The guardian guides you into a chamber where you see the sleeper: The guardian stays by the entrance and watches as you approach the sleeper carefully. Be still, be silent and allow the power of the sleeper to wash over you. It will become obvious to you what you should do. You may feel that you have to lie down and sleep awhile with the sleeper, to keep them company or to help them sleep. You may have to sing them songs, lullabies, or comb their hair for them.

Or they may begin to awaken as you sit there, in which case you will have to help them release. To do that, you will have to either help them to their feet and climb out, or you will have to cradle them in your arms and carry them out.

They will need to be released through the directions or through a flame. One way to do this, if you cannot build a fire, is to have a candle lit in a jam jar and place it atop the mound. As you carry the sleeper out, you would see a gateway in your vision opening in the flame and let them pass through it.

Once they have released, go back into the chamber and see if anything was left there. If there was, take it and pass it through the flame also, or put it in running water. When you have finished, use rocks and earth to close up any hole that you made so that the mound is sealed. Ask the guardian if he needs your help to leave/release and help them if they ask for that help.

Be still and listen to nature around the mound, feel the peace and stillness, and when you are ready, open your eyes.

18.5 The future

Now that so many sleepers are being removed or released from the Earth and none are being replaced, what will happen? And what can we do to help?

Well, our culture does not have a structure for such a problem, and I think ritual deaths and burials would not go down well with the Western community these days. And yet something must be done to try and address the imbalance, particularly as the planet needs all the help it can get right now. Our communities and cultures are crumbling as we destroy our environment and ourselves.

One option is active dreaming. Rather than becoming a sleeper through death and burial, we can become active sleepers through visions and dreams. At the end of the day what is needed is for some humans to act as intermediaries between the earth and humanity, between the Underworld and the people.

One way of doing that as modern living humans is to commit to a length of service in which we agree to do regular visions with a certain area of the land, and we agree to sleep with intent.

Sleeping with intent is where you lie down and go to sleep, not your normal nighttime sleep, but a daytime sleep where you allow yourself to be pulled deep down into the earth where you commune with the consciousness of the land. The land will impress upon you things that need doing or will warn you of things coming.

With that information, you actively pass on the information to those who work magically with you, or you act upon the information yourself. A sleeper will often work to rebalance a patch of land, or unblock an energy flow, or direct humans to work that needs doing with the forest or the birds.

You basically become a bridge between the land and the people. Actively sleeping opens you up slowly to such work, where you will dream deep dreams about the land and the spirits, and you will be warned of things coming.

When I lived on the burial mound, I did a lot of active sleeping where I would wake up in the morning and be promptly told an hour later to go back to bed and dream.

When I did this, I would be shown some amazing things, introduced to powerful beings and asked to do visions for faery beings: mainly bridging work in the Underworld.

This has happened to me many times. I didn't choose to do this, nor did I agree to a term of service specifically to sleep. I think it became part and parcel of my wider service as a priestess. It was also a matter of the fact that I always said yes to any inner request before I took the time to find out what I had just said yes to...which went along with my love of pressing buttons just to see what would happen. Amazingly I'm still alive!

In today's modern decaying world, one of the things we need to do is to become flexible and able to adjust quickly. Things are changing fast and we have to run to keep up. Old ways of working no longer really apply, and yet the ancient flow of power needs to be maintained. It is up to us as modern humans to find new and effective ways of working magically for the good of the land and the people.

18.6 Bridging

The other important way to work with sleepers in this modern age is to work with them as bridges to the ancient past. Sleepers are often one of a long line of sleepers, and contacts are passed from one sleeper to the next, so their connections stretch deep in into the distant past. They are often connected, through this line, to deities or powers that are no longer worked with or contacted in modern times.

18.6. Bridging

Sometimes, a power or deity is so far back that we cannot reach them as we know nothing about them or how they presented themselves. For example, we know how Horus presented and even though his temples and priests faded out in real terms millennia ago, because we still have his image, his history and his stories, we can reach him.

But older deities become harder to reach. Tefnut for example is a much older and lesser-known deity in the Egyptian pantheon, and is harder, but not impossible, to reach. But what about the deity that was before Tefnut? What female divinity of the water, what power, kept the forest alive and the land balanced? To find this out we must contact the oldest sleeper we can find in that culture and start there.

From that starting point, you commune with that sleeper to establish a connection. Work with them to see what they need, what tasks they have for you, and what communications they wish to have.

Then, you would converse with the contact to ask about the sleeper who went before them. Once they have told you about the previous sleeper, you can use that information to track back through time to commune with that sleeper. You repeat this work until you reach the earliest sleeper you can find.

Upon reaching that first sleeper, you would commune with their spirit and ask if they need anything. Don't forget you would be communing with them in their own time, not yours. So they may ask you to do things that are no longer possible. You have to make sure that the sleeper is aware that you are from the future.

If you know of disasters that will happen in their near future, as a priest/ess you must tell the sleeper about the coming event. The sleeper then converts that information into a language the local community of that time would understand, and then conveys that information to the tribal seer.

This is one of the major ways in which a sleeper works. They work with contacts from the future who warn the people of the past what is coming. They also work with the land, the faery beings, the animals and the trees in an effort to make sure that the tribe is aware of what calamities lie ahead.

Time jumping, or bridging, in magical work is common and is indeed one of the major tribal ways of working with ancestors. We

18. Working with Sleepers

know what is coming, they don't, and between the information passed to a sleeper, the information gleaned from the behaviour of the land and the animals, and information passed on in dreams, again the dreams are information whispered to them by workers of the future while they sleep. With that collection of information tribal peoples can ascertain what is coming and take evasive steps.

We had a really good example of this recently. A fascinating story came out of the tsunami disaster that hit the Andaman and Nicobar Islands in December 2004: the survival of all the members of the indigenous Jarawa tribe. This tribe is one of the most ancient in the world, with DNA studies indicating that their generations may have spanned back seventy thousand years. The tribe fled into the jungle in plenty of time, hours before the tsunami hit, and remained there for several days before reemerging.

When approached by the Indian Authority tribal agent, the tribesmen refused to say how they had known in advance. My guess is that it was a combination of signs and warnings, with ancestral bridging included. Now that the tsunami has happened, their seers can go back through time in ceremony and warn the people. So which came first, the event, or the after-knowledge?

This throws us back to the issues regarding time and how time works. When doing work with sleepers, it is better to approach time in a different way. Do not think of time as before and after, but as over here and over there. That way your brain doesn't get chewed when you try to figure out how it all works. I gave up years ago! All I know is that it does work and should be worked with.

The other service that emerges from this type of work is the bridging between sleepers. As living humans, we have immense capacity to bridge between time and people. One of the important services that should be offered to sleepers is to bridge between the first sleeper in a line and the last or present one.

That allows the ancient knowledge and power that always gets lost between the generations to be reconnected to the present. The first sleeper in a line will have inherent knowledge regarding the land powers and divinities that stretch back into the distant past behind them. By bridging between the oldest and the newest sleepers, you connect the present day sleeper with the ancient knowledge that would have become diluted by the time they began to sleep. You are also connecting the oldest sleeper with the acquired and matured knowledge developed by the tribe over the millennia.

This strengthens the connection, deepens the powers of the sleepers and begins the process of transforming the original sleeper from human sleeper to Titan.

Working with a sleeper is something that every magical worker should undertake at some point in their magical training. It is a service to the land that gave you life and a service to the humanity that flows through you. Sleepers are wherever people settled. Start by searching in your own area for one, and if you don't find one, then look further afield.

Or you can travel to find one and make the connection. Once the connection is there, then you can go in vision to work with that sleeper from a distance.

Chapter Nineteen

Death and Birth

The Mysteries of death and birth, and the powers that work within these transitions, have slowly been eroded from Western culture by the monotheistic religions. All three religions are based upon a foundation of submission, fear and abdication of responsibility.

This castration of the human spirit has, as a side issue, disabled the once splendid transitions of birth and death, and replaced them with pain, fear and helplessness. If you attend a hospital birth in the Western cultures, you are most likely to see the woman in a space of 'not knowing': she doesn't have any control over her birth. She has no idea how to give birth and has to rely on paying an 'expert' (often male) to tell her how to do the job.

Women often emerge traumatized, torn and exhausted. They are thrown back into the community almost immediately where they are expected to just figure it out, read a book or rely on yet more 'experts' to guide them through.

The social engineering that has shaped our modern life has also served to further separate us from our mothers and grandmothers. We no longer tend to live in the same community we were raised in, sometimes not even in the same country we were born in. There is no spiritual input for the mother or the child, and no spiritual guidance. We are truly 'cast from the garden' to give birth 'alone' and in pain.

And then there is the other end of the spectrum. Death has also been made into a medical money spinner. I have had to stand by and watch doctors insist on invasive and painful procedures to be conducted on dying people, not for the patients good, but for the insurance money and their own curiosity. Dying people are dragged to hospitals, pumped full of drugs and they die in a spiritually void institution: how disgraceful.

19. Death and Birth

Death has been made so disgusting and terrible that most Americans have never seen a dead body let alone tended to the dying and the dead. Death must happen away from the home, it is unclean, it is a reminder of your own fate: these are all the nightmares that so many people live with.

When I was a child, there was always someone dying. I come from a large family with many generations still living. So there was always someone old and dying or someone young and stupid who has crashed their car, taken too many pills, etc. When a person died, we would cleanse and dress the body while talking to the soul. They would be kept in vigil in the house until burial time. This happens in various ways around the world in countries that have not yet been contaminated by the soulless greed of Western living.

So how do you find that way forward for yourselves, your family and your community?

You have to learn to be with birth and death. As an esoteric worker, the best and most solid way to learn the methods of these transitions is first to learn the visions that accompany these transitions, and then begin to work with them. Once you have become proficient with these methods, you will find that the universe puts you in situations where you can be of use to humanity. The other important thing is to go through your own death vision while in life. This is, important to someone on a spiritual path: the death within life is one of the oldest recorded Mysteries from various ancient cultures.

19.1 Death

The method of working within death that is compatible with the Western culture is the Vision of Death. There are many different versions of this vision/story and some cultures have even produced a Book of the Dead for their priests to recite from.

The death vision creates the scenario of a journey that includes a river, mountains and plains. When you die, this is not what you see but the images covey to the living what the dead person is experiencing. So the living human can access death by passing through the imagination into the Inner Worlds.

The vision is divided into sections that chart the progression from the separation of the spirit from the body, to the separation of the consciousness from the spirit. This enables the spirit or soul to progress into transformation without carrying any baggage from the recent life. Then the spirit awakens and moves on either to a new life, an inner service, an inner healing or to a merging with the Divine Being, which manifests as the Void.

19.2 So what happens when a person dies?

It depends on the circumstances of the death. If the person dies quickly, they are often catapulted into a state of unconsciousness of the spirit. This is a form of defense mechanism to protect the spirit just as the body will switch off the mind to protect itself while under extreme stress. It doesn't happen all the time but it happens most of the time.

While in this stage of nothingness, the spirit is still heavily connected to the body, and while passing through this short phase the person experiences this situation in the same way they would if they had briefly fallen asleep. They awaken slowly as if from a deep sleep. So be aware of this connection if you are around the body. *They can often still hear you.*

The person then begins to emerge out of their short sleep to find themselves in a place of nothingness. This is the most superficial form of the Void and is like a 'passing through' stage for the spirit. The person must have the will to move forward so that they can begin their death journey.

If they do not move forward, they need to be helped and coaxed to move forward. This is done by going in vision to this place and imagining a door. Once you have formed the vision strongly they will start to see the door for themselves and will be more willing to move.

In the state of death, the personality that you are dealing with is the threshold personality: that is to say, the part of the person that acted as a fulcrum between the body and the soul. Images can be conveyed through your 'imagining,' and the imagination is a common ground that you both share.

When the person moves through that door, you must not follow. This is very important to understand. Once they move through that door they are fully committed to death and if you go through that door, the same rule applies to you. You can work deeply in the death vision but how you get there is different if you are still in life.

Once the person steps through that door, it may be anything from day or two to an hour or two before they emerge in the death vision itself. If a person has died slowly and is preparing for that death, they just seem to appear in the death vision immediately. I have known some people who have prepared spiritually for death to just go straight through everything immediately, which is really how it should be.

But in today's spiritually bereft modern world, that rarely happens. The death process has become a long, drawn-out painful passage that is like having wisdom teeth pulled without anaesthesia. And that is so unnecessary. Death should be a stillness: a letting go and surrendering to the natural forces that you know will wash you up on the beach of life many, many times. And the fear should not be a consuming terrible darkness: rather it should be the excited fear of a new marriage or a new child.

Life is not our natural state. Timelessness and stillness out of life is our natural state. This is why when people discover the depths of the Void in their meditations, they do not want to come back from it: this is our soul's natural state. That is not to say that we should turn away from life as some religions would have us do. Life is a wondrous, beautiful and powerful thing that is a special gift to us all. But at the end of the day our real state is an infinite timeless and conscious communion with Divine Being.

19.3 The death vision in detail

The death vision as we see it begins with a long walk across a hot dusty Desert landscape. In the distance is a river which the dead person is drawn to. Other people are often walking too, and some are sitting by the river. The dead person will be thirsty and they rush towards the river to drink of its water. As they drink it begins to affect their ability to remember their newly lost life. The more they drink, the more they forget.

This is why Initiates in some of the Eastern Mysteries were trained to control their thirst and to control their inner actions. It was drummed into them from the beginning of their advanced training: do not drink of the River of Death. By doing this, they could cross through death and retain the memories of who they were. They can then pick up on their work that they left behind in the previous life.

I do not think that is all too healthy: some forgetting and letting go is important for the soul's development. The continuance from one life to the next in a conscious line of work becomes corrupted quickly, as can be seen with the Lamas of Tibet. Their obsessive clinging to power through linear reincarnation was the beginning of the end for their priesthood.

Such a practice for them is relatively new in terms of the age of their priesthood. It used to be that different enlightened souls would manifest each time through the incarnation of the senior Lama, thus bringing a wide variety of skills and wisdom to the leadership of the priesthood. Approximately three hundred years ago that practice was changed through magic to make sure that the same souls came back again and again. This is a degenerate practice that has brought about the destruction of an ancient spiritual lineage.

The balance for an adept is to drink only a tiny bit from the river and retain enough memory to recall your hard-earned wisdom and knowledge. But the tiny sips would have wiped away most memories of partners, loved ones, etc. which will allow the soul to move forward and understand the deeper rules of attachment.

The rules of attachment are that one must not be attached to anything or anyone. Once you die, all the people you loved no longer exist for you. For your sake and theirs, you must let go and move on. And by letting go, you will eventually be able to reconnect with these people under different circumstances and different forms of relationships, if it is appropriate.

At this stage of the vision, at the side of the river, the person ponders their lost life and begins the process of shedding and accepting. Often angelic beings will make themselves available to help people through this stage of the transition. These beings guard

19. Death and Birth

the bridge and the river, allowing only those who should cross to cross.

These beings will often cross-dress to help people accept them better. For example they will often appear as your aunt Betty, or as Jesus, Buddha, or whichever form of God, saint, or family member you would reach out to. This is not to deceive you: this is only to help those who are so traumatized that they cannot move forward without real practical help. And angels appearing in their own guise would frighten the socks off most people, so they dress up.

A good example of this is a story from some inner work I did for a family a few years ago. A young friend of my daughter had a snowboarding accident and ended up with severe injuries. He was in a deep coma and the hospital informed his parents that he would not recover. They planned to wait a week and then turn the machines off that were keeping him alive.

My daughter asked if we could sit down at the time of the turn off and do the death vision for him. I said yes. The day before the turn off was due, I suddenly was told by inner contacts to sit down with my daughter and do the death vision straightaway, so we did.

I saw the boy standing by the river. He was in shock. He refused to move in any way. He would not believe he was dead, and refused my efforts to get him to move forward to cross the bridge. Crossing the bridge would enable him to move to the next, deeper stage of death.

In desperation I asked one of the angelic beings for help. A few seconds later a beautiful young girl with rather large breasts strutted over the bridge towards the boy. His eyes nearly popped out of his head. He forgot everything he was afraid of, and immediately agreed to take her arm and walk across the bridge with her, so off he went. The angelic being had dressed as a beautiful young woman to assist this boy.

We later found out that he died naturally just as we were doing the death vision, thus saving his family from the terrible trauma of having to 'turn him off.'

But back to the side of the river. At this stage people are often confused, bewildered and angry. They are angry that death was not what they expected: there was no choir of angels to herald them into 'heaven' and no endless supply of ice cream, sunshine and all the other trivial things that were promised to them.

They sit at the side of the river and wait. Some at this stage realize that their imagination can take them back to the people that they left behind. Some become skilled at this and refuse to move further into death, choosing instead to 'haunt' their lost loved ones or their lost property. The longer they stay in death, the more the living world becomes a sort of 'inner' world to them: that is to say where they are becomes their total reality and the living world is accessed through imagination. For us, it is the reverse.

It is at this stage that you also sometimes find people who are in deep comas. They have a foot in death and a foot in life. They hang between the two and while their body is still alive in the living world, their spirit sometimes begins the death journey and they end up at the side of the river. They cannot go any further until their body is dead. So they hang out, confused and afraid.

They have to make a choice, either to go back or to let go of their body. If they cannot go back, i.e. if their body is too damaged, then they must learn to let go and allow their body to die. If they wish to go back, help them by looking for the umbilical line that connects them to life and follow it back to their body.

19.4 The Bridge

The bridge is a crucial part of the death vision: if they don't cross the bridge one way or another, then they cannot continue with the death process. They will remain frozen in the half-life world that is somewhere between life and death. Crossing the river by way of a bridge is our way of seeing a process in which the spirit severs connections with life and commits to moving forward in their cycle of development.

The bridge can appear to us as being guarded by angelic beings. They stand on either side of the entrance and act as gatekeepers, keeping out those who must not cross for one reason or another. As a priest or priestess, we can cross the bridge safely, though it is best not to return that way. Once we cross the bridge, if we wish as living beings to come out of the vision, we have to exit either from the top of the mountain or continue and complete the whole cycle of the vision. Another option, if you wish to come in and out of the vision, is to pass through one of the angelic beings.

The reason for not returning over the bridge is that there is always the possibility of some being that does not belong in life hitching a ride on you unnoticed. To avoid such happenings, which do indeed happen, care has to be taken to make sure that you always pass through an angelic being, or a threshold that is protected by, and created of, angelic consciousness. This can be done by approaching one of the working beings in the death vision and asking them to allow you to pass through them to get home. The thresholds of the mountain and the Abyss are protected thresholds which only allow those who should pass, to pass.

19.5 The Plains

As the spirit begins its journey towards the mountains it enters into a phase of letting go at a much deeper level. The physical form and all that was attached to that form begins to dissolve as they walk across the plains towards the high mountains. This often appears to us as things falling from the person as they walk. They may appear to drop baggage, clothing, heavy weights, even limbs as they draw closer and closer to the mountain.

While they are in this phase, they will begin to forget who they are and what they are doing. Some will be disorientated and will be drawn by instinct to the mountains before them. During this walk, it is the priest's/priestess's job to walk alongside them and be a companion until they are ready to let go of companionship and face being alone.

This is also an important lesson for this phase of death: that we are truly alone and that the love that we had for our children, parents, lovers and friends was love that was conditional love and as such is limited. Eventually the spirit passes through the letting go phase, understanding that such relationships were bound to that life and they begin to cut the emotional ties.

Eventually the understanding that such love is unconditional and flows out to all begins to dawn, not in a fluffy New Age sense, but in a real solid sense. Life flows in cycles and patterns and the love connected to that life flows in the same way. Someone whom we once loved as a lover may cross our paths again as a sibling, offspring or parent. Or that soul may never cross our paths again...The point being is that we really do not know, so potentially everyone around us has been connected to us at one point or another for good or bad. That brings a whole new meaning to 'love thy brother as thyself,' because you really truly do not know how much of a connection you really have with the person down the street.

People do reconnect and interconnect, and learning to let go between is so important: we must start the surface connection each time with a fresh outlook and an open heart. That way we truly learn to be one with the rest of humanity: because we really are all one family in one way or another.

The quicker that the person understands this, the quicker they reach the mountain and begin the next phase of their journey. If you are still accompanying someone, this phase is the last one where you can walk alongside them. By this stage there is often not much communication happening anymore, and as a worker you can walk along and observe, but not much else.

19.6 The Mountain

The mountain is the final hurdle that the soul must encounter within the death vision. The mountain is the deep spiritual programming that has happened to a person during their lives. Any religion they have been raised with, any cultural baggage they may have and any deep-seated ideals are challenged at this point.

This manifests itself in a couple of ways: the more the dogma is entrenched within a person, the higher the mountain is and the harder it is to climb. Once a person begins to climb, they will begin to hear many voices, some reciting sacred text, some praying, some political voices, some cultural voices and some of their own ponderings. The voices will be loud and annoying as they try to climb beyond the programming that happened during their lifetime.

When the person hears the voices, they will begin to be aware of them as something that is outside them: this is something they acquired during their lifetimes when they had a body, but it is not a

19. Death and Birth

part of them. The awareness that such thoughts are not of the spirit, but are a product of humanity, can be a shock to some people and the harder the shock, the harder the climb.

Such a letting go is probably the hardest: it is releasing everything you have ever held as being real, as being right. It shows a person the falsehood of their society, their religion and their own reasoning. It is a frightening and exhausting experience that weighs heavily upon the shoulders of a person who is struggling in such a difficult transition.

Once the spirit reaches the top of the mountain, they are exhausted and are ready for sleep. There are many beings who work in this section of the death vision and their duty is to guard, nurture, and prepare the soul for the renewal of life or for the service of the Inner Worlds.

The top of the mountain appears as a plateau with a grassy flat area where people lie down to rest. The beings wander in among the sleeping people, singing to them and stroking them as they sleep. The spirit lies down and the angelic beings arrange them so that they can sleep comfortably. They are laid out in a ritual position of one arm outstretched and the opposite leg outstretched. The other leg and arm are bent into the body. This position can be seen on some traditional tarot decks as a man curled around the wheel of life. It is also mirrored in some decks in the hanged man. It is a ritual position of preparation for life.

Spirits who are not going to reincarnate but are going to pass into the Inner Worlds in service as an inner contact or teacher, do not lie down. They are urged to a far, dark side of the plateau where the mountain falls away down a bottomless crevice or Abyss. The spirit stands on the edge of the Abyss and makes the ultimate initiation move by stepping off the cliff. Each spirit that is pulled to this place will have practised this action many times during their life in visions. The spirit steps out into the Mystery of the Abyss and vanishes into the mist. They will emerge in the Inner Worlds, ready to teach and guide humanity in a spirit of service.

This is also a get-off point for you as a visionary should you wish to exit the death vision with esoteric purpose. By going through the death vision to this point and then stepping off into the Abyss, you fully complete the death initiation of the ancients. You will emerge in the sanctuary of the Great Library.

The spirits, who are left sleeping and regenerating, are surrounded by song: the angelic beings sing to them the secrets of human life so that the spirit should not forget what human life is. This will prevent a spirit from forgetting that they manifested through humanity so that when they come to choose a new life, they will choose humanity over some other being.

19.7 The awakening into rebirth

At some point all the angels face east as the sun rises and they begin to call out the names of those spirits that they have guarded to awaken them. The spirits awaken and are immediately pushed down the opposite side of the mountain, which is a gentle grassy slope.

The spirits roll around and around as they tumble down the hill towards an Abyss that is guarded by an archangel. The angel appears as a woman with hair that flows in all directions and long arms that reach out to slow down the spirits as they roll down the hill.

Once they come to a halt, the spirits uncurl themselves and walk to the edge of the Abyss. The angel holds a protective arm out to stop them falling as they explore the power of this place. As they look over the Abyss they slowly become aware of potential lives that could relate to them. There is no past or present, as such concepts have no place where there is no matter. But all the lives that are within their field appear on the other side of the Abyss and they can watch them.

The spirit fixes on one life that seems to connect more than others. It is not a conscious choice, but an instinctive one. All the cultural and religious programming that would have affected such a choice has long gone and all that is left is deep spiritual reaction and instinct. Once the life has been chosen, the angel removes her arm and the spirit falls into a whirling mass of air that appears like a whirlwind. This is also an archangel that carries the soul from the depths of death to the threshold of life.

19. Death and Birth

The soul falls down and down, swirling around the directions as it falls towards a couple who are making love. And such is the inner mechanism of conception.

19.8 Practical working methods

To work with the above vision, construct a vision using the elements above. The safest access point to begin the vision is the Underworld: go down into the Underworld until you hit a river. Stand beside the river and call for the boatman. Slowly a boat will appear with a boatman holding a flame light—give him a coin which after the vision you later throw into water, and step into the boat. It will float along the underground river until it emerges in the realm of death and you will get out of the right hand side of the riverbank, which is the area that newly dead people come and gather before crossing the bridge.

Once you have constructed the vision, you can use it to reach newly dead people, or you can recite it as a story to someone who is in a coma. Most of the time when people are in comas you will find them near the edge of the river: They will be confused and unsure what to do or what is happening. You can talk to them if you visit in vision and ask them what they want to do. If they want to let go and die, then you can help them by taking them over the bridge, and then physically holding their hand which allows your energy to flow into them: it takes a lot of energy to die.

If someone is dying and they are receptive to it, you can do the vision with them so that it prepares them for what is to come. The more prepared they are, the less frightened they become and the smoother the passing is. You can then go in and track them on a daily basis: going through the inner death process takes many days usually, and you can go in each day to work with them and monitor their progress. Usually, by the time they have reached the top of the mountain you will be told by the angelic workers to stop coming in as help is no longer needed.

If you are emotionally connected to the person, you have to be careful not to hold them back by your own longings or wishes for them to stay around longer. You have to work from a place of non-emotion so that you can do your job. I worked with my father for ten days when he died. After the second day, he had no idea who I was as he had let go of his earthly life: I found that hard but it was good for me to learn how important it is to be focused and not let emotions intrude.

If you are working with a dying adept who wishes to stay around a bit longer to continue some work, then go over the vision with them a few times even if they know it. And once they die, be ready for them changing their minds and wishing to move on. They may also pass into a different space after crossing the bridge: there is a place over the bridge where adepts go to become inner contacts.

If someone is stuck by the side of the river and is not moving on, and has learned to stick around and access the human world, then they need to be taken over the bridge. This is a form of haunting and you have to explain to them what they are doing. If they still will not cross, and they are haunting people, then you need to work with beings to forcibly take them over the bridge.

19.9 Physical practicalities

When you are working with someone who is dying there are certain things to keep an eye out for. If they are in a coma, sometimes they will awaken just before death. Sometimes, when you are feeling them energetically, you will feel that they die slowly from the feet up, one leg at a time. This once happened to me when I was working on someone who was in intensive care: one day I couldn't feel their right leg anymore and I became confused. A being told me later that the man in question 'had one foot in the grave.' It made me think a little more about old sayings and what they had grown out of.

When working with the dying, be aware of the energy needs of a dying person and of the beings around them. If they have a parasite keeping them alive, take it out. If they are frightened, do the inner vision quietly to yourself because even if they do not consciously do it, your action of it has a stretching effect upon them.

You can also help them by working within the spiritual construct that they are used to: Christian, Muslim, it doesn't really matter. Recite sacred text at their side, as some of the sacred texts are designed to draw angelic beings to the dying to help them in the passing. If they are not religious, call upon the angelic beings yourself for the death preparations. You can do that quietly, with eyes open as you sit and keep vigil.

Working with the newly dead is the most important work. These are the people who are least cared for and the most in need of help. Lots of structures are in place for those who are left and are grieving. To work with the newly dead, just be with them for each day that they need it and keep a vigil candle burning for them as they are going through the process.

If the family is receptive to the idea, you can let one or two of them join in the vision with you leading, so that they can become a part of the overall process. This can be an incredible healing tool for all concerned.

19.10 Birth

Upon conception, the spirit of the new life spreads out throughout the body of the mother, affecting her moods, her body and her character. The mother's personality will often change. This is just a side effect of the mingling of the two souls: the mother will often display the personality traits of the future child.

As the pregnancy progresses, the new spirit slowly adjusts to the growing body of the child and slowly withdraws from the safety net of the mother. By the time the birth is imminent, the child's body will hold almost all of the spirit and that transition is completed with the cutting of the cord. The inner cord is cut by the angelic beings who attend a birth, and the outer cord is cut by the midwife or doctor.

Once that cord is cut, the spirit is totally housed within the body of the infant and the mother's body begins its adjustment to returning to a pre-pregnancy state. Just as the physical body adjusts to the sudden departure of the baby, so the inner body has to adjust to the departure of another spirit that was housed there. Both changes take some time and have their difficulties.

Many beings attend a birth to help with this adjustment phase. They will appear as angelic beings who 'stroke' their fingers through the mother to readjust her energy and realign her inner landscape.

19.10. Birth

What fascinates me more than anything about the birth process is the inner connection with the stars. I obviously knew about the astrological significance of the moment of birth and the planetary alignments, but I fell across something else by accident, which, in theoretical terms, was obvious. But for true understanding, the real experience just blew me away.

I was busy working in vision with angelic beings and the stars. Suddenly, all the angelic beings that were the consciousness of the planets and stars began to sing. It was a strange, beautiful cacophony of sounds that stirred my soul. As I listened, I watched: the angelic beings slowly moved in harmony and when they reached a certain point, the song reached a strange crescendo and a light appeared to rush past me. Out of curiosity I followed.

The light entered a woman's womb as she was making love to her partner. I was stunned. The angelic beings that were the stars had created or had aligned themselves to an opening that allowed a soul to pass from the Inner Worlds into physical manifestation. The soul had waited, or had been held back, until the planetary pattern was correct, and the angelic beings who were the consciousness of the planets worked in harmony to create a window of opportunity for that soul. It was fabulous to watch and listen to.

I then realized that when I was in the death visions and looking at the souls tipping into the Abyss to fall into life, I was seeing the 'outer' picture of conception. But what I was seeing here in the stars was the deeper, more profound picture of conception. And it was the most beautiful thing I had ever seen or listened to.

It suddenly occurred to me that the most important part of a child's astrological chart is the conception time and date. It was also as though the moment of the child's birth was set at the point of conception and that the two events tied harmoniously into each other.

That then raises questions regarding induced births: how much does an induced birth interfere with the harmony of a child's life pattern? And if an inducement has to be done for safety reasons, rather than the usual convenience reasons, is there any way we can work magically or spiritually to help redress the imbalance?

19. Death and Birth

It also raises questions regarding test tube babies and forced conception. I think it will take us a few more generations to unravel these questions and concerns.

Chapter Twenty

Using tarot as a working tool

Tarot can be used for a great many things besides looking at someone's love life/career/ingrowing toenails. In magical practice, tarot can be used to look for the best way to approach a magical problem, to identify the source of a particular energy, to preempt the effects of a particular magical action, to identify hidden matters and to ascertain if a body impact is magical or a physical illness. The limitations upon what a reader can see are dependent upon what boundaries the reader puts up as we make our own limitations when it comes to seeing. If a deck is poorly thought out however, it can hinder a reading, which is another matter.

Such self-imposed limitations are not only the ones we consciously adopt, such as "oh you cannot read unless they are on red silk, laid east facing," or "you cannot read for yourself": we also limit ourselves through our inability to see something without prejudice. Sometimes the answer can be staring us in the face, but if you are unwilling to look critically at yourself, then often the answer can be missed. By the time a reader comes to using tarot as a magical tool, I would presume that the phase of 'only seeing what you want to see' has passed.

The choice of deck is immaterial really, so long as the deck has the range of beings needed for a wide view of the worlds. The layout is probably more important because the layout is how we put pattern and focus to the information: if the layout is clear and precise then the information will be clear and precise. The best decks are the ones that are designed around and within the layout, with the positions and the beings interacting and interlacing. To find a deck like that to work with, you need to look for an author who has a good understanding of how everything works as opposed to a good artist. A beautiful deck

20. USING TAROT AS A WORKING TOOL

can be useless if it is not structured properly, but a spartan deck will work perfectly if it is constructed properly.

This is why it is a useful magical exercise to make your own deck: get blank cards and coloured pens, and structure your own deck to work for you.

So how is a deck constructed properly? Well, the first step towards putting a proper working deck together is need. If you have a real need for a working tool, then you will be a lot clearer about what you need and why. Phase one would be marking down the worlds that you go to and need to be aware of, and then within those worlds, asking, "What functional areas of these worlds affect my work?"

Look at the past, present and future, look at the magical, emotional and practical parts of life, look at the help and hindrance, the inner and outer expressions, the relationships, the home, the temple and the deeper worlds. With that mapping of the worlds and how we live and operate within those worlds, then you have to put in the people. What types and quality of beings do you interact with? Where do they belong in the universe? What powers flow through these beings and what are the effects of those powers. And so the list goes on.

You can see that, by constructing your own deck, you begin to think about the magical world around you in a more focused and connected way. By building a layout/mapping the universe and then putting the beings and powers in their positions on/within that map, you begin to see magical patterns arising that have implications upon your life that you had not thought about. Certain interrelations start to emerge as do flows of power and progressions of states. The whole exercise can be a massive magical education even before you pick one card up to do a reading: it also teaches you the depths of reading.

But using a deck can help you gain information quickly and efficiently if you learn to approach it as a simple working tool, and again, the success of that depends upon the layout as much as your ability to read.

20.1 Layouts

Looking at two layouts, one which most people will know is the Tree of Life layout which is a useful simple layout that can be used to ascertain what is going on with a particular situation, or to look at the results of work. The cards are laid in the following numbered Tree of Life sequence:

The following mapping of the layout is not deep, mystical, Kabbalistic or anything else like that. It is not for meditation, for introspection or backflips. It is just to get simple answers to straightforward magical questions.

Now before all you Kabbalists jump all over me for shifting things a little: in this context, it is just a useful pattern that works! It has simplified the powers right down to get straight answers and if you look deeper about how the layout operates, you will see that it actually makes sense.

For example if you are a magical practitioner who has a variety of skills and you have to attempt an important and maybe dangerous magical act, and you are not sure quite which system or being to use to facilitate the action, then you can look using a reading, asking 'which system should I use?' You would pay particular attention to what is in positions five, eight and ten. For example, if the Knight of Swords is in position five, then it is saying don't use the angelic powers/magical instruments of air. If for example the 5 of Wands is in position eight, then that is saying that the inner contacts that you were considering will be weak and disorganized. If the Magician is in position eight then you have a good magical inner contact, probably human, if the Tower is in position ten then you are screwed, etc.

Looking at magical actions and the differing ways that action can go, depending on what tools/contacts you work with, can teach you an enormous amount about how the power works and how you work within that power from an inner point of view. So you can use the readings to pinpoint the exact best way to approach an important working and find out which contacts, etc. would be the best to work with.

A downside to this, which we have to be aware of and balance against the benefits, is that the simple act of reading for a situation

20. USING TAROT AS A WORKING TOOL

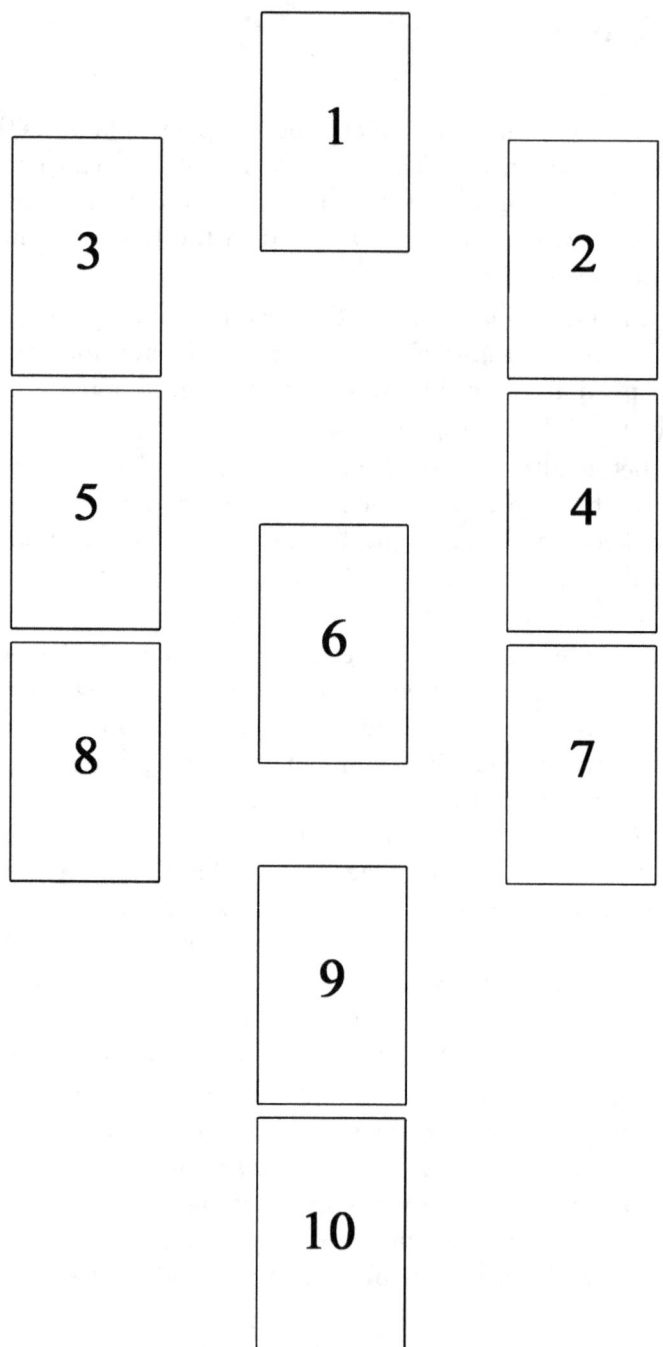

Figure 20.1: The Tree of Life tarot layout

can change the path of that situation. Too many readings on a particular subject or incident can narrow the options available to the worker, so it is important that you do not use decks indiscriminately. Use your own knowledge and common sense to eliminate certain possibilities and then approach the unknown aspects using the deck but be clear and precise about what you ask.

This is the other problem that surfaces when reading for a magical situation: how do you phrase the question? The question has to take into account the limits of a deck in its vocabulary. So for example here are two ways to ask a question:

1. "What will happen if I do X and use Y tool?"

2. "Show me the outcome of the working if I use Y tool."

The first question would bring about an answer that could potentially show you about the dropped candle, the toothache that you get in the middle of it, the untimely knock at the door, the neighbour dropping dead in the middle of the working or your zip bursting when you stand up. By asking what will happen you are opening a field of visions that is potentially wide indeed.

The second question is specific: it will show you the consequence and outcome of using a specific tool. If you are using the reading to see if that tool will be the right one, then you will get a clear and straightforward answer. *It's all about the focus of the question.*

The other thing to think about is the allocation of characters within a deck. If you are working magically with faeries, ancestors, angelic beings etc., you need to sit and think about how court cards and major cards are going to represent the various beings that you work with. Doing such allocation with a deck ends up being a joint effort: you allocate a specific card for a specific being, but the deck consistently spews out another card repeatedly for the same being. So the deck has made the choice and you have to make the connection, but by beginning an action of allocation, it opens a door for that process to begin. As in all magical work, starting the ball rolling allows all the other invested powers, beings and contacts to step up to the plate and do their job.

20. USING TAROT AS A WORKING TOOL

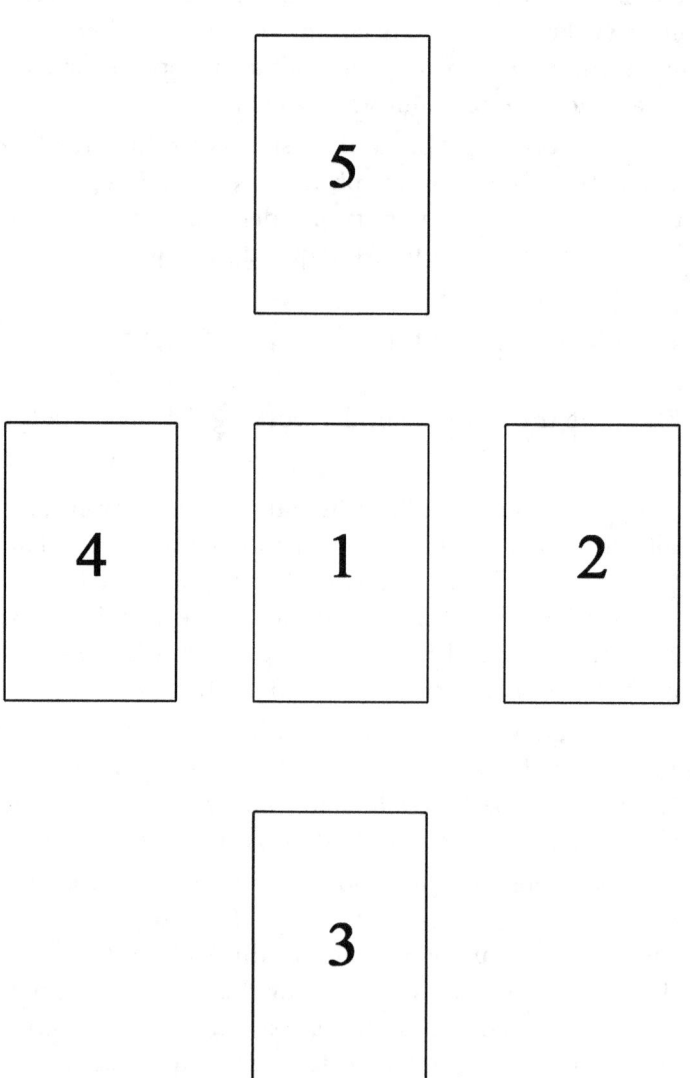

Figure 20.2: The four-directional layout

A second layout that can be useful for a simple view of power is a layout of the four gates. These are general magical attributes that can be used not only in magic, ritual and vision, but also in divination. Once you have a basic idea of the powers that flow from these magical directions, you can use that knowledge to work with the directions for tarot readings.

1. Centre. Body, self, land, starting point, present time. Always start at ground zero: you are seeing from this perspective and this is what all of the directional powers are affecting.

2. East. Air, swords, words, spring, morning, birth, intellect, training, mind, utterance, books.

3. South. Fire, summer, midday, wands, success, rulership, kings, gods, immune system, future.

4. West. Water, autumn, dusk, cups, emotions, relationships, psychic ability, bridge of death.

5. North. Earth, winter, nighttime, pentacles, substance, ancestors, death, elders, queens, goddesses: female.

6. Relationships. This position is about how things, powers and people directly affect you and your relationship with them.

There are many more directional attributes, and as you develop as a magician you will learn far more subtleties, interlinks and connections. But it is unwise to swamp yourself beneath a ton of lists: start simple and go from there. These are a basic list of magical directional powers and how you use them in readings will depend largely on what you are reading about and what you need to know.

This layout can be versatile and can be used for a lot of different types of questions if you work within the parameters of directional attributes, for example east = spring, starting, air, utterance, books, incoming. If you are reading to look to see if a magical attack is incoming, if it is active and forming, it will show in the east (and south). If you were looking for the best timing to do a particular working, the strongest card in the east would indicate dawn/spring, and so on.

20.2 The use of tarot in healing

Tarot, as we know, has many applications, and one of the more interesting ones is as a tool for looking in depth at the human body. Not only does it tell you what is going on with the body, but you can, with the right layout, look at the influences that are bringing about changes in the body, be they organic or inner.

Before we go any further, I have to point out the commonsense thing that everyone knows but it has to be said anyway: using tarot as part of healing is not a substitute for going to a doctor.

You can use an ordinary deck but, if this is something that you are going to use often, I suggest that you make your own deck using your own health and magically related key words written on blank cards. Creating your own deck is not easy as there are a lot of things to think about, such as what key powers, words and dynamics are necessary for a healing deck. But the journey itself is revealing and can teach you a lot not only about the sickness/healing process, but also about how a deck can truly work powerfully.

When you look at the body using tarot, you begin to see some interesting things that relate to illness, body changes, and minute reactions to things that have long-term consequence but little outer symptoms. You start to see the impact that inner work has on the body, how magic sometimes changes things within the body, and how various parts of the body react to power in various ways. It also maps out the passage of inner power through the body, which in turn gives the magical worker clues about how to care for the body while doing powerful work.

The other interesting thing that begins to emerge is the pattern of illness: normally we see only the outer symptoms, which are treated and we get better. Using tarot, we start to see the profound implications of a virus or bacteria, how it can change things at a deep level, and we also start to see the inner manifestation of the outer virus. Every living thing has an inner expression, and through the tarot, we can look at these illnesses to see their inner 'personalities.' This in turn can change how we approach an illness and how we get rid of it.

20.2. The use of tarot in healing

One of the first things that emerge when you start to track the progression of an illness using tarot is that some illnesses, while they may make us miserable, have positive uses for the body. I used to hate the occasional cold: I rarely got them but when I did they made my life a misery. But when I started to look at them from an inner point of view by using the tarot, I saw that the body was using the cold to 'dump' a whole load of toxins that it had in storage. The cold virus was actually a positive thing for me, so I stopped trying to treat the symptoms, and let the body get on with it.

In fact, the more you look at the body and illness using tarot, the more you see positive sides to minor illnesses that the body can use to avoid deeper and more troublesome problems. You also start to see the positive and negative effects of certain types of magic and how the body copes with such power: it changed the way I did magic.

It also began to become clear that the endocrine system processed the heavy impact of magic and too much heavy work, or the burden of a serious attack/curse could seriously damage the endocrine system. This was something that Dion Fortune wrote about from her own body observations, and to see it laid out within a spread is fascinating.

I also began to look closely at the immune system and tracked how magical attacks trigger the immune system: the body treats the energy as an invasion, which, in reality is what it is. The immune system kicks in and tries to fight the attack. If it cannot succeed, the reaction becomes chronic. No amount of treatment can cure it because it is not an outer illness i.e. there is no virus to subdue: it is purely an inner attack and has to be dealt with using inner work.

It really helps if you are doing a lot of magical work to differentiate between ordinary illness and illness that is a manifestation of magic. Too many people think their body problems are the result of magic and the reading will clearly point out if it is or not. Mostly it's not: but it is always good to check, particularly if someone is just not getting better. If someone is sensitive, then their body will react to all sorts of things and you can track that reaction all the way through the body: it's fascinating!

The layout is the key to working in this way. The layout has to be specific so that you can pinpoint certain things that you need

20. Using tarot as a working tool

information about, and the layout has to have no ambiguous parts to it: it must be precise. I put together a layout that I have used for a few years now and it works in tandem with a healing deck, which is focused specifically upon the human body.

You can track the progression over the days of an illness, seeing if it alters the deeper parts of the body in anyway. I have watched things in my children, seeing how an illness has caused a change and then watching that change emerge over the years. At first I used to panic and try to put back whatever had been altered using homeopathy, cranial work or inner work.

Eventually I learned not to do that: we are the sum total of constant change within ourselves and the changes that come from the viruses are all part of our maturation and growth. Nothing stays the same: everything is always changing and moving.

As a person who uses a lot of homeopathy, this method of using tarot to look at the body became invaluable. I was able to look at the possible progression of a specific remedy to decide the potency or even if it is the right remedy. What I learned over the years is that sometimes even though it's the right remedy picture, the remedy would wreak havoc in the body if I took it or gave it. For me, that was not too much of a revelation: when you do a lot of magical work, the 'body' changes. The way that the body processes power and substance becomes inextricably altered so that normal everyday remedies, medicines and herbs do not work, or have an different or opposing effect. You have to approach a magical body in a different way and take the magical changes into account.

It also becomes useful to look at a person's body rhythm: by getting familiar with someone's processing pattern, you can the make better decisions regarding recovery/treatment. By a person's rhythm I mean the way that the particular body in question processes power, food and illness. Everyone's body has their own unique way of doing things, and that 'way' is borne out of the body's previous experiences, its miasms and its personality. By tracking certain behaviours through the readings, you begin to see the individual pattern of action/reaction in the body and such information can be invaluable when trying to help them.

To sum up, be clear with your questions is always the cornerstone of good reading. Develop the work to fit what you do: quite a few doctor friends of mine have taken this layout and quietly used it in their diagnostic work with some adjustments. And finally, allow your curiosity free rein: that is how we discover things!

20.3 The health layout

The health layout is just that: it is a layout that gives you a snapshot of what is happening in the different areas of the body, and how they are affecting each other. This is an excellent place to start when looking at a magical impact that is physically manifesting, or an illness that is rooted in magic.

This layout looks at the interaction of three forms of energy: emotion, inner energy coming from outside the body, and the energy the body derives from whatever it ingests. These three dynamics are inextricably linked, and the layout shows how those interactions affect the body's various functions.

1.

The first position shows what magic, power, and energetic influence is coming from the Inner Worlds in order to manifest in the body. This is where any magic that could affect the body will show up: for example an inner contact, current inner work, or a magical attack. It is also the position where you will be able to see any future patterns of fate or action that have not yet fully begun to manifest. If the only negative influence in the reading occupies this position, then the destructive pattern is still forming and can be obviated or avoided, as it has not yet reached the individual's inner landscape.

2.

The second position shows any inner influence that has already penetrated a person's sphere/has entered their inner landscape, and is now present in their immediate future pattern. Something that turns up here is already having an energetic influence on how a

20. Using tarot as a working tool

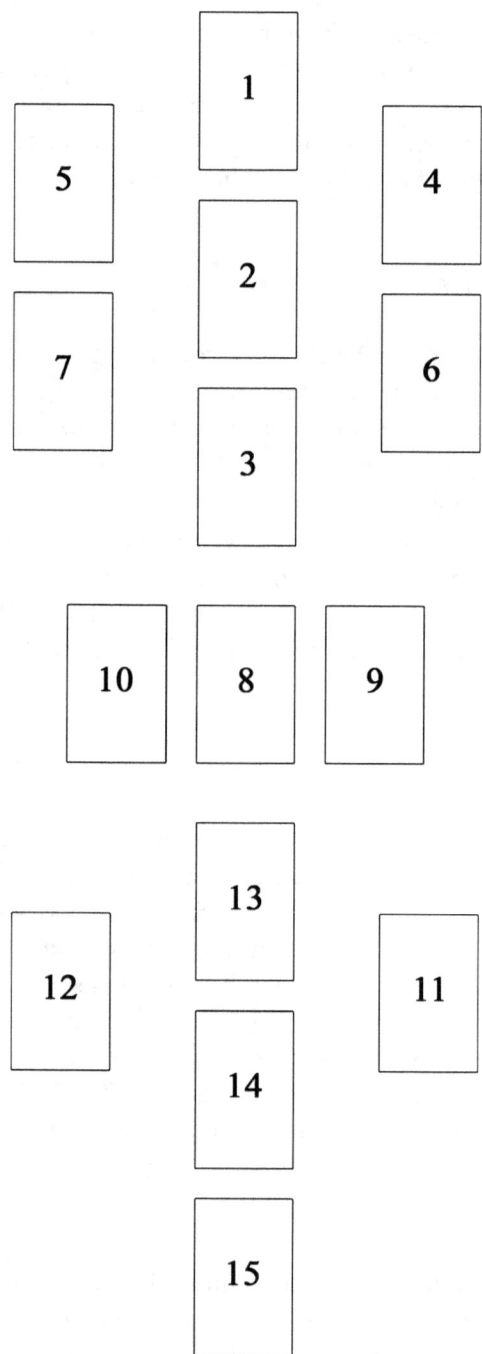

Figure 20.3: Health layout.

body is operating, but it has not yet fully manifested as a full-blown condition.

It is in this position that we see the consciousnesses of viruses and bacteria, along with beings, magical attacks, impacts, etc. Whatever occupies this position is already affecting the person's energetic body, and if left unchecked will descend into their physical body and cause symptoms.

Learning how to discern the meaning of the card in this position will really help you to understand what type of magical impact or injury you are suffering from. If something major shows in this position, do a follow-up reading using the Inner Landscape or Desert layout to gain more detail.

3.

The third position tells us what is physically happening regarding the health of the head. That includes the brain, sinuses, lymph glands, endocrine glands in the brain,[1] ears, nose, eyes, and the throat including the thyroid gland—basically everything above the base of the neck. If something untoward shows in this position, and the physical symptoms presenting are not enough information to pinpoint the exact problem or what area of the head is affected, then narrow things down using a simple layout. To do that I use the Tree of Life layout and ask questions like "is the problem infection?" "is the problem inflammation?" and so on. Remember, the health reading only gives you an overview. After that, you need to focus in on specifics.

4.

The fourth position shows us the solid energy going into the body. Anything that you are eating, drinking, smoking, or otherwise ingesting will show here, and the type of card that falls in this position will also indicate whether it is affecting you badly.

---

[1] The hypothalamus, and the pineal and pituitary glands.

20. Using tarot as a working tool

5.

The fifth position shows the state of the emotions: how the person feels. Often the emotions can be good indicators of what is going on deeper within the body. The emotions can drive the immune system, and when looking for a treatment make sure that it brings about favourable emotional energies. If a person is in physical pain, it will also show in this position.

6.

The sixth position shows what the short-term or primary immune system is currently doing. If it is fighting something or it is in overdrive, it will show here. What we put into our bodies directly affects the front line of the immune system: hence this card sits directly under the 'solid energy' position. Look at the relations between the two cards: if an ingested substance (food, drugs, etc.) is contributing to, aggravating, or causing the illness, then both positions four and six will show aggravating or aggressive cards.

7.

The seventh position shows the deeper immune system, and this is connected to the function of the thymus, an endocrine gland. The thymus prepares and trains T and B cells for a front-line attack on an intruder, and it is deeply affected by emotional wellbeing, which is why card seven sits beneath card five in this spread. This position also shows the secondary immune system that wraps up, locks up, or breaks down threats that have already been overcome.

When the querent is already on the winning side of an illness, the aggressive cards will often move from position six (primary immune response) to position seven. This is where disease threats are processed and put into 'sleep mode.' The person's emotional wellbeing will affect how well this process works, and if they have recently experienced terrible grief, this area of the immune system can become compromised. This position also tells us how our immune system is functioning. It indicates how well-balanced the immune responses are, and whether the body's T- and B-cells are being produced in the right quantities and are operating as they should, and are not attacking the body itself. (Regarding inflammatory diseases: when one is in active mode, it will often show in both immune positions. When the disease is dormant but has potential, it will show only in the seventh position.)

8.

The eighth position shows the central core of the body, which houses the vital organs. If there is a problem with those organs, it will show here. If a major aggressive card falls in this position, then the reader needs to do further readings to see which specific organ has been affected.

9.

The ninth position shows the male sexual organs, testosterone, and the bladder. Testosterone is also present in females, and if the reading is for a woman and a difficult card turns up in this position, then it will probably be necessary to look in more depth at her endocrine system and hormone balances. If they all look fine in separate readings, then a reading needs to be done to look at her hormonal response to being around males.

10.

The tenth position shows the female sexual organs and the bladder. Again, males also have estrogen in their bodies, so if the reading is for a male and a difficult card turns up here, check their hormone system. A difficult card here can also indicate the presence of a member of the opposite sex who is hormonally disruptive. So for example, if a woman magician is out-of-balance and a reading shows an aggressive card in the ninth position, it could either indicate a testosterone imbalance within her own body, or a male around her who is disrupting her health simply with his presence or energetic influence. This usually happens unconsciously, and it is the result of the many hormone signals our bodies put out—sometimes we can have a bad reaction to hormone signals coming from another person. Depending on where a woman is in her cycle, she can be attracted by male pheromones—but she can also be made aggressive by the presence of the same. In female magicians, this is far more pronounced than in the general population, depending on what streams of inner power and contacts they work with. So be aware of those possible dynamics when reading those positions: hormones are the dynamos that run our moods and emotions, and as such they have a powerful influence over everything that we do. The other thing that can show in these two sexual reproductive positions is bladder issues, so bear that in mind.

11.

The eleventh position shows the digestive system, and it reveals how the large and small intestines are processing everything that came in at position four (food, etc). But be aware that a lot of magic can also be processed through the digestive system, particularly when we are given energy or information to take in. This area of the body can also be read in conjunction with position five (the emotions): there is a direct relationship between digestive health and mental and emotional health. For example, neurotransmitters like serotonin play a major part in mood, muscle health, and digestion.

12.

Position twelve tells us what is happening to us in our sleep. Many magicians put too much emphasis on controlling their dreams in order to have 'lucid dreams.' This is a mistake and it can interfere with true magical events that can happen in sleep, plus it also interferes with the body's own repair system that swings into action when we sleep.

Any magical intrusions of any real power will surface naturally in dreams, and dreams are also an opportunity for protective beings to warn us of impending trouble. Our sleep is also a time when our deeper spirit can partake of magical service, and it is unwise to interfere with the natural flow of our deeper selves. The dreams/sleep position is directly below the emotions and the deeper immune system in this layout, as they are all inexorably linked, and these cards can be read together to get a deeper understanding of what is happening in our subconscious, our brains, and our immune system. This position is also linked to positions one and two, and if disturbances show in positions one and two, and there is a volatile or difficult card in position twelve, then you are most likely looking at a magical attack, a difficult period of fate changes, or at least a magical disturbance. The quality of your sleep is important to both your health and your strength, so pay good attention to what is going on in this position.

13.

Position thirteen looks at the 'structure and movement' system of the body, which means bone, muscle, and nerves. Any inflammatory reaction, central nervous system disturbance, or bone/muscle impact will show here. If there is a difficult card in this position and also in position three (head/brain) then you are more likely to be looking at a problem with nerve issues. If there are fiery cards in this position and in the eleventh position (digestion) then it may indicate an inflammatory disease active with roots in bacterial imbalance or inflammation in the small intestine.

14.

Position fourteen is the skin. The skin is the most externalized organ and also the biggest organ of our body. It is through the skin that the body can safely deposit toxins and dead matter, and process irritants: this mechanism keeps such problems away from vital organs, and also gives you an obvious heads-up when there is a problem.

Issues with food sensitivity or allergy, recovery from viruses and infections, and reactions to magical power will all show on the skin: the skin is a good weather indicator about how our bodies are coping, and what they are coping with. If the magician is badly attacked and gets ill as a result, one of the healing objectives should be to bring that imbalance up to the surface to present itself on the skin.

As soon as the rashes start to show, you know the healing process is working. Because of this mechanism, never be tempted to suppress rashes that appear: rather it is better to keep an eye on them and let them be. If it is an allergic reaction or a sensitivity reaction like eczema, find out the root cause and eliminate it if possible.

20. Using tarot as a working tool

15.

Position fifteen tells us the immediate future of the body's health. If a damaging card turns up in this position, then work still has to be done to help to body come back into balance. Consider this card in relation to the time limit you put on the reading: if the reading looked three weeks ahead, and the card in position fifteen is a difficult one, then redo the reading to look at a span of six weeks, to see if the body just needs a bit more time to heal. If at six weeks the card in position fifteen (or other cards) is still difficult, then you need to reassess what action you are taking.

When to use the health layout

Use this layout when the body is showing obvious signs of distress after magical work, or if your body suddenly nosedives and you suspect that magic has been used. It is also a good layout to keep an eye on your general health and it can be used by energy healers to look at a client to get a deeper picture of what is going on inside their body.

Keep a record of the readings so that you can track recovery over time, but also so that you can spot potential longer-term problems that are not so apparent in the first readings. Often an imbalance in an area of the body starts like a grain of sand rubbing in your sock, but then grows over time to become a major issue. If that happens, you can go back over the readings to pinpoint the beginning of the problem and locate the area of the body that first went into decline. It also helps you to see how a particular body copes with problems: each body is slightly different and will have its own healing pattern. Through tracking various bodily reactions through readings, you can ascertain that body's own method of self-healing.

20.4 Making a contacted deck for magical seership

When you design your own deck for divination, there are many ways in which it can be done which will decide what type of deck you will end up with. Doing a vague copy of the Rider-Waite will give you a

20.4. Making a contacted deck for magical seership

Rider-Waite deck. Working within the structures of archetypes and psychology will give you a deck that speaks from the complexity of the human psyche. But if you do a lot of magical work and you use your deck as a tool to assist you in your work, then you need a deck that will bend and flex with the demands that present in the type of work that you do.

Such a deck will be the most useful if it is connected to the contacts that you work with, or the types of beings that you regularly encounter. This way, the beings can talk to you clearly through the deck which can save a lot of faffing about when you need to get a job done swiftly and successfully.

In conjunction with the contacts within the deck, the layout should reflect the realms and places that you work in or that are a part of your life, or the places that you go to when you are working with a particular order of beings. This way, the cards and the layout are read together, and begin to form a natural flow of communication that you can plug into.

If you are making a contacted deck, then you need to make sure that every being, place and power that you put in the deck is real: it must be beings and places that you have experience of, however brief the encounter. This ensures the clarity, depth and honesty of the deck: it cannot be a contacted deck if the beings are not real!

What can happen however is that, if the beings are not real, they can occasionally act as filters or windows for real beings to come through. The only problem with this is that the filter can interfere with the natural qualities of the being—it will literally filter them and they will only be able to express the power that is represented in the image.

Then you need to look at the sorts of 'actions' that need to express themselves through the deck. These 'actions' are the equivalent of the Minor Arcana in the tarot deck. They must express all the different depths of emotions, actions, happenings, etc. and it is a good idea to use the elements as a basis, but it is not essential. The way to decide the actions section of the deck is to write a list of emotions, happenings, actions, etc.

For example: power, work, travel, past, balance, imbalance, illness, creation, accident, gift, accumulation, etc. It does not matter

20. Using tarot as a working tool

how many you have, though I tend to work on seven or ten for each element. Using a single word or only two words takes away the deliberate and terribly annoying whimsical obscurity that is found in the minor cards in some decks. I want straight answers, not a philosophy lesson!

Once you have all your actions charted, then you need people for your deck. Again, I usually steer away from the traditional court cards, which can be as equally annoying as the obscure minor picture cards.

How many of us have wanted to tear up page/child cards that litter a reading and have nothing useful to say!

Look at the different aspects of womanhood and manhood. Some people are rulers, others are seers, some are workers, so you would need a king, a queen, a priestess, an old person, a young person, a mother, a father, consort, a wise elder, a young lover, etc. You need to represent one of each of the various expressions of womanhood and manhood. I usually end up with about 20 court cards, 10 for each sex. But you can do as many or as little as you like: you are the only person who imposes limits on yourself!

When it comes to layout, you must decide which realms you wish the deck to work in and what elements of your own realm you wish to include: home? temple? work? Within your own realm, you will need positions to allow the powers to define a specific influence e.g. dreams, warnings, struggles, what is coming in, what is going out, what is past, what is future. If you want clarity within your readings, then the positions of the layout must be in harmony with each other and the pattern must make sense, rather that being decided upon by a design/aesthetics decision.

One of the strongest ways of working with a contacted deck is to design the layout in fellowship with the major cards. Each major card is also a position in the layout: for example if you have twenty major cards, there will be twenty positions for the full layout. Each position will be named after and will be the home of a major card. When you are doing a reading with the full layout, the card and the position will be read together.

When approaching the layout design, write the realms that you work with, and then think about the major cards and where they would live, what realm they reside in. The actual pattern of the layout reflects the realms, and the positions reflect the powers and beings that are the major cards. The positions and cards interact to create a pattern that flows through the reading once the deck is in use.

Once you have got a basic pattern for your layout, look at it again from a geometric point of view: the universe that we live in is mathematically coherent and its patterns are clear, beautiful and make perfect sense. Your layout needs to reflect that harmony, so it also needs to make geometric sense. The best pattern of all to use is the patterning of the universe.

20.5 Minor layouts

The full layout of your deck would be for major magical readings. For smaller readings where you need straight answers and to identify powers, action, etc. you will need a more work-friendly layout that can be used quickly and efficiently.

Think about the basic environment you are in: past, present, future, home, work, and temple. Think about positions that will express a space for an answer to come in: i.e., dreams, obstacles, support, and relationships. The layout will then be built around a basic structure that will enable the cards to talk in a clear way to you for simple communication.

20.6 Creating your major cards

Once your basic mapping of cards and layout is done, then you need to start creating the deck from an inner point of view before you begin to create the outer deck. The orders of beings, the individual beings and the places that are represented need to be connected up to images that you will create. This is the most time-consuming part of the whole process as it cannot be rushed and needs to be done systematically and carefully.

Find a space where you can leave out parts of the deck where they and you will not be disturbed, and where you can keep a safety candle going all the time. Starting with the first being or place of the deck, go in vision to that place or to meet that being and commune

20. Using tarot as a working tool

with them. Ask for a sigil, pattern or image and when you come out of vision, write it down and then make that card. Repeat the process until all the major cards have been made.

You may find that during the process, some of the beings or places want their layout positions changed or modified: the first map of your layout should be a starting point, not a finished production. Be flexible and able to listen to the beings as they guide you. Ideally, the major cards and the layout are created together and are a part of each other. They should have a close working relationship with the layout and with each other so that it becomes their own little world.

Then you can then go onto make the minor and court cards. When you make the minor cards, again stay flexible, as you may find that some actions become unnecessary and you will most likely realize that you have left out a crucial action. You can use the harmony of numbers to allow powers to flow through the minor cards too, in which case you must make sure that the actions and emotions are relevant to the harmonics of the number patterns.

Sometimes you will find that the minor cards become lower octaves of some of the major cards, showing that life patterns are often octaves of higher and more powerful fate patterns that flow through the consciousness of the time and the culture that you live in. It can get very interesting and this is where some of the astrological symbolism comes into play on the minor cards: the planetary symbol can be put in the corner of the card if it is useful to show the deeper pattern of the power that you are expressing.

One word of caution though: don't fall into the trap of putting lots of obscure magical symbols on your cards just to make them look more magical as you will clutter the filter, confuse the reading, and you will start to walk down the road of glamour. Magic is about real powers, real work and a real world: it's not about black clothes, funny symbols and looking magically cool.

On that note, you don't have to be an artist to create your own contacted deck, words, symbols and basic images will work and allow the power to flow through, just make sure that there is nothing on the cards that does not belong there: don't fill them with junk!

If you are an artist, then you are especially lucky: some of the inner world beings are stunning in their representations, and to

20.6. Creating your major cards

recreate them with all their colours, lines and shapes would be awesome! The power would truly flow through unhindered and such visual beauty is wonderful to work with.

As you are working on your deck, make sure you have a living flame burning to tune the space in as you work. It can be really useful if you tune the flame into the Void: this means that help can flow out of the Void as you create.

Once the deck is created, let it sit for twenty-four hours before you start to work with it. This is like a settling-in period to let the powers settle: it's the cooking of the deck! Make sure you have a safe place to put it so that it cannot be played with: contacted decks can affect people if they mishandle them. Having a warrior goddess coming face-to-face with your three-year-old toddler is not always a good idea: it could get messy (though in my household it would have been debatable about which one would come out on top).

When the deck is ready to work, start by laying out the major cards in their layout positions and just sit and hang out with them for a few minutes to look over the connections, patterns and relationships. You might start to see new ones that you did not know about, or hadn't thought about. It also helps to get a visual of the card in its position so that when you come to do a reading, you can see the major card position in your head and read the card that fell in that position in tandem with the positional meaning, along with the position where that positional card landed. (Confused? Ha!)

So for example: say you have two major cards, the Pathway (future) and the Old Gods: the Pathway falls in the layout position of the Old Gods while the Old Gods is in the position of the Mountain (challenges you must face). This would indicate that the way forward for you is to look into/work with the powers of the old ways/gods, but it will be a hard struggle that must be faced. If it still doesn't make sense, just drink a few beers, it will all get clearer...

Once you are familiar with the layout positions/powers, then it is time to start to play with the deck. Work with a notebook and write your questions. The first one to do, which will open your deck up and align it to you, is to look at your long-term magical/spiritual work/life, or something of that ilk that is connected to your magical work and you, and it should be a long-term or lifetime view. This is

20. USING TAROT AS A WORKING TOOL

like charging a phone battery: you have to give it a long charge the first time around, as that sets the power levels for future fills.

Write down the reading so that you can go back to it in the future. This is a good training habit to get into: always write readings and your interpretations. If you are wrong, you can go back and see why, and you can see how it really unfolded.

Once you have seen the disaster that is the rest of your life, then you can start to look at other things of power to exercise the deck, and to train you to understand its idiosyncrasies. Don't put any limitations upon what you look at or why, just be curious so that you can learn.

Look at the work of political figures: look at the inner influences that flow through them, for good or bad. Look at religious and magical figures, look at historical figures and their powers. Look at deities and their powers, their histories and their stories now. Look at magical places and realms: ask how they work and why.

The secret to the focus of the deck is the focus of the reader's questions. You have to be clear and to the point with a question. For example, if you ask the deck to show you your magical work now, it will probably show you your magical work at that precise point in time. So think about your questions and be simple, for example: show me the magical powers that ran through Crowley from his teens until his death, show me the magical influences that were around him from birth until the age of twenty. You can see how specific the questions should be.

Once you have done one deck and have become proficient at working with it, then you can start to look at creating decks with specific purposes. If you work a lot with herbs or are a healer for example, you can create a healing deck where the cards are slanted towards body issues and powers, and the layout reflects the systems of the body.

There is no real limit on what you can do in deck design: we create our own limits which we have to learn to move beyond. If you spend enough time pressing the red button and blowing the world up, you will begin to learn your real limits, as opposed to the ones that are inflicted upon you that are there simply to keep you in your place in the magical pecking order.

Chapter Twenty-one

Working methods for leading group visions/workings

When you are in a situation of leading groups into visions, there are many powers and techniques that come into play both to protect the group and to facilitate the inner contact/connection.

In this chapter, I will be dealing with visions that are 'contacted' i.e. going to real places and interacting with real beings as opposed to psychological guided journeys that are written in advance and explore the deeper part of the self. That is therapy and is not dealt with here.

When you are leading people in a vision, you are basically telling them what you see: you take them by the hand and lead them to a place where they can interact with a contact. So the first step is to make sure that the vision you are using is flexible enough for that purpose so that the group can pass from imagination to reality pretty quickly. For that you need a structure that is well used so that you do not have to do any 'hacking' into new territory, unless that is your aim.

To approach it this way, you begin the structure from the minute you light a candle in the centre of the gathering. People have been lighting candles to precipitate inner work for hundreds if not thousands of years, so the minute you light a flame with intent, you begin your walk down a well trodden path.

The vision that you use will need to have the basic gateway structure that gets people to where you need them to go. It also needs to have the 'unfolding' energy that stretches the people from an inner point of view to make them more 'flexible.' There is a great deal of power in approaching a contact slowly by going through a series of processes: first the people need to become focused, then they

21. Working methods for leading group visions/workings

need stilling and to be made aware of their own environment before embarking on a journey that will take them away from themselves.

By instilling the details of their environment, it is easier to bring them back after a particularly deep vision. What they will need is a sense of the directions, of themselves in relation to those directions, and the focal point of their own power within. Then connect that to the central flame that will act as a beacon for when they begin their journey back.

One piece of advice at this stage is that throughout the vision don't be tempted to describe too much, or to be creative in your language or to add things in to 'make' the surroundings, as these details cloud the natural vision of the listener and can be distracting. Simple and straightforward is much better and allows the listener to 'see' things for themselves. If you describe too much, you end up blocking their sight, so the less you describe the better. The basic rule of thumb is to say only what is needed to get them somewhere and to introduce them to the contacts.

Once you have crossed into the vision from the imagination, you will basically be telling them what you see, except don't give too much detail regarding the contact. Just outline the power and basics of the contact, and let them experience it for themselves. Give them a period of silence so that they can commune with the contact themselves. And then when you start to bring them back, you will find it is much easier and quicker to bring them back than it is to take them there.

21.1 Contacts

When you are reaching for a contact to work with in vision, they will often be lining up for you once you have decided what it is you are going to do. This works if you are working within a framework, rather than random visions where you are looking for anyone who is an inner contact: that is like wandering the streets for someone to talk to. Be focused and know where you are going and why.

Don't fall into the trap of visionary tourism: going somewhere just to look/connect with a contact but not actually doing anything useful. This is a dead end road to go down and will slowly close your contacts up over a period of time. When you go into the Inner Worlds, particularly with a group of people, you have the chance to do something useful. Ask the contact if they need you to do anything for them: they will jump at the chance usually and it is better for groups to be doing rather than looking.

21.2 Energy dynamics

The energy dynamics of group vision is interesting. You can go further and open things out more with the group energy, but you also have the strain of carrying the weaker members of the group to some extent. If it is a fairly large group, it is advisable to have experienced workers in each direction and they have the responsibility of holding the energy in that direction. This intention of action automatically begins a load-sharing between the workers and shares the strain out, enabling the group to do much more powerful work without blowing anyone out.

The protection of the group comes from the framework that you are working in. If you are using a vision path that has been walked many times over the generations, then certain beings will be operating within that structure and will automatically keep you safe. If you are working on a new path, or hardly used path, then you will have to be a little more attentive.

Be on the alert for beings that you had no intention of working with ("hey, I can work with you, I will take you here, I am the high priest" etc.), as they are mostly hungry parasites out for a quick lunch. If you are doing exploratory work, have a clear intent of where you want to go, what you want to achieve and who you want to meet. Don't move out of that framework and don't get taken down the garden path, so to speak.

If for example, you are aiming to connect with a certain deity, then they will probably have protective beings within their structure that will come into play the minute you begin the vision. If you are stretching for a person in time, or another type of being, then it is advisable to work within your own structure if you are a part of a coven/lodge/priest line, etc. Use your own contacts and guardians to warn you and keep you safe.

21. Working methods for leading group visions/workings

As you get to be more experienced at exploratory work, you begin to recognize the beings that will just be a pain in the ass or could be a threat to your group. If you stay on your intended path though, such things tend not to happen.

When the group is looking at a particular set of beings, places, people, deities, the best way is to always go meet them in visions first, and then talk about them afterwards. This way, you do not colour the person's experience, or preempt their vision in any way. The effect is the opposite: if you do the vision and then have a talk-around to share experiences and then talk about the theoretical stuff, you will see things dawn on people's faces as they come to realize what it was that they just saw. Hearing other people describe something that you thought only you saw is a wonderful feeling: you realize you were all really there.

21.3 Reality or imagination?

This takes us to the age-old beginner's question: what is real and what is the imagination? Well, both really. You use the imagination as a vehicle to get you into the Inner Worlds and then it crosses over into visions of what is actually there, not what is imagined there.

People have to experience this for themselves: no amount of explaining will do it. I have been doing this work for a long time and I still get shivers of happiness when I get inner conformation of the reality. When a person has a silent experience in a vision (i.e. they see something that was not described, or the contact tells them something directly) and then at the talk-around after the working someone else describes exactly the same thing, you know you have all been in the same place.

My all-time favourite example of this happened in Bath UK and Ulster. Many years ago, while teaching in Ulster, during a vision I offered a precious ring that I had to the Dark Goddess. She took it with thanks and I made the promise to put the actual ring into the river in Bath where the hot springs of Sul pour into the river's edge.

As soon as I got to my home in Bath I got my ring, put it in my bag and went off to the river. I couldn't bear to look at the ring (it was the most precious thing I had besides my kids, and dropping little kids into the river as a goddess offering tends to get you arrested these days...) so I just put my hand in the bag, got it on the end of my finger, and with my eyes shut, dropped it into the water. All was well.

Until a week later when I was leading a group vision into the cave of the Dark Goddess, where she lunged at me in fury demanding to know where her gift was. To say that I was shitting myself would be putting it mildly. I stammered that I had given her the ring but she held another ring up to my face: a ring I recognized but wasn't 'The' precious one: it was an Egyptian ring, antique gold, but not the one she wanted. I was confused.

When I got home, my then partner reminded me that he had put my Egyptian ring in my bag to remind me to get it fixed (the turquoise was loose). When I put my hand into my bag I had pulled out the wrong ring unknowingly and the Goddess had not got her gift.

I immediately found the precious ring and took it straight to the river and deposited it. That is one of many examples of the reality of visions, and a good example of my unerring ability to be a dork.

21.4 Snatched energy

One sad thing to be cautious of in group work is to be on the lookout for energy snatchers. These people try and harness some of the group energy to use for their own agenda which, just by nature of their action, will probably be unhealthy.

The way it is done is a rock, little bag, trinket, amulet, etc. is quietly placed under or around the altar in the centre with the intention of siphoning off power into it to be taken away at the end of the day. It can also be done by holding the object and gathering up the group power as the others work. Do not allow anyone to put anything by, on or near the altar, and don't let them hold anything. There are often many excuses given but none are valid: there is no reason for anyone to need an object while working. The protections are in place and they need to work like everyone else. It is sad in today's magical world that such things happen, but they do.

21. Working methods for leading group visions/workings

On a side note, if you are part of a visionary magic group or at a workshop type gathering, look for the leader doing the same thing. I have had experiences of watching teachers and leaders use workshop energy to fuel their own private agenda even to the point of using group workshop energy to launch curses and magical attacks. Under those circumstances the unwitting participants become sucked into the energetic structure of the attack and take the repercussions as if they were the initiator of the attack. This is a sneaky way for the attacker to use the group as a scapegoat for the backlash of energy such attacks generate. I hate writing about this type of thing, but it happens more than you would think and people need to be aware of it.

21.5 Different strains for different places

When you take groups to different places, there are different body impacts that such visions bring. The closer the vision is to your own realm and time, the less of an impact it will cause. The further away in time and the deeper the realm, the more of a bodily impact you will get. If you are taking a group way out in the stars at a planetary consciousness level, they will get hammered. If you are taking them to the depths of the Abyss, they will get hammered, but in a different way. Going up seems to precipitate nausea and going down has the beaten with a baseball bat feeling.

One of the things that can help to lessen such impact is to build up to such heavy workings slowly by doing a few gentler ones first. If you are planning to go far out in any direction, do at least two visions that take people a part of the way so that they become stretched along that path. Then when they come to do the heavy one, they have already been down a section of the road and their body has had time to adjust.

Take frequent coffee breaks and make the group talk in turn about their experiences after the visions: this helps people to come back, it helps jog memories that become lost in deep vision, and it also helps to hear other people's experience in relation to your own.

After a particularly heavy vision, do a light rebalancing meditation or take them into a Void-type setting to rebalance and restore them. Don't finish the day on a powerful working either, finish on a gentle note: people have to drive and find their way home. That is not easy if you head is stretched in fourteen different directions.

21.6 Picking up maps from written visions

When you read a written vision that was created through true vision as opposed to being a constructed vision—i.e. what is written was the direct experience of a seer rather than a vision put together theoretically—then you are looking at someone else's experience. But it can still be used as a basic map to get you somewhere without being affected by the author's individual sight/experience, if you know how to read what they wrote.

When you look at a written vision (such as the ones below), look without getting drawn into the vision. Look at the mechanism used for getting into the inner realms, look at the path used, the contacts worked with and the way out. You can extract a basic skeleton map that you can work with to allow your own vision to emerge. This ends up being a deeper experience than following another person's writings word for word. Following other people's visions to the letter will limit your own ability to reach into the Inner Worlds for visions and contacts.

When you look at written visions, be on the lookout for things put in there that are mythical or psychological: you want neither. What you want is the true map and nothing else, so don't get sidelined by descriptions or declarations.

An important point to think about within group working is don't filter who can come and who cannot: when you work with deep inner contacts, they line up the group before you do. They pull in people they need to work with and will reject people they do not wish to work with. If you have an open door policy, then the filtering is done for you providing the work is conducted within the right ethics i.e. it is not a commercial affair.

The strangest people, who you think might not be able to handle the work, often turn out to be the strongest of the group or they take on some very important role that you hadn't thought of. The more I have worked with groups over the years, the more I have realized

21. Working methods for leading group visions/workings

that I really haven't a clue what I am doing and I just turn up and tune in. The inner contacts plug in after shaking their heads at the dork that life has thrown at them, and we are off and away.

The same goes for written work: I have found that if you just put out the work, it will inform those that need the info, will not interest the ones who don't, and will be totally incomprehensible or unusable to the people who really shouldn't be doing it anyway.

21.7 Clearing up

After you have finished a day of working, it is wise to clear up the room after yourself. You can do this as a group working, the last working of the day where people in the directions gather up the energy that has been generated and the vision imprints that are left in the room and they put the energy into the central flame, sending back into the Inner Worlds where it came from.

You then in vision fold up the room where you were working, like folding up a skin, and take it into the Void to disperse it, or put it in the flame. This way, you leave no imprint that can disturb or affect any future users of the room.

21.8 Creating a vision from a personal experience

When you have a powerful personal vision or experience, it can be good to share or expand the contact for use by a group. To do that you need to construct a vision that will safely get someone to a place and get them back.

The first stage of the construction is the opening and reaching for the contact. Intent is everything in magical work so when you light the flame, have specific intentions about where you want to go and what you want to do. You can draw the opening sequence from your own magical structures. I use the Void as a gateway to many places, while some people use a four-directional gate system, and others go down into the Underworld as a gateway to other places, and so on.

For example, say you had a powerful experience at a stone circle and you wanted to take a group there. You would open the vision using your own structure and then see yourself walking out of the mists towards the circle from some distance away. As you walk, call upon the guardians and contacts of the stones to grant you access to the circle, and you may have to as a group stop at a threshold and give gifts to the guardians. If you do this, warn people that if they give something that exists, they might have to throw it into a nearby river as an offering. This transfer of energy is important: if you are going to access a powerful place, it is only right that you contribute to the site in some way.

Once you have left gifts on the threshold, go down the path that leads to the stones and tell the group of any contacts that you see and introduce them to them. Once they are in the stones, give then silent time to commune for themselves with the stones and contacts. Then you can ask the contacts if they need anything from you as a group: sometimes they will need a job doing. In return you can ask them about the power of the site and how to work with it properly in the physical realm.

When the work is finished, guide the people back away from the stones and towards the mists. Pass them through the mists and into the Void or whatever threshold you use. Then remind them of where they are, where their directions are, and give then a minute of two to orientate themselves before asking them to open their eyes.

I am hoping that some of this information in this chapter will be useful to people embarking upon the role of vision leader. To help with ideas, and for material to extract skeletons/structure from, I have included below a few visions for people to work with and use. All of the visions are contacted visions and can be used to connect with those connections.

21.9 The vision of the goddess Tefnut in Ethiopia

Light a candle and close your eyes. Be aware of the flame within you, burning at the edge of the Void, and be aware of the candle flame before you. With your inner vision, you look at the candle flame and it grows into a column of fire. The fire is inviting and you edge closer to it.

21. Working Methods for Leading Group Visions/Workings

As you look at the fire, the room in which you are seated falls away and you find yourself walking down a hot dusty road with the sun burning in your face. There are many people around you, walking with you as you walk towards a walled city ahead of you.

As you get closer to the city you see that the wall that surrounds the city is made of dried mud and upon it are many beautiful frescos of birds, animals and strange-looking beasts with many wings and many eyes.

The air hums with bees, and flowers are all around you as you walk. The procession that you follow enters the city and heads straight to a low-built temple made of mud and brick. Many people are bearing gifts and male priests stop all women as they reach the temple: the women are not allowed to enter, they may only leave offerings at the threshold.

A deep instinct tells you to assume the look of a man and you draw a large cover over yourself to mimic some of the men who are swathed with robes and covers. No one looks at you as you enter the temple. To the far side of the temple is a narrow corridor and you walk down this corridor towards a large door.

No one seems to be interested in this door: they are busy celebrating something in the main temple. Pushing the door open you find yourself in a small dark sanctuary with a black rock in the center of a six-pointed star that is laid out upon the floor in grain.

Your hands are drawn to the rock and you reverently place your hands upon the black stone. A power builds up all around you and the room begins to hiss.

A face appears before you: a face of a lion who is also human. She is weeping and is angry. She has been trapped here in this temple by priests who wish to control her powers of moisture and life. She asks that you free her without alerting the priesthood.

A priest walks in and you pretend to be leaving an offering. Without wasting time, you leave the sanctuary and the temple, heading west to the river. Frantically you look around for a rock that looks similar to the one on the sanctuary. Finally you find one and hide it among your robes.

Returning to the temple you walk swiftly to the sanctuary and wait until it is empty. While no one is looking, you switch the rocks,

21.9. The vision of the goddess Tefnut in Ethiopia

picking up the sacred back stone and replacing it with the one from the river.

Once you are free of the temple and walking towards the river, you begin to be aware that the rock in your arms is beating like a heart. The voice of the Goddess swirls all around you: "yes, you hold my heart within your hands...take care and place me gently in the river that runs to the sea."

Once at the river, you walk into the water and find a good spot where she will not be disturbed. You place the rock among other rocks so that she is hidden. As soon as the rock leaves your arms you are overcome with a great tiredness.

Reaching the bank of the river, you lie down on the grass and immediately fall asleep. You dream of lions running free upon the land and of rivers bursting with life. Someone shouts your name and you wake with a start.

Before you stands a woman with the face of a lion. She is clothed in a cloak of many colors and around her neck are many bone beads. Aside her are two male lions without manes, and bees swarm all around her. She smiles as she shows you the life in the river that flows from her heart. She shows you how the life of the river flows down to the sea, flooding the land around it with life-giving moisture. Forests appear alongside the river and plants begin to grow.

She walks towards you, grass sprouting wherever her feet touch the ground, and she reaches out her hand. In the palm of her hand is one drop of moisture. She offers it to you and you carefully lick it from her hand.

The power of life flows through you, energizing you and filling you with strength and vitality. The Goddess tells you that with your willingness to help her, she will always help you and that wherever she is worshipped, drought will never appear.

She touches you upon the head and her touch fills you with a blinding light. All that you can see in the light is a flame: your flame. You move towards the flame and find yourself stepping through a flame back into the room where you first started. You sit awhile, absorbing what you have experienced. When you are ready, you open your eyes and blow out the candle.

21. Working methods for leading group visions/workings

21.10 The vision of Metatron and the Abyss

Be still and light a candle. As you become silent, so you begin to lose awareness of the room in which you are seated. The external noises fade, your mind settles and your breathing becomes relaxed and natural. Using your inner vision, you look at the candle flame before you. The room in which you are seated falls away and you find yourself looking through the flame to a landscape beyond.

Instinctively you reach through the flame and pass into the landscape—a place of sand, earth and wind. The wind whips around you and the sand gets into your eyes. For a moment you are blinded and yet you become aware of someone walking alongside you.

As your eyes clear, you see a human-type being, neither male nor female, walking alongside you, and yet their feet are down in the earth, so their legs are only visible from the calf up. They walk through the earth as though it was not there. Their hair is long and trails along the ground behind them, swishing away their footprints. No mark is left of their passing.

The being reaches out to touch you, and as their hand contacts your skin, a force flows through you with such strength that you fear you may fall. You become aware of the landscape in a different way. Life reflects from everything around you. The stones, the grains of sand, the plants and the wind, all are lit with the light of Divinity—all life is visible to you.

Looking around you see people come and go: they are unaware of you as you observe them. The perfection of power manifest in substance is evident in every person you look upon, and as you look to your own hands, you see divinity within your own flesh.

The angel moves you on and you walk deeper and deeper into the Desert, leaving the people behind. As you walk you become more and more aware of the mistakes you have made in this life, and the things that you have to learn. You find yourself assessing your life and you become so absorbed in this task that you arrive at the edge of a cliff without realizing. The angel puts out an arm to stop you falling over the edge.

You look out over the cliff and see that it falls down so far that you cannot see the bottom. It looks like a tear in the universe with no

21.10. The vision of Metatron and the Abyss

end. You look up and the sky is the same. The tear rises up through the stars also.

On the other side is a land swathed in mist. Something draws you to the other side but there is no way to cross. As you look around for a way across, a sound like no other echoes around the Abyss. The sound gets louder and louder until you put your hands over your ears. The angel who has walked beside you kneels down and lowers his head.

Out of the Abyss rises a being that looks like a man but is so large he fills the Abyss. He places one eyeball up to the cliff edge so that he can see you. He strains to see something so small but when he sees you he smiles and places out his hand. He whispers for you to step onto his hand but his voice is so strong it sounds like a hurricane strong enough to demolish the earth itself.

Carefully you step out onto his hand and he holds you up so that he can see you better. He cannot speak to you lest his voice destroy you, so he reaches over and places you on the other side of the Abyss.

As soon as your feet touch the floor the power of the universe emerges before you, building up to an uncomfortable pitch that makes you feel like you will explode. On instinct you turn around and look back over the Abyss and you see your many lives all happening at once. You see powers weaving back and forth interacting with your lives and you feel them within your own body as you watch.

The angel motions for you to look down and you peek over the edge. You see many different kinds of beings, with steps and ledges that lead to tunnels that vanish off into the darkness. Some of the beings look up at you and you recognize some of them. The beings start to look more familiar to you than the lives on the other side of the Abyss which means it is time for you to leave this side.

Metatron lifts you back over the Abyss quickly before you can lose your sense of humanity: to stand upon the realm of God, one must lose who one is.

Now that you are back upon your own side of the Abyss, the visions of your lives fade but you can still look over the edge. All the polarized beings that manifest into the physical realm are down in the Abyss, and all the non-polarized beings are up. You see that you can come back here and explore further, and that the first ledge down the Abyss is a sleeping place for your ancestors.

You are placed gently back on the ground beside the kneeling angel. The archangel Metatron holds a hand over you before withdrawing back into the Abyss. That action fills you with fire and heat, so much so that you feel you are stood within fire and yet you are filled with stillness.

The stillness stays with you as you remember being seated before a candle flame. Your focus returns to the candle and you see the Divinity and stillness flow through the flame. Carefully, you blow out the candle, allowing your breath to mingle with the fire and the flame passes from this world to a deeper one. Remain seated and quiet for a while, allowing the stillness to deepen within you before you rise.

21.11 Vision of the elders

Light a candle flame and close your eyes. Be aware of the flame within you, feel the peace and serenity flow through you as you settle into silence. As you look at the candle flame with your inner vision, be aware that the flame grows into a fire and the room in which you are seated falls away. You find yourself sat outside on grass.

A strange noise comes from the sky above and as you look up, you see a giant bird swooping down towards you. The bird lands near you and encourages you to climb upon his back.

The bird flies up into the sky and you cling onto the feathers on his back as he climbs higher and higher into the sky. The bird flies at great speed and as you look down, you see that you are passing over the great ocean as you head east.

While flying, you notice that you are also passing backwards through time. As the bird flies over the European landmass you see civilizations rise and fall. The bird flies lower over the Mediterranean Sea and you watch boats appear and vanish as you pass backwards through time.

The Bird begins to circle over land, falling lower and lower towards the earth as he circles. You watch as the hills and valleys get closer and still you are passing back through time. On landing, you jump off of the bird's back and offer him a gift. Reach into yourself

21.11. Vision of the elders

and pull out something sweet from your childhood memories, offer it to the bird and step back. A single feather falls from his back as a gift for you.

Before you stands a large craggy hill that is cleaved down the middle creating a narrow passageway through the hillside. A priest emerges from the passage and asks you to follow him. You realize that there are more people with you who have travelled from all the corners of space and time. Together you follow him down through the passageway.

As you walk through the passageway you look up the steep cliff sides that almost obscure the sun. You can hear the tapping of tools and distant voices. You emerge from the passageway into a clearing with a tall stone cliff before you. Many men are working on the cliff face to create an impressive façade. The priest guides you around the workers and through a small doorway that is covered by a heavy cloth. You emerge on a ledge at the entrance to a large city that is in the early stages of construction. Looking around, you see many temples, houses, baths and other buildings in various stages of construction. In the center of the city is a strange-looking compound that houses a decaying step pyramid.

The priest guides you down through the city and to the threshold of the old temple compound. The priest tells you that he cannot go any further, as the compound is the territory of the 'old ones.' He tells you to enter the compound and climb the pyramid.

Stepping over the threshold into the compound, you notice that everything sounds different. The building sounds of the city do not penetrate the air of the compound and everything is quiet. You stand a while in the silence and stillness, gradually becoming aware that the compound and its contents are partially in another time. An overwhelming urge to climb the steps of the old pyramid flows over you and you begin to climb slowly.

With each step you take, a brief vision flashes before you of a previous time when the pyramid was in use. Sights and sounds of ceremonies, gatherings, conversations flash before you as you climb to the top.

Part of the way up the pyramid, you put your foot on the next step but your foot seems to vanish into nothing. You retract your foot

21. WORKING METHODS FOR LEADING GROUP VISIONS/WORKINGS

and try to touch the step. Your hand falls into nothing. Something deep within you urges you to walk forward as though through the steps. Moving forward, you pass through the image of the steps and find yourself walking through a dark stone tunnel cut deep into the pyramid. A small flame urges you forward until you reach a strange-looking door.

Reaching out to touch the door, your hand again passes through the image into nothing. Stepping forward, you pass through the doorway: power swirls all around you as you pass though the image. The doorway is a threshold guardian: a being of fire that guards the inner sanctum. Their flames lick around you, probing into every part of your thoughts to see if you are worthy to pass through.

As you pass through the flames, the fire withdraws and you find yourself in a small octagonal room with a fire bowl in the center. The fire bowl is empty and surrounding the fire bowl is a group of Priests and Priestesses. An old priestess steps forward to greet you. She tells you that before you can commune with the assembled company you must pass the test of the inner sanctuary. You must light the fire bowl in the center using only your inner flame.

Closing your eyes, you reach deep inside to the inner flame at the edge of the Void. You pass into a state of stillness and peace. Your flame burns brightly at the edge of the Void within you. Reaching inside, you cup your hand around your inner flame and allow a fragment of the flame to settle in the palm of your hand. Pulling your hand out, you hold up the tiny flame to light the room.

Lowering the flame into the fire bowl, the fire bowl lightens with fire and the room illuminates. Looking around you see many priests and priestesses standing in all the directions. The old priestess reaches out and holds your hands. Her energies feel strange to you and she picks up on your thoughts.

She smiles and speaks to you:

> "We are the last of our world, the remnants of what has passed into the Void. We are waiting for you and people like you, the seed carriers. Please take our wisdom and our secrets, and carry them forward into the future. The people who have come into this land and built their cities

21.11. Vision of the elders

are deaf and blind to our ways. But these treasures must not die. They must be carried forward to the edge of time and seeded out to the future waves of humanity. Are you willing to carry these treasures out to the future to pass onto whomever is able to access them?"

The priestess waits for your answer. If you answer yes, four people step forward from the four directions. If you answer no you are guided back out of the room to wait at the steps of the pyramid.

The four people who step forward ask you to approach them one at a time. The first person lays their hand on your shoulders. An immense power of fire flows through you, reaching every cell in your body. With your inner senses, you see volcanoes, fire upon water, fire within cells and finally electricity. Your home and the electricity running thorough it appears in your mind. The electricity shows itself as a conscious being flowing constantly through your home and you become aware of how you could work with this being in a more harmonious way. The knowledge of the power of fire enters your consciousness and you feel the wisdom reach every part of your body.

The second person touches you on the chest, and your thymus gland, seated in the deep center of your chest, responds. The firepower flows into the gland and energizes your immune system. You feel its action flow into you and its power building up in your hands. It is at that point that you realize this is the power of healing. The power flows out of your hands and into the person stood before you. Awareness builds of your connectedness with the land and how the power flows from being to rock to air to water and back in a continuous flow of sacred life.

The third person touches you upon the lips and immediately you draw in breath. You find yourself at the edge of the Void looking out over the universe. The planets and stars are all around you. Air builds up within you until you feel as though you are going to burst. When you can take the pressure no more, you breathe out.

Many beings pass through you and out on your breath. They fall to the planets and you fall with them. As they fall closer and closer to the planet they take on recognizable forms. Some are animals, some

21. WORKING METHODS FOR LEADING GROUP VISIONS/WORKINGS

are trees, insects, plants, humans of many different types: some are part human and part animal. You fall with them to the land.

On touching the surface of the planet, the beings spread out in all directions and you find yourself in a forest among the trees and the animals. Many of the animals are also part faerie part human. They commune with you and you feel their wisdom and light.

A strange noise carries upon the air and the beings start to change. The animals and faeries separate from the humans and the humans are cast out of the forest to live in isolation. You watch as the humans walk into darkness: they find themselves walking through a Desert. You can hear the cries and feel the tears of the animals and faeries as they weep for the humans. Something nudges you and you find yourself back in the temple room.

The fourth person touches you on your abdomen. Something passes into you from their hand and begins to sting your eyes. Your eyes water from the pain and you rub them hard. When you try to open them you blink in the flame light and begin to see strange things. Everything seems to be connected by patterns or threads. You see the building around you, not as stone and wood, but as fire and air. Beyond the fire and air are the stars, which have threads reaching down to the planet surface. Each person is connected by the threads, which seem to weave into a complicated but beautiful web pattern. Looking down at your own body, you see it as made up of a combination of elements rather than flesh. Everything around you appears in its true from and you marvel at its beauty.

The old priestess asks you to take these secrets out into the world and allow them to flow from you naturally in your everyday life. You do not need to teach them or activate them: they will sit within you and will pass, at the right time, to whomever needs them. With that she reaches into the fire bowl and picks up the fire with her hands. She throws the fire at you and the flames consume you. Cleansing you, the fire surrounds you and you feel it as a powerful being who is transporting you through time. The fire has many eyes that watch over you as you pass from one world to another.

The fire within you grows so that you can see nothing but the flames. You feel the stillness of the Void within you and the vision of the elders falls away, leaving you in stillness and silence. When you

21.11. Vision of the elders

are still and ready to move, you step forward with the intent to return home.

Finally you emerge back in the room where you first started, passing though the candle flame. You remember yourself seated before the flame and when you are ready, you open your eyes.

Chapter Twenty-two

The inner aspects of consecration

In today's magical world which has become so heavily commercialized, offers of consecrations, initiations and ordinations abound, from serious spiritual and magical groups to the silliest New Age faery Saxon Celtic Wiccan Church of the Shamanic voice of the Archangel Michael. If you filter out all the silly stuff, there is still a good solid tradition alive in today's world where power, lineage and connection is passed from generation to generation.

The words consecration, ordination and initiation mean different things to different people. Even dictionary definitions are vague so the picture can become complicated and arguments often break out between magical and witchcraft groups about who has what and when they got it, etc. For the sake of looking at this from an inner point of view, I want to talk about consecration from the way I perceive it, received it and have handed it on. I am not approaching this from any particular magical system: rather it is a reflection from personal experience of how it works outside those systems i.e. what it is in its own right without dogma and structures.

For me personally, initiation is the magical/spiritual acceptance into a magical/spiritual family and the initiation both marks you as a human individual, and opens you to a family connection that stays with you for that lifetime or for however long you stay in that group. Consecration on the other hand (for me and the way I pass it on) is the marking of the soul pattern. It connects the soul into a stream of consciousness that it becomes an inseparable part of.

22.1 Born or touched

When someone is consecrated, they are woven into a stream of consciousness, becoming one with that stream whilst their own

22. The inner aspects of consecration

personal qualities are added to the stream to effect change and mature the consciousness as a whole. If that particular stream is about change, then you will become a vessel for change in your world. If it is about service, then your life will walk down that path, etc. Once you are connected into a line at this depth, it flows through you and you flow through it life after life.

It may go dormant if unused in this life, and reemerge in another life, or it may go dormant in another life only to reemerge in a few lifetimes. I have consecrated many people over the years and there have been times when people have stood before me and I see that they are already consecrated into a line, they are just not aware of it. But I and other consecrated people can often see it in them or upon them: they carry a mark that follows them from life to life. They had it when they came into life and my job in consecrating them was simply to reawaken it within them.

It may be a line that is not the same as what I am passing on, but their own line must not be interfered with: as a priest/ess the job is simply to lift the veil so that they can see again. When this is done, they very often become immediately aware of the line and they can see how it has always been with them.

The most commonly known line of consecration historically is the Apostolic Succession which is the Christian line of connection from Apostle to Apostle going back to the original touch by the Holy Spirit (though in my opinion—and in my experience—it is a much older line). That line is all one and they become all of each other (hence a bishop is 'we' rather than 'he' or 'she'): they become a composite consciousness that comprises Christ plus all the Apostles who have been before and will go after.

When you consecrate someone who does not already have the consecration, you tie them into the stream that you work with, blending them with that line so that they become a part of that weave with full access to its benefits and connections.

22.2 Pros and cons

Most people are not aware of what they are getting themselves into when they are consecrated. This is why, in times past, it took a long time and a lot of study, work and commitment to build up to a consecration of any form. Unlike initiation, consecration passes through all of your lives, which immediately takes it to a serious and heavy commitment. It is the time in your existence where you stop playing, put away your toys and commit to an inner path of fate that cannot be gone back on. You can stop working with it intentionally, but it will continue to affect your lives and the decisions you make: once you are changed, there is no going back.

The benefits of such consecration are many: you become a part of a huge collective consciousness, being able to connect and reach out to all the other priests/esses in the line, drawing upon their knowledge, strength, wisdom and skills. If you use it properly, you have the keys to the Library.

If the consecrator has agendas when passing it on, then there is a chance that he will limit or interfere with the communication of the line in order to control it and you. This doesn't happen often, but it does happen: some priests will tie you in such a way that you become a part of their structure, i.e. you become their scapegoat and carry the consequences of their actions. So it really pays to look, think and meditate carefully on the choices you make!

The unfolding of the consecration brings with it a sense of being a true conscious part of a large number of people: you never feel alone. You become aware of the constant nudges, voices, gentle guidance and the speeding up of your fate: this is one of the most noticeable things: everything goes and comes a lot faster.

There is none of this karma, fate unfolding slowly as you learn: when you are consecrated your fate will swing out of the sky and smack you like a baseball bat. You do something bad or silly knowingly, here comes the bat. This is why unscrupulous priests rig the scapegoat effect at a consecration. Because fate is speeded up, they have to behave which they do not want to do, so they construct the ultimate scapegoat: you become the scapegoat to them by becoming he who takes all the sins and sufferings into the Desert.

This is why when you are consecrated properly, the angelic structures are brought into play so that other types of consciousness cannot be tied into you or you to them—which brings me into the practical aspect of how it is done.

22. The Inner Aspects of Consecration

When the consecration is done from within a structure, there are certain rules, witnesses, codes of dress, oils, etc. that the particular structure/lodge defines as their ritual of consecration. In reality there is little needed, but the ones that are needed are important. The rest of the dressing defines the particular magical family and enfolds the people attending in a sense of ritual.

The following is a simple breakdown of what I do and how I do it. I cannot speak for any other consecrator nor would wish to. The method I use works and has been stripped down to its basic simplicity so that it is nondenominational: it connects people to the ancient line without the dressings of a magical order/lodge etc.

I work with the four elements and the four directions, with or without a living priest and with or without altars (I have consecrated on the edge of the sea with nothing other than an implement). I draw in an inner contact that carries the line into each direction of east, south (unless I have a working priest in there) and west, and I work in the north.

Working with the contacts in the directions and angelic beings I have called in, I begin to 'weave' using inner vision, a web of connection using strands from the line and with the strands from the other contacts. The web is woven to create a veil that is also a doorway that will go over the person consecrated and they will 'pass through' that veil by having it pass through them: it passes through them and becomes a part of them and they become a part of it. All of this is done silently.

Once I have woven the veil, I begin working. Sometimes I will have a couple of priestesses to work with as upholders on either side of me who will keep the gates open. From the north, I draw angelic beings to me to work with me and also the priestess inner contact from the north to work through me.

As a person comes up to me, I ritually strip them of anything or any being that does not belong with them (so no parasites, etc. get consecrated too!) using angelic names and contacts as part of the stripping so that the person is a clean slate to work upon. Then I lower the inner veil over them silently by lowering my hand onto them and I wait until the inner contacts have done the same thing. Then the inner contact behind me steps through me and connects them into the line that she originates and that flows in me. Sometimes more than one line passes through. Then I verbally consecrate them, using angelic and sacred names to seal it, and mark upon their heads the sacred seal in consecrated oil.

Then they go and stand to the other three directions and commune with the contacts who put their inner lines of consecration into the person. Then it is done.

It carries a lot of power with it, so it is exhausting for the consecrator and if I am doing a few people I can often end up with burns on my hands. I have never figured out how to stop that happening.

22.3 Physical and magical effects

The physical effects for someone who has been consecrated can vary from a subtle shift in consciousness to the feeling of being hit by a train at high speed while choking on a gobstopper. The first thing most people notice is that they have to treat their body differently: it will often not put up with trash anymore and you may find yourself having to change your diet, give up certain things, and change how you do things. It varies from person to person depending on that person's health and their current lifestyle. And the changes that one person makes are often not the same that another person needs to make.

This is why I feel it is important that there should be no real rule books, formats, or one-size-fits-all systems: it varies so much according to what your path should be and what your role upon that path is. So one person might have to give up meat, and one person might have to start eating it: it's all about what your task is, what tools you will need and how you need to protect your body in the meantime.

The magical effects can be quite profound: you are plugged into an ancient line of consciousness that wants to work through you and the more sensitive you are, the more they will push through you and nudge you upon your path. Over the years I have come to the conclusion that the idea I had of life, i.e. that it is all about the choices we make, all goes out of the window. I feel these days that I have no real choice, even when I think I do. I find myself pushed into situations, lifestyles and lands that are not my choice: I just end up relaxing and going with the flow. I gave up trying to rationalize my life years ago, and just tighten the seat belt and try to enjoy the ride!

One of the interesting things that happens magically, is that you begin to stack up power for the work before you even know you are going to be doing it and then often find that you have connected in with a much bigger 'happening' that you were unaware of. You are called to work whenever you are needed and many times you haven't a clue what you are doing, it just flows through you and happens regardless of your intent or lack of it.

22.4 Training versus nature

This is something that is a sore point with many pagan, magical and spiritual organizations: it is projected that only 'they' can uphold your consecration, and that you cannot leave them and if you do, your consecration will no longer work. The inference that you cannot be consecrated unless you have undergone a series of trainings, tests and rituals is total bullshit: what they mean is that they will not consecrate you unless you jump through their hoops. There is a big difference.

I do not really advocate consecrating someone who is unprepared, but saying that I have done it anyway because it was right for that person at that time and basically I was told by the inner lot to get on with it. But in general, I believe that people need to have a full understanding of what they are getting themselves into and preparing themselves appropriately. The training can provide this, but then so can the individual if they are mature and focused enough: hoop jumping is not necessary, but preparation is a good and sensible thing. Sometimes someone has walked alone on an intense spiritual or magical path for a long time and they are put in your path to consecrate them into service.

The problem arises when the organization tells the people that the consecration will not work unless X is done, paid for and studied. This is harnessing and putting fake conditions on something, which I feel is a dishonourable action. It would be better to say, the consecration may cause problems for you if you are not fully prepared and X is designed to prepare you properly over a period of time.

The other myth that is heavily propagated is that if you leave the group, your consecration will be taken from you and you will have no access to its power or connections. That may be true of a simple initiation in which you are 'marked' with a badge that can be taken off on the inner, but when someone is consecrated, that is it: it is an irreversible change within the person's soul that can never be taken from them, regardless of their actions.

Some people are natural vessels for the consecration and they are ready from the word go. If I have come across someone like this in the past, I have tended to throw them in with the lot who are about to be consecrated and let them run with the pack. The consecration takes fine, but I often worry about the effect it can have on them. Some are fine, but some might need help in the future. Over the years I have moved more and more away from set rules, structures and definitions to just doing what I 'know' is right regardless of what rules it breaks. By taking that stance, the inner contacts then filter who gets put before you and who does not.

But the responsibility to all the people that you consecrate is a heavy one. When you consecrate a person, you become a type of partial parent or guide from an inner point of view. Because the veil woven from all the directional threads is woven by you, you are responsible for what flows through those threads and how it affects them. It is something that really needs to be thought about before you decide to start being a consecrator.

Once you consecrate someone, you are inextricably linked through the Inner Worlds. If that person is in severe need, near death or under terrible threat, then you will be called upon to help them. If they have drifted away from the group and no longer do magic it doesn't matter, you are still linked and you are still responsible. And it is not a conscious helping: your strength, knowledge, contacts and action will be plugged in and working automatically when they are in such severe distress.

It has happened to me many times that I have suddenly become overwhelmed with a sense of disaster, or of passing, or of need and I have had to stop what I was doing and tune in. Often it ends up being a priest or priestess in need and as consecrator you have to call upon all powers that are needed to help them or even just to load share with them. In time, you get to know on the outer what it was that was happening.

22.5 Lines

One of the things that consecrators become aware of early on in their work is that all lines that flow through them also flow through the consecration: you cannot separate out the magical threads that flow through you. The person you are consecrating gets all the lines within you all braided in together. I have three lines that run through me and when I consecrate someone, they get all three lines. I cannot block any single one of them; nor would I wish to. But people who are on the receiving end need to be aware of what it is they are getting and why.

These lines often sit well together and create a pattern within you that weaves in harmony to a much bigger web that is the universe. We are so used to a modern culture of segregation and separation by nature of how we live, eat and work, that we expect the same in our spiritual life. It doesn't really work like that and the inner consecrations often reflect that. When a priest has a few lines within him and he goes onto consecrate someone who came into life with other lines already within them, we begin to see a large weave of lines slowly converging together in a wonderful harmonic.

So essentially, instead of becoming a consecrated priestess of the line of blah, you become a mongrel which makes for a healthier genetic structure.

22.6 What is the future for such consecrations?

I think that the less rigid, less 'members only' group-orientated way of working will slowly develop within our consciousness as we mature and loosen our ability to work in the Inner Worlds without major dressing and rules.

22.6. What is the future for such consecrations?

Consecrations should be there for people who are truly dedicated to the work, who wish to devote themselves to something bigger than themselves, and are willing to take on the work burdens and challenges that they may face as part of their inner service.

It should not be dangled as something that will give power or status, nor should it be tied forever to a particular line of work: it should be a tool that is given at the right time to a worker who needs it, and who will use it wisely in their own field of work, whatever that may be.

I think truly that the way forward into the future for magic is to not work within consecrations, but to work naturally within the fate that flows through you, and the connections that are reached through years of working with inner contacts. Truly, consecrations are man-made and are not necessary for walking a powerful magical path: some of the most powerful and profound magicians I work with today are not consecrated or initiated, but have developed and gained the skills and lines of contact they need through hard work and dedication to magic. *If the magic is within you, life and fate will draw it out for you.*

Chapter Twenty-three

Afterword

The life of an Initiate can become increasingly isolated as fewer and fewer of the things around you in everyday life make sense, and the popular magical community loses its glamour: it begins to look like a giant therapy dressing-up box with weird sex.

Being able to connect with and befriend like-minded people, even within your own lodge/coven/community can become harder and harder the deeper into the inner realms you go. This is not because such work causes depression, but the deeper into the Inner Worlds you go, the more obvious the bullshit around you becomes. Your tolerance levels for silly things goes down rapidly and the little things in life that used to fire you up are no longer significant in the face of grappling regularly with demons, angels and the like.

This is a blessing and a curse: the path is hard and sometimes lonely, but it is immensely rewarding, uplifting and educational.

This life is not by choice: you are called, like all magical and spiritual paths; and if you are called then you are a brother or sister and you join a large, powerful, insane group of isolated magicians all over the world. Thank the gods (or the devils) for the internet!

Above all, remember that as an initiate you are bound by duty to stretch the boundaries of life and magic that other people cannot. We open doors, close doors, clean windows, ferry parcels and sweep roads: the magicians/priests are the maintainers of balance within a temple/city culture just as the shaman is the maintainer in a tribal culture. You can try and walk away from it, but it will always be in front of you waiting at the next destination you have run to. And when you realize that deep down you are relieved to see it waiting for you, and that it has not abandoned you, then all the power and beauty that is the world will open up to you.

Appendix A

The directions in Western magic

A brief journey through history

The following is an extended essay looking at the use of directions in magic at various points in history. It can be of interest to magicians to see where modern day magical concepts of directions, attributes, usage and power came from, what was behind them, and how they traveled down through time.

> Personal experience is the genesis of true learning
> — Aeschylus, *Agamemnon* (c. 458 B.C.)

In modern Western magic and also in some religious patterns, the directions are the thresholds and boundaries that define and focus the power and contact that flows from inner to outer, from non-physical realms into the physical ones. How we use those directions and why we use them differs according to the tradition or system we work within. In this essay, I want to look at certain points in magical history to look at how different people in time approached the directions and directional concepts.

Using that overarching subject matter of the directions, I also want to look a bit closer at some of those people and their cultures, to get a better understanding of who they were, what they were interested in, and to understand why they did what they did.

A.1 Background

The main difference in the use of directions is the difference between religion and magic. In religions the directions tend to be used in order

A. The directions in Western magic

for passive prayer and ritual to be 'sent' to the deity or to celebrate the deity, and for the passive acceptance of what flows from the deity. In magic the flow from the magician is active, and triggers the powers, deities, and spirits of that direction to an active interface which is then combined by the magician for a specific purpose.

In the last hundred and fifty years or so in the West, magic has slowly opened out to a wider number of people, and in the last century various traditions have come into form, often drawing from a wide variety of older practices. Some of those magical practices have subsequently branched and developed down a path to form pagan or mystical religions. Others have stayed as purely magical traditions and have similarly morphed and evolved into specific systems and traditions: how we approach magic and the Mysteries is a constantly evolving process.

This is important to think about when we look into the history of these practices, as someone approaching the directions in a magical sense is going to be different from someone approaching those same directions from a religious stance. It may appear similar or the same on the surface, but the inner dynamics are often going to be different, even when the religion relies heavily upon magical expression.

In modern magic, practitioners are often influenced by the culture they grew up in and the religious pattern that is most prominent in their society. While this is slowly changing in younger generations, the generations who formed or informed a lot of Western traditions were highly influenced by Christianity and Judaism. This can make for an interesting mix when it is done with full awareness, but more often than not, the founders and developers of those traditions were unaware that what they brought to their magical table drew heavily upon their Christian upbringing.

This is a complex subject all on its own, and may warrant its own essay in the future, but for now it is simply useful to keep in mind that our cultural lens and filter can sometimes cloud what we are looking at if we are not careful. Sometimes our embedded religious and cultural patterns are so deeply buried within our psyches that we are not aware of the influences they bring to bear upon our magical work.

A.2 The magical directions

The confinement of directions (east, south, west, north) in a magical working space appears in most Western magical forms, and is worked with either as a foundation ritual pattern or as a simple focus for intent.

I am often asked why a magician must face a particular direction, and why the directions are approached in different ways in different systems. To answer those questions, we must dig deep into the past and also pause to think about how we view magical actions today.

For the most part, Europe today has a culture that has been heavily influenced by more than a thousand years of Christianity, and that influence plays a major role in how we think, act and analyse everything around us. Similarly, since the fifteenth-century in Europe, rediscovered Classical Greek philosophy, particularly the work of the Platonists, also played a major part in influencing how we approach learning and thinking, not only in education in general but specifically in magic.

The only problem with this cultural and educational lens is that once we start looking at the ancient world itself, we find that our current model of thinking does not often match the model of thinking of ancient cultures. Nor do our modern mystical concepts often match those of ancient cultures. It is really important to realize this: if we are not careful, we can end up trying to shoehorn an ancient way of looking at the universe into our own modern way of thinking, and *vice versa*.

This becomes apparent when historians and theologians move out of their comfort zone and start to look at ancient cultures like Egypt, which was a culture that was vastly different to our own today. It can be painful to watch someone trying to fit the religious complexity of dynastic Egypt into the neat box of monotheism; and while this does not appear on the surface to have anything to do with magic, in real terms this is of the greatest importance to magicians. These ancient complex cultures were the cauldrons of what we call magic today: as is mentioned in the Jewish Kiddushin[1] 49b:

---

[1] The Jewish marriage betrothal: the first stage of the Torah-mandated wedding.

A. The directions in Western magic

> Ten measures of magic were given to the world: Egypt received nine, and the rest of the world got one.

Magic is about drawing power and contact into a defined pattern (ritual, vision, magical action) and giving it boundaries that the magician can operate within. Those boundaries can be anything from a drawn image or words, to utterances, vessels (statues and tools) or a defined space such as the directions. Such boundaries in a space make it a vessel that can 'receive' in a contained way, and the acts of the magician as a bridge of power from inner (non-physical) to outer (physical) create a pattern of action or intent. That pattern is woven and harmonized by the magician using his or her tools, utterances, vision and action. The pattern (the magical act) is then released into the flow of time in order for it to go do its job.

A.3 The current magical use of the directions

There are a dizzying number of magical systems today, with new ones or recycled ones emerging on a regular basis. Some of this is driven by innovation and the evolution of magic, and some of it is driven by marketing and ego.

When you look at modern systems, the first thing that can often become apparent is the use of 'boxes': everything is slotted into lists and categories. While this can be useful, it can easily 'lock down' the understanding and practice of the magician if it becomes too dogmatic. What can happen is that the magician rote learns lists of attributes connected to specific directions: knowledge without understanding. Or to put it another way, the person has a recipe book but doesn't know how to turn on an oven or blend ingredients together.

This has become far more apparent in recent years by way of the internet: there are an abundance of websites and E-schools where the directions are presented with lists of attributes, and these are copied over to other websites *ad nauseam* with mistakes also copied over, but no one actually learns anything in a practical sense.

In different magical systems the directions are used in different ways for different reasons. Some systems use the directions to focus

A.3. The current magical use of the directions

upon a mythic land construct connected to the elements and solar cycle. In these systems, the most common 'list' is east/air/morning, south/fire/midday, west/water/dusk, north/earth/winter. This is a northern hemisphere land cycle and can be used to draw upon the inner dynamics of the elemental and solar powers.

Some systems dig a little deeper and also lap over into Christian and/or Jewish patterns to draw upon specific angelic beings in the directions, such as east/Raphael, south/Michael, west/Gabriel, north/Uriel.

Other systems draw upon the 'four winds,' planetary dynamics that flow with the winds, and some draw upon specific planetary powers, 'earth-belt' spirits, etc.

Sometimes all of the different layers of powers are used directionally depending upon what the magician is doing. In more commercially formed systems, everything but the kitchen sink is assigned a direction along with a product to buy for each direction.

Keep in mind the earlier comment I made about religion versus magic in terms of the directions, and that the directions are used magically in an active way, which means contacted ritual, inner contact, vision, and so forth. Learning attributes is simply like learning an alphabet. You have to actually *do* something with the letters to make poetry, song, or stories: just learning and reciting the alphabet is meaningless.

As you dig around history, you will come upon points in magical history where systems devolve down to intellectual exercises or dogmatic lists that move the directional 'alphabet' from being a useful starting reference, to being an endpoint of knowledge.

Just for your reference, when we look at magic in the nineteenth and eighteenth centuries, there is a huge amount of historical writing that has already been done, so I do not need to go into too much detail: use the information in this essay as a starting point if you wish to dig deeper for yourself. It is a rich, complex, and at times messy period in magical history.

A. THE DIRECTIONS IN WESTERN MAGIC

A.4 Nineteenth-century Europe

The Hermetic Order of the Golden Dawn (founded 1888)

The biggest (though not the only) influence on twentieth-century magic in Europe was the Hermetic Order of the Golden Dawn. Founded in 1888 with three temples in Britain, it created a structured education system for magical training, its three founders being Dr W. Robert Woodman, William W. Westcott, and Samuel Liddell Mathers.

As a cohesive organization it fragmented within a few decades, but it became the grandparent of many spin-off magical groups and subsequent new schools. It influenced many of the great magical thinkers of the late nineteenth and twentieth century either directly or indirectly, from Gerard Encausse (Papus) and A. E. Waite, to magical thinkers such as Aleister Crowley and Dion Fortune.

The system used in the Golden Dawn was a mix of, or influenced by, Freemasonry, Rosicrucianism, Kabbalah, and Theosophy. It was a broadly Christian system with added influences from other cultures which were likely brought to the table by one of the founders, Dr. W. Robert Woodman. Woodman had wide-ranging interests such as Kabbalistic philosophy, Egyptian antiquities, and Rosicrucianism as well as being a Freemason.

The Golden Dawn system is essentially a patchwork of different strands of magic brought together, and when you look closely at the various parts of the system, you can spot the actual books that Mathers had studied in the British Library collection.

The founders of the Golden Dawn were true innovators of their time, and did the best they could with what they had and with what was within their capabilities. Their system was deeply shaped by the Victorian industrial mindset and the need for order, ceremony and coherence. It also came out at a time when 'revels' were becoming popular, where reenactments were fashionable, and where a stonkingly good costume was everything. All of these influences brought to the group by various members made their mark in one way or another.

The magical system itself was formal and highly organized. The directional system that was used reflected that sense of coherence, and is largely a pattern that is still worked with today:

    East   air   sword
    West   water   cup
    North   earth   pentacle
    South   fire   wand

Each of these directions was assigned an archangel: Raphael, Gabriel, Uriel and Michael. Colours and letters were also assigned to the directions, as were planets, zodiac signs, and names of God.

The Golden Dawn approached the ritual pattern by use of theatrics, scripts and symbolism: it was a heavily externalized pattern that had its roots of action and symbolism in Freemasonry and Rosicrucianism. These were drawn from the experiences of its founder members, who used what they recognized in order to build a magical system. It was approached in a systematized, structured and hierarchical manner which reflected the times and society it was created in.

The directional attributes were also apparent in the tarot symbolism used by and recreated by members of the Golden Dawn; and this act, more than anything else, in my opinion, anchored the pattern deeply in subsequent generations of magical seekers who came after. The tarot deck developed by A. E. Waite and painted by Pamela Coleman Smith (published in 1910), known as the *Rider-Waite Tarot*, became a major tool for people seeking magic.

So where did those directional concepts and attributes come from? To answer that question, we have to keep digging further back in time, and observe how ideas, concepts and learning morphed from generation to generation. I will not take us through every step in the developmental journey, as that is not the point of this exercise; however let us look at a small number of people who cast an influence over their subsequent generations.

Eliphas Levi (born Alphonse Louis Constant 1810-1875)

Eliphas Levi was a French occultist with a strong, enquiring mind and an eccentric personality. Levi's writings had immense influence on

A. The directions in Western magic

various members of the Golden Dawn including A. E. Waite, along with other occult groups and individuals, such as Papus, in Europe.

Levi initially trained as a Catholic priest, but failed to take holy ordination when he fell in love and left the seminary in 1836. Levi began to delve deeply into socialism as an expression of true Christianity, and considered the Roman Catholic Church to be spiritually and morally corrupt. It is worth pointing out here, particularly for readers in the USA, that what Levi considered socialism was very different from the popular understanding of socialism today.

Without digressing too much, it is worth being clear about this, as it gives us insight into not only the mindset of historical and contemporary occultists, but also how easy it is to misunderstand something in history due to a lack of history education. In popular media in the USA today, socialism is often equated incorrectly with Hitler and the Nazi party. Nationalsozialismus (German for 'national socialism') was an extreme political experiment that became Nazism, and it has little in common with the vision that Levi and subsequent thinkers ascribed to.

Socialism and social democracy as Levi and others saw it can be described thus: *a political and economic theory of social organization which advocates that the means of production, distribution, and exchange should be owned or regulated by the community as a whole.* It was experimented with by various nations in the twentieth-century, and to this day many European capitalist nations have elements of social democracy within their national political structure (Germany, France, Spain, Britain etc.).

Understanding the time that Levi lived in can also help us understand his marriage of politics and magic. France was rapidly changing politically and economically from its first revolution less than fifty years earlier, where the people of France overthrew the monarchy and nobles—and subsequently threw their nation into a bloodbath of executions, restrictions, and war.

After that revolution, France went through a series of rapid changes from the First French Empire (Napoleon I) of 1804–1815 to the restoration of Monarchy, and then to the second revolution and Republic (1848–1852). The time of the Second Republic was when Levi, still using his birth name of Alphonse Constant, became strongly active in socialist thinking and also magic. In 1848 he wrote and published *Le Testament de la liberté*, and by the 1850s he was openly giving talks on a mixture of socialism and Kabbalistic philosophy.

He was immersed in occult studies and in Kabbalah, and mixed them together with Catholicism and socialism. By the 1860s he was writing magical books and was probably the first person to incorporate the use of tarot into magical training. He was a major influence on magical thinkers in the late nineteenth century onwards. Today he is still considered one of the grandfathers of modern magic.

Levi wrote extensively on ritual patterns and occult philosophy, and revelled in lists (of powers, attributes, directions etc.). His actual magical writing is odd in that in places it hits on points of wisdom and insight, and elsewhere is disordered and fragmented. When looking closely at his work, it becomes obvious that mostly he didn't know what to *do* with the magical lists and information he had acquired from various sources: he was mostly a theorist and a thinker rather than an actual practising magician.

We will look at his version of the directional attributes, as his work was subsequently taken up by other magicians, and it provides some major insights into the influence he brought to bear upon modern occultism.

Levi's directional system

In his extensive work *Transcendental magic: its Doctrine and ritual* (1854) Levi outlines directional theories and powers, which can be summed up for the purpose of this subject matter in his treatment of the directional powers in the section 'Conjuration of the Four Elements.' They are as follows—and I have included his various elemental, emotive, and talismanic attributions, as they throw an interesting light on the methodology which subsequently influenced generations of magicians:

A. THE DIRECTIONS IN WESTERN MAGIC

East	Air	Sylphs	Eagle
South	Fire	Salamanders	Lion
West	Water	Undines	Aquarius
North	Earth	Gnomes	Bull

East	Bilious (Argumentative)	Gold and Silver	Morning
South	Sanguine (Optimistic)	Iron and Copper	Noon
West	Phlegmatic (Unemotional)	Mercury	Dusk
North	Melancholic (Sad)	Lead	Night

Aquarius as listed in Levi's work is the 'Man of the New Dawn' i.e. the 'developed' man in a mystical sense. It does not stand for the zodiac sign Aquarius, as is often assumed today.

The attributions of the emotive states are interesting, and many would (wrongly) assume that these are emotional powers that 'rule' the direction, and would thus try to use those emotions in directional magical work, or expect that type of person to find a natural home in that direction. However, to do so would be to misunderstand why those attributes are there and what the list is telling the magician (and the emotive qualities for west and north are mixed up in Levi's listing: they should be the other way around). They show how the powers flowing from each direction can trigger and amplify certain emotions within the magician.

The listing of the emotive responses triggered by elemental powers in the directions is there to inform the magician what to watch out for in their emotive responses to the magical work: if they begin to manifest a specific emotion strongly during or shortly after their magical work, it is to be taken as a symptom of a magical imbalance or stasis somewhere in their work, or within themselves. The magician can then, by nature of the emotive response to the work, identify which directional power working might be unnecessary or unbalanced. It can also be an indicator of a major power imbalance within the magical system itself.

For that information alone, Levi sent a great gift down the path of time for us today (and likely has its roots in the writing of Luria, whom we will look at). I have observed this emotive response issue countless times during my decades of magical practice with groups and teaching, and learning to pay attention to such details and responses in magical work enables the magician to adjust and adapt their work accordingly.

Such power issues are part and parcel of working with external powers in a defined containment, and while it is virtually impossible to do magic to any great degree and avoid such issues, there are many things we can do to adapt and evolve our practice to mitigate such emotive triggers in our work. One such adaptation, which I use extensively in the Quareia training, is to create a filter for the magician themselves by placing them in the stream of time while they work.

This method directly draws upon the magical wisdom of the Egyptian pattern, which we will look at later in this essay. Essentially it makes the magician 'sovereign in their space': it is akin to putting a fuse box on the power inlet. Let us return to Levi and see what else he has to say in his directional listings.

In his elemental listings, he also includes magical tools to be used to 'command the spirits,' and they are:

North	Bull	Sword
South	Lion	Forked wand
West	Aquarius	Cup of libations
East	Eagle	Pentacle

This list caught my attention in his work, as one little detail in the list is a fragment of a much older magical tool that hides a potentially interesting history. His lists and consequent conjurations reveal quite clearly that he did not have full understanding of either the lists nor the ritual: he was using another source, a magical book, and using the lists and rituals like a recipe book.

Here is an excerpt of the explanatory text, and then a part of the ritual:

> We most observe that the special kingdom of the Gnomes is at the North: that of the Salamanders at the South: that of the Sylphs at the East: and that of the Undines at the West. They influence the four temperaments of men (i. e., the Gnomes, the melancholic: the Salamanders, the sanguine: the Undines, the phlegmatic: and the Sylphs,

A. THE DIRECTIONS IN WESTERN MAGIC

the bilious). Their signs are as follows: the hieroglyphs of the bull for the Gnomes, and we command them with the sword: of the lion for the Salamanders, and we command them with the forked wand, or the magic trident: of the eagle for the Sylphs, and we command them with the holy pentacles: finally with Aquarius for the Undines, and we evoke them with the cup of libations.

When an elementary spirit comes to torment, or at least to annoy the inhabitants of this world, we must conquer it by means of air, water, fire and earth, blowing, sprinkling, burning perfumes, and tracing on the earth the star of Solomon and the sacred pentagram. These figures should be perfectly regular, and made either with coals from the consecrated fire, or with a reed dipped in diverse colors which we mix with pulverized magnet. Then, while holding in the hand the pentacle of Solomon, and taking by turns the sword, the wand, and the cup, we pronounce in these terms and in a loud voice the conjuration of the four.[1]

Let's just take a little time to have a look at this text and see how it equates magically, and also what its roots may be. Most magic that comes to us from the last few centuries has its roots in a mixture of Greek, Egyptian and Persian thinking, and the various concepts were picked up, mixed about, passed on and ended up in various magical texts.

North: Earth, Gnomes, Bull, Melancholic (sadness) lead, night.

Gnomes are earth, and magically earth is equated with the north in the northern hemisphere. Why? From a magical perspective, earth is the element that houses all that has long since died: the dead are buried, and all that lives upon the earth eventually is absorbed by the earth. It is also the direction of winter, the direction where the sun never peaks as it does in the south, and where the further you go

---

[1]Eliphas Levi (1854) *The Conjuration of the Four Elements from Transcendental magic: its Doctrine and ritual*

north, the colder and often darker it gets. Winter is a time of death and struggle, so when you put all of these practicalities together, you start to get a pattern where the directions are equated with certain qualities of life and death, and of the elements.

Mythically the element of earth is connected to the north, probably by way of Greek and Egyptian mythology. In Greek mythology, Boreas, the god of the north wind was one of the four Anemoi (gods of the four winds) and he was the god of winter. He was also the north wind that blew down from the northern mountains of Thrace, bringing the cold of winter with him.

So where does the bull come in? Most people when looking at magical roots trace the bull to one the four holy creatures (Chayot)[1] from the Book of Revelations and the Book of Ezekiel, and that would be correct to a certain extent, except that those creatures have much older roots, and also have non-Biblical roots. The bull as the power creature/angelic being of the north likely comes from Egypt.

Since the first dynasty of the Old Kingdom in Egypt, the bull has played a major part in the state religion (bulls in general were considered magical power animals in the ancient world). The early appearances of the bull in the Egyptian state religion were based at Memphis (the most northern 'power city' of the time in Egypt) in the form of the Apis Bull. The Apis Bull was considered a form of the king's courage, power and vitality (I am simplifying this to be brief) and as the Osiris Apis, the bull was the triumphant king power in the Underworld/realm of death. Memphis was mostly the ancient centre of administrative power in Egypt, and was close to the royal necropolis of Saqqara. Memphis/Saqqara was 'north' in Egypt, which also had connotations of the long dead/the Underworld, which we will look at later in this essay.

Osiris Apis was something that was embraced in Egypt by Alexander the Great once he invaded Egypt in 332 B.C. and threw the Persians out. Osiris Apis as the Bull in the Underworld, and Apis as the *ka* of the king, had a strong draw for Alexander as a kingship symbol which he took up and used to great effect. Apis was also a major deity in the town of Rhacotis on the north coast of Lower

---

[1]Bull, lion, eagle and man: from Book of Ezekiel, Merkabah texts and the Book of Revelations.

A. The directions in Western magic

Egypt, a town which later became the site of the city Alexandria. The subsequent ruler after Alexander, Ptolemy I, also took up the Apis[1] and particularly Osiris Apis, and eventually the concept of the bull was fused with a humanesque deity which was subsequently called Serapis.[2] Serapis became a major feature in the cultic community in Alexandria,[3] a community that was a mixture of Greeks, Hellenized Jews, Egyptians, and others.

When Alexander died in Babylon in 323 B.C., Ptolemy, his general, had his body taken to the temple of Ptah at Memphis for embalming, the same temple where only a year earlier, he had been crowned king. Also bear in mind that the temple of Ptah was also the home to/enclosure of the Apis bull: the power of the king. Alexander was then entombed in Alexandria, the city where Serapis eventually became the main deity.

So you can see how the image of the bull became connected with power, kingship, death, and the north. It is likely that the cult of the Apis bull is also the root of the bull in the Chayot, something we will come back to in a moment.

The connection of the sword with the north and the bull had me puzzled for a while, as magically, historically, and mythically, the sword tends to be a tool of the east. East, magically, is connected to utterance, the dawn of new powers/actions, and the power of protecting/limiting/prophecy, and that probably comes into magic from Biblical sources where we have instances of the sword guarding in the east, or the sword and word being 'one.'[4]

I have come across such things before where tools and powers are in directions you would not expect, and often there is no magical logic nor historical context for such placing (where there is a magical logic, you can learn a great deal by analysing what someone has done). When I come across such things and it is clear that the writer is not a practising skilled magician, I have to assume they used common

---

[1] Diodorus Siculus (first century B.C.) Book I *Bibliotheca Historica* 84.8

[2] Mckechnice P, Guillaume P, (2008). *Ptolemy II Philadelphus and his World*. Leidon, Boston.

[3] Bevan E. (1927: reprint 2015) *A History of Egypt Under the Ptolemaic Dynasty*. Routledge.

[4] *Revelation* 19:15 sword/utterance, *Genesis* 3:24 sword in the east of the Garden of Eden.

sense to place the tools if the original information was not available to them or is missing, or they are copying from another text. In terms of the Bull and kingship, it would make rational sense to place the sword there, but it doesn't make magical sense.

When you work with directional powers in magic, certain tools and powers do switch on strongly in certain directions, hence it is important to place things carefully and make informed choices about how to work directionally. I do not fully grasp whether these natural homes for powers and subsequent tools are the result of human focus over millennia, or if there is some other deeper dynamic going on: I just don't know. But what I do know is that when the sword is used in the north, it has a different and lesser effect than if it is used in the east.

If you apply working magical logic to the tools in directions and the natural powers that flow through magical directions, then for example with the sword you would trigger:

> East: sword: limitation/guarding of utterance, new action, new power.
>
> South: sword: limitation/guarding of the future, or the fire of battle.
>
> West: sword: limitation of harvest/people, or the act of culling.
>
> North: sword: limitation of ancestors or a past power, or the sword pinning that which is in the earth.

Going back to the directional elements list, there are whole rabbit holes you can vanish down should you wish to work on tracking the roots of each one: I will leave that up to you so that this essay doesn't turn into a book. However, it is worth noting that a lot of what appears in grimoires from the eighteenth and nineteenth centuries can be traced back to Alexandria in Hellenistic Egypt, where the old Egyptian religion, the Hellenized Jews, the Persian influence, and later the Romans and early Christians all rubbed shoulders.

For example, if you are looking for a source for the four creatures/Chayot in magical and Biblical texts, it is a curious point to note that the temple of Ptah in Memphis, which played such

A. The Directions in Western Magic

an important role in the founding of the Ptolemaic dynasty, was a temple that also featured Sekhmet (lion) the wife of Ptah, who in Old Kingdom Egypt was considered to be the mother of the King[1] and was a protector/consecrator of the King in the New Kingdom.[2]

At that time, Ptah himself was often equated with Imhotep (the 'perfect man'), the Old Kingdom architect and scholar who later became glorified as a demigod. His statue would appear in shrines to Thoth and Ptah, and in shrines of Thoth Hermes later during the Ptolemaic period. He was considered the 'greatest among men' for his wisdom and knowledge: a man of Aquarius indeed. Another god that featured at the temple of Ptah was Nefertem, son of Ptah and Sekhmet, a deity that would also have featured as the 'Aquarian man.'

Horus, the raptor bird (falcon) was considered Lord of Lower Egypt. During the Ptolemaic period, the second biggest temple in Egypt after Karnak was built to Horus. Horus was also strongly connected with kingship, was the protector of the king, and was the dawn/sun/eastern horizon/future as Ra-Horakhty.[3]

And finally you have the Apis bull, whose cult was centred at Memphis, in an enclosure at the temple of Ptah, Memphis.

I find it curious that the lion, the bull, the falcon and the man figure so strongly in magical and mystical symbolism, and that these figures would have also played a major role in symbolism in Alexandrian Egypt, which later became the centre of magical, religious, and philosophical thought for seven hundred years. Alexandria became a melting pot for Greek, Egyptian, and Roman thought, and was a major early centre in Christianity and early Christian Gnostic thought. It was also the melting pot that gave us texts that have now become magical classics, like the Greek Magical Papyri.

This could be pure coincidence, and when you look for patterns, you are likely to find them. But knowing the complexity of the community in Alexandria at the time and for the next few hundred

---

[1] West Gable of the Antechamber, Pyramid of Unas, Utterance 248. Faulkner R.O. (1969) *The Ancient Egyptian Pyramid Texts*. Oxford University Press.

[2] Ramses II's mortuary temple at Thebes: the smaller hypostyle hall wall relief of the king burning incense to his guide, Ptah, and protector/consecrator Sekhmet. New Kingdom, 19th Dynasty.

[3] Ra-Horakhty, "Ra, who is Horus of the Two Horizons."

years, and knowing that a lot of magical texts and ideas that travelled across Europe emerged out of Alexandria, it is an interesting hypothesis.

Levi's listing and system has many such interesting correlations to Dynastic Egypt, Ptolemaic and Greco-Roman Egypt and it would be an interesting exercise one day to take it all apart and trace each concept back to its roots.

Just to demonstrate this, for example, Levi's listing of *Undines water, west, Aquarius, cup*, is interesting and when you know the dynastic Egyptian religious and magical system you spot something interesting straightaway. The mixture of west, the perfect man, the cup, and water brings to mind one of the central pillars of the dynastic Egyptian magical religion: The justified one (human who has conquered death and been judged before the gods) who resides in the west, and the cup that provides his 'cool refreshment' (water).

In the funerary texts and in particular the *Book of Gates*, as a person develops more and more through their death transformation process, they are offered *cool refreshment* in the form of water, along with bread and wine, as part of the Osirian transformation (which sounds Catholic). This was also done at the mortuary temple of a dead person: water, wine, and bread would be offered to the spirit of the dead.

The connection with water pouring or offering and the dead also appears in some areas of Islam and is likely a pre-Islamic practice:

> Jabir narrated that the Prophet's grave was sprinkled and that the one who sprinkled the water over his grave from a waterskin was Bilal bin Rabah. He began where the head was and sprinkled it to his feet.
>
> — Imam al-Bayhaqi (A.D. 994)

And just before we move on, there is one last thing that caught my eye in Levi's listings, which was the mention of the forked staff. That confirmed for me that Levi had been reading the *Grand Grimoire*, a magical grimoire that was doing the rounds in the early part of the nineteenth century. The forked staff appears in Chapter III of the *Grand Grimoire*:

A. The directions in Western magic

> On the eve of the great undertaking you will search for a rod or wand of wild hazel tree that has not yet born fruit, at the highest point of the sought-after branch there should be a second little branch in the form of a fork with two ends: its length should be nineteen and a half inches.[1]

It is likely from his work that he read the *Grand Grimoire* and the *Grimoire Verum*, both early nineteenth-century texts that purported to be much older than they in fact were. Declaring great age and mysterious sources was highly fashionable in 'magical society' from the sixteenth century onward. Thankfully, although Levi obviously immersed himself in whatever magical texts he could lay his hands on, instead of simply copying them and giving them a new name and even greater age, which is something that happened a lot, Levi picked out bits here and there and tried to create a more coherent magical structure with them.

So why did the forked staff catch my eye beyond dating Levi's work? Because it is an ancient tool indeed and has an important role to play in magic. When we see ancient fragments emerging in later texts, it tells us that someone along the line had access to information or texts with roots in an ancient source. Whether they understood them or not is irrelevant; what we are seeing is how magic can move down through time, hiding in plain sight. And where there is one fragment, there are often more lurking around.

Later on we will come to understand quite how old the forked staff is, and what it harks back to, so take a mental note of this tool for later.

From the sixteenth to the nineteenth century we see a glut of grimoires. A few are magically interesting and hide a real magical practice, but the majority are mainly collections of folk spells with smatterings of Hebrew, Latin, and made up words (some of which draw from what their authors think is Hebrew and Latin). They are interesting in terms of magical history and folklore, but in real magical terms they are mostly simply babble. Their popularity waxes and wanes with fashions, and they are no different from today's glut

---

[1] *Grand Grimoire* a.k.a. *The Red Dragon*: Chapter III, Book One

of fake 'channelled' books or ones that are cobbled together from various sources and given a shiny pedigree in order to sell them.

Then, just as now, these books were presented to make money, open doors of influence and to prey on the magically illiterate. Saying this is deeply unpopular but is something that needs saying, and I am likely to attract a lot of howls of protest and yet more hate mail as result of this stance. A female magician poking at the most treasured toys in Western magic is definitely not going to be popular.

For the purposes of this historical analysis of directions and magic, it is vitally important that students learn to separate the wheat from the chaff not only in practice but also in historical studies. Discernment is an important skill in magic, and learning to look closely beyond glamour is an important exercise in developing that skill.

Although we cannot know what went on in the head of Eliphas Levi, we can see from his writings that he undertook what was then the herculean task of moving magic's focus away from empty glamour, and attempted to inject a more serious and in parts mystical treatment of magic. For that, we must always be eternally grateful to him.

A.5 The sixteenth century

If we step back in history before Levi, the next big waving flag in regards to assignments in the magical directions can be found in the work of Luria, and just before him, Agrippa. The sixteenth century was truly a blossoming time for magical texts, and although it is an absolutely fascinating time to read about, for the purpose of this essay we can only consider it briefly. It is not necessary to include every retrospective step in the development of directional magic, as this article is about the actual magic itself, not the history of those who developed and passed things along.

Isaac Luria (1534–1572)

Isaac Luria, also known as Yitzhak Ben Sh'lomo Lurya Ashkenazi, and also known as Ha'ARI Hakadosh (the holy lion), was a highly learned and deeply visionary Jewish mystic who essentially

A. The directions in Western magic

overhauled how Jewish mysticism was approached. When we as magicians look at the Tree of Life, the powers of the Sefirot, and the powers of the directions (among many other things) we are looking at the Divinely inspired work of Luria.

Luria brought the loosely connected knowledge that was scattered across the Zohar and put it into order, Reflection, and correspondence. It is important to point out at this time that Luria was not a magician but a Kabbalist, and his whole being was focused towards the Divine expression through mystical understanding. His most famous gift to modern magicians today was the Tree of Life and the Sefirot as an organized pattern.

His work appeared at a time when the magical minds of Europe had spent decades digesting the Greek philosophical and Hermetic texts that had been translated and narrated by Marsilio Ficino (A.D. 1433–99) and the mass of inspired magical books that had emerged in Italy, Spain and Germany. From the mid-fifteenth century onward in Europe, there had been a massive influx of magical, sacred, philosophical and mystical texts that been carried into Europe as a result of the strengthening new Ottoman Empire and the eventual conquest of Constantinople by Mehmed the Conqueror in A.D. 1453.

These texts varied widely in age and content, and were mostly Greek and Greco-Roman Egyptian texts that had come from Alexandria and the Near East. They were in Greek, Latin and Arabic: many texts of classical and ancient origin had been translated into Arabic a few hundred years earlier, which preserved them. The great libraries at Constantinople were basically grabbed and shipped out as much as possible, in the face of the advancing Ottoman army.

There was also rather a glut of cynically produced magical grimoires that essentially were cobbled messes of correspondences, demon names and mysterious sigils. For those who searched deeply through the dross, and found the magical and philosophical writings that touched their magical souls, the work of Luria shone a bright light for those who had laboured in the shadow of confusion. Here is just a small a glimpse of Luria's work:

> It is important to know that all worlds and all creatures that inhabit those worlds were created through

permutations of the holy names. The supernal root of all the names is the name Havayah.[1]

It has 4 letters and 12 permutations, 3 for each letter. Thus, from 4, we obtain 12. Corresponding to these, there are four banners (angelic camps) in the Supernal Merkava (Chariot). They are: Michael, Gabriel, Raphael and Uriel. Each of these 4 consists of 3, again making a total of 12. Corresponding to these, there are 4 basic directions (South, North, East, West) from which 12 sub-directions emerge. Each basic direction has two sub-directions.

Luria's directional correspondences:

South	kindness	chesed
North	discipline	gevurah
East	harmony	tiferet
Up	perseverance	netzach
Down	submission	hod
West	connection	yesod

Bringing the four species towards the heart: communication (malchut).

Luria's work remains a major part of Kabbalah to this day, and in the following comment, quoted from an article on the Jewish custom of extending the lulav and etrog[2] to the directions, we can see a faint fragment of the magical ritual pattern of facing east and working the directions.

> Our sages explain that the manifestation of the Divine Presence in this world—the Shechinah, stems from the

---

[1] "And Elokim G-d spoke to Moses and He said to Him, I am Havayah!" (*Exodus* 6:2)
HaVaYaH: the Tetragrammaton, G-d's Divine Name of the four Hebrew letters yud-hei-vav-hei, expressing His transcendence of time and space.

[2] The etrog is a Citrus fruit/lemon/lime (Etz Hadar) and the Lulav is palm branches (Kapot t'marim): used during Sukkot.

A. THE DIRECTIONS IN WESTERN MAGIC

west.[1] If the Shechinah is in the west, figuratively, when facing east, south would be to its right and north to its left.[2]

Facing east as a default magical position in ritual tracks back much further (probably a great deal further back than Christianity) and we find mention of it in the writing of an early Christian author Quintus Septimius Florens Tertullianus.

> Others with a greater show of reason take us for worshippers of the sun. These send us to the religion of Persia, though we are far from adoring a painted sun, like them who carry about his image everywhere upon their bucklers. This suspicion took its rise from hence, because it was observed that Christians prayed with their faces towards the east.
>
> — Tertullian (A.D. 160–220)

For those of you reading this essay who have practised Hermetic magic, you will start to see the roots of some ritual actions and patterns used within various Hermetic systems. The Kabbalistic patterns that emerged in Hermetic magic all stem from the work of Luria, and were passed on by various writers, thinkers, and practitioners such as Levi.

His work was revolutionary, and in keeping with the European magical communities of that time, his concepts, ideas and developments were absorbed, digested and incorporated into the swiftly growing corpus of magical knowledge.

Henry Cornelius Agrippa 1486–1535

The work of Agrippa, in his *Three Books of Occult Philosophy*, can in many respects be viewed as one of the cornerstones of modern

---

[1] Midrash Rabbah on *Numbers* 11:2. The Talmud (Bava Batra 25a) points out, from the verse (*Nechemia* 9:6) "and the hosts of the heavens bow down to you" that the heavenly bodies move westward because they are bowing down to G-d whose presence is manifest in the west.

[2] Chabad—Rabbi Eliezer Shemtov: the Chabad-Lubavitch emissary in Montevideo, Uruguay

Western magic. Agrippa was a German theologian and occult writer, and one of the great polymaths of his time.

He studied at the University of Cologne as a young man (thirteen to sixteen years old) where he was deeply influenced by the work of Albertus Magnus (1193–1280).[1] Magnus was a German bishop who had a deep interest in a wide variety of subject matter from philosophy and theology to alchemy, astrology, botany and mineralogy. Magnus translated Aristotle and a variety of Arabic writings, and delved into the writings of the Neoplatonists.

In his early twenties Agrippa studied with Johannes Trithemius (1462–1516) a Benedictine Abbot, cryptographer and occultist, at Würzburg in northern Bavaria.[2] This was also the time that Agrippa began working on his first draft of *De Occulta Philosophia* (The Occult Philosophies). When you look at Agrippa's work, you see straightaway how much it consists of lists, categories etc. Indeed, although Agrippa studied intensively every text he could lay his hands upon, he was not a practising magician. This pattern repeats heavily in the history of Western magic, and is important to bear in mind: magic is often passed along in texts from one generation to another by people who did not really practice magic and didn't really understand it, and it was often married to mystical texts, such as Luria.

However, although mysticism and magic often meet upon the road, their actual power systems are different, and it is easy for oddities and blind alleys to be introduced accidently into magical systems when mystical or religious elements are woven into magical systems without practical understanding or forethought from direct experience. I am sure that comment will elicit howls of protest from many quarters, but it is something that magicians need to seriously keep in mind and think about carefully.

To get back to the directions, here is a table from book II chapter seven of Agrippa's *The Occult Philosophies*.[3] It looks at the numerical pattern of four and the directional attributes. You will see immediately where subsequent magical writers and grimoires drew

---

[1] Nicholas Goodrick-Clarke, *The Western Esoteric Tradition* (2008)
[2] W J Hanegraaff, *Dictionary of Gnosis and Western Esotericism* (2006)
[3] http://www.esotericarchives.com/agrippa/agrippa2.htm#chap7

A. The directions in Western magic

their attributions from, and also the names, powers and Hebrew patterns.

The Scale of the Number four, answering the four Elements

THE NAME OF GOD WITH FOUR LETTERS.	י	ה	ו	ה
Four Hierarchies	Seraphim. Cherubin. Thrones.	Dominations. Powers. Vertues.	Principalities. Archangels. Angels.	Innocents. Martyrs. Confessors.
Four Angels ruling over the corners of the world	מיכאל Michael.	רפאל Raphael.	גבריאל Gabriel.	אוריאל Uriel.
Four rulers of the Elements	שרף Seraph.	כרוב Cherub.	תרשיש Tharsis.	אריאל Ariel.
Four consecrated Animals	The Lion.	The Eagle.	Man.	A Calf.
Four Triplicities of the tribes of Israel	Dan Asser Nephtalim	Jehuda Isachar Zabulum	Manasse Benjamin Ephraim.	Reubin Simeon Gad
Four Triplicities of Apostles	Mathias Peter Jacob the elder	Simon Bartholemew Mathew	John Phillip James the younger	Thaddeus Andrew Thomas
Four Evangelists	Mark	John	Mathew	Luke
Four Triplicities of Signs.	Aries. Leo. Sagittarius.	Gemini. Libra. Aquarius.	Cancer. Scorpius. Pisces.	Taurus. Virgo. Capricornus
The Stars & Planets, related to the Elements.	Mars, and the Sun.	Jupiter, and Venus.	Saturn, and Mercury.	The fixed Stars, and the Moon.
Four qualities of the Celestial Elements	Light.	Diaphanousness.	Agility.	Solidity.
Four Elements.	אש Fire.	רוח Air.	מים Water.	עפר Earth.
Four qualities.	Heat.	Moisture.	Cold.	Dryness.
Four seasons.	Summer.	Spring.	Winter.	Autumn.
Four corners of the World.	The East.	The West.	The North.	The South.

Continued on next page

A.5. The sixteenth century

Continued from previous page

THE NAME OF GOD WITH FOUR LETTERS.	י	ה	ו	ה
Four perfect kinds of mixed bodies.	Animals.	Plants.	Metals.	Stones.
Four kinds of Animals.	Walking.	Flying.	Swimming.	Creeping.
The Elements, in Plants.	Seeds.	Flowers.	Leaves.	Roots.
What in Metals.	Gold, and Iron.	Copper, and Tin.	Quicksilver.	Lead, & Silver.
What in stones.	Bright, and burning.	Light, and transparent.	Clear, and congealed.	Heavy, & dark.
Four Elements of man.	The Mind.	The spirit.	The Soul.	The body.
Four powers of the Soul.	The Intellect.	Reason.	Phantasy.	Sense.
Four Judiciary powers.	Faith.	Science.	Opinion.	Experience.
Four moral virtues.	Justice.	Temperance.	Prudence.	Fortitude.
The senses answering to the Elements.	Sight.	Hearing.	Taste and smell.	Touch.
Four Elements of man's body.	Spirit.	Flesh.	Humours.	Bones.
A four-fold spirit.	Animal.	Vital.	Generative.	Natural.
Four humours.	Choller.	Blood.	Flegme.	Melancholy.
Four Manners of complexion.	Violence.	Nimbleness.	Dulness.	Slowness.
Four Princes of devils, offensive in the Elements.	סמאל Samael.	עזאזל Azazel.	עזאל Azael.	מהזאל Mahazael.
Four infernal Rivers.	Phlegeton	Cocytus	Styx.	Acheron.
Four Princes of spirits, upon the four angels of the world.	Oriens.	Paymon.	Egyn.	Amaymon.

As you look at Agrippa's chart of the powers of four, you can immediately see the various sources that have been drawn together, Christianized, and then shoehorned into a system. And you can also see what an influence this listing had on subsequent generations of

A. THE DIRECTIONS IN WESTERN MAGIC

magicians up to present day. Agrippa's work also cemented the idea of 'lists' and tables in magical work, something that continues to this day.

Rather than continue back further in time, as we have what we need now to see the basis of the modern directional patterns, I think now is a good point to look at what is actually going on here in magical structural terms.

A.6 The modern structural approach

When I say modern, I include everything from the present day right back to thirteenth-century Europe, which in turn has its roots in Greco-Roman Egypt.

This approach in its foundations works from the perspective of everything *outside* of the magician. This reaches from the landscape, the elements, the stars and planets, the Underworld and so forth, and this externalization between the magician and the 'four' has informed and influenced Western magicians over long periods of time to the extent that it has become the orthodoxy of directional ritual patterns. If you look at any Western magical system today, you will see some or all of the 'four' powers and qualities emerge into the ritual pattern.

The 'four' as a patterned structure is very much about the earth, the Kingdom (Malkuth) and the universe in relation to the magician. The magician stands as the controller of the orchestra: there is a clear separation between the magician and his magic.

When you jump back much further back in time, further back than Greece or Greco-Roman Egypt, and start to look at Dynastic Egypt, you start to see a different pattern emerging, but one that subsequently influenced, informed and underpinned the later patterns that emerged as a result of what I call the 'Alexandrian Soup,' which is a mixture of Semitic, Egyptian, Greek, and Persian influences. (Its Egyptian influences were not uniquely Alexandrian: it clearly shows the influence of other areas, such as Thebes.) It was the 'Alexandrian Soup' that was the parent of what we call magic today, but the great-grandmother of the Alexandrian Soup was Egypt.

What I will say is that one of the major ingredients in that soup was the cultural and religious pattern of Dynastic Egypt, remnants of which made a base for the magical and religious patterns that emerged out of that time period. A lot of the elements that survived from Dynastic Egypt were heavily misinterpreted or misunderstood, and those misunderstandings carried forward into the newer religions and magical patterns in various obscure ways. However, some fragments also remained true to their roots and continued to be passed down from priest to magician, to alchemist to priest, and so forth.

Let us look at one small aspect of that of those surviving fragments: the use, knowledge, and understanding of the directions in Dynastic Egypt.

A.7 Dynastic Egypt

Before we delve into the directional patterns of Dynastic Egypt, it is worth pointing out to you that in Egypt, magic was part and parcel of the religion and culture. Magic was used within the temples to maintain the laws of Ma'at, to protect the king and nation, and to heal.

It was also used to heal and protect everyday people. Healer priests (male and female) operated out of the temple 'House of Life,' which was the library, archive and place of training and knowledge. Some, *swnw*, were general doctors, and some were *sЗw*, who were the magical doctors. This role was later taken up by the *ḥkʿy* ("magician") in the first millennium B.C.. The lector priests also played a major role in magical activity, as they were the ones who could read and recite the magical texts.[1]

Protection spells were worked not only by priests but also 'wise women' and seers who were usually connected to temple life in one way or another. Many of the priests, both male and female in a temple, often served only for a few months of the year and the rest of the time they worked out in the community either in a trade, or as a scribe, or as a healer, seer and so forth. This likely laid the foundation for the much later 'community magicians for hire,' a dynamic that we have

---

[1]David, R. *Religion and Magic in Ancient Egypt*. Penguin Books, 2003

A. The directions in Western magic

no evidence for until the Ptolemaic and subsequent Roman period of Egypt.[1]

One thing that all the Dynastic Egyptian magic had in common was how it used the directions. On the surface it can appear to be similar to Western magic in many respects, but in fact it is a whole other dynamic that separates it from later directional magic, and from the directional magic of the Greeks, Romans and Persians.

The big fundamental difference in the directional system, is that Dynastic system was based around the human and the Divine within the human, not so much the universe around them, which is the system that the West is more used to: the magic of Dynastic Egypt *was magician-centred and not environment-centred*. You can argue the point that the modern magician in general Western magic is indeed the centre, the Divine within, but that is simply one of the fragments of the Dynastic system that survived.

Because this has such a strong bearing on magic today, we will look at this in detail. If you understand those ancient fragments, and subsequently how they remain in modern magic, and then understand it within its own context, you will have a much greater understanding of the magic of today, and of yourself as the magician.

This in turn enables you to make choices: in a way, we as modern magicians have inherited two core principles: the magician as controller, and the magician as the centre of magic. That allows us elbowroom to decide what to use, when and how: we have a freedom of choice that was not so much of an option in times past.

Magic, Egypt, and the directions

This section of the essay is long and at times convoluted. Because Egyptian history is long, complex and at times completely different in its concepts to modern thinking, there need to be various digressions in order to establish context, content and meaning. However, I have attempted to approach this in a way that will also give you the reader a wider understanding of Dynastic Egyptian magical and religious/cultural thinking, and shine lights in corners of the Egyptian

---

[1] JF Borghouts. Witchcraft, Magic and Divination in Ancient Egypt. In: *Civilizations of the Ancient Near East.* ed. JM Sasson, Charles Scribner's Sons, 1995.

'Mysteries' that will help many readers reflect upon how these ancient concepts appear in various forms to this day. These concepts were carried out of Egypt by various waves of new religious thought and embedded in various ways into new magical and religious streams that still influence us to this day.

It is wise to bear in mind that unlike later Greco-Roman and much later Western magic, Egyptian magic and its texts as such were not recorded for the common man. The Egyptian sacred magical texts do not have bullet points, recipe lists (spells), and easily understood references: if you were trained and active, you were expected to understand the basics of what you were looking at. If you were not trained and active, but were a noble looking for a funerary text for your tomb, then a pre-prepared funerary scroll with your name inserted in it was essentially handed to you to place in your tomb or coffin, a text that most likely you would not understand.

Saying that, when you look at funerary texts over the huge span of Dynastic Egyptian history, you can tell when the education levels in the priesthood went up and down, or when such texts were used for the tombs/coffins of rich nobles who had little or no education. The complex texts start to acquire pictures, or are at times almost all pictures, though you would need to understand the process and Mysteries to decipher what was happening. But by the end of the New Kingdom, the Late Period and beyond, we do see basic 'picture book' funerary text that is about as simple as you can get for such concepts.

It is also worth knowing should you wish to research further, what form of Egyptian hieroglyphs you are looking at, as in terms of spotting magical signifiers, that there are big differences in the texts at certain periods in time. Anything from the Old Kingdom will be in Old Egyptian,[1] which is markedly different from Middle Egyptian which emerged c. 2050 B.C. in the Middle Kingdom period.

Middle Egyptian continued to be used as a form of high literature through the New Kingdom right up to Roman times for sacred and important texts, stelas and funerary writings, but its spoken form was only used for hymns, spells and important utterances once Late Egyptian emerged around the Amarna Period (c 1300 B.C.). And then

---

[1] For example, the Pyramid texts.

A. The directions in Western magic

there are other forms of Egyptian scripts such as Hieratic,[1] Demotic[2] and Coptic.[3,4]

Knowing what script it is you are looking at tells you a great deal about the information contained within that script, whether it was administrative, secular, sacred or magical. It can also tell you roughly what period in Egyptian history it was from. And also bear in mind the common misconception that the culture and religion of Egypt was one coherent history throughout its four-thousand-year history: nothing could be further from the truth. It was a mixed bag, just like any other nation of such age. Most of what we will be looking at has its origins in New Kingdom Egypt and the Third Intermediate Period.[5]

By looking at texts, images and wall paintings, we can discern from the directional positions and symbolic nature of the imagery, what was going on and often, why. As the magic was embodied within the magician/priest/king, the positions of the body in images tell us what dynamic they were working on, and also if they dead or alive or working in death or life. Left leg forward is striding into life or through life, for example, and right leg was striding through death. And ankh in the left hand is life in life, and in the right hand, is life in death.

So you start to see the subtle but major difference in how magic was approached in Dynastic Egypt. The Western magician seeks outside him or herself to draw in the power, the Egyptian magician generated it from themselves outwards.

Most Egyptian writings are multilayered in their meaning, so that high priests, kings and magicians could read one thing, and the lesser priests and scribes read another: hiding it in plain sight. And I presume that, knowing the pragmatic culture within ancient Egypt, those who knew, knew, and didn't need to point it out or need it pointing out to them. When a modern Western person looks at a

---

[1] Simplified cursive form of Old and Middle Egyptian

[2] Cursive variant of Hieratic that developed in Lower Egypt during the 25th Dynasty (c. 600 B.C.).

[3] Based around the Greek script (c100 B.C.).

[4] Allen, James P. (2000) *Middle Egyptian: An Introduction to the Language and Culture of Hieroglyphs.* Cambridge: Cambridge University Press.

[5] New Kingdom and Third Intermediate period (c. 1550-712 B.C.).

A.7. Dynastic Egypt

map, they automatically assume the top of the map is north, because that is how we align our maps: it rarely needs pointing out.

The first dynamic to understand before we look at directions, is a pattern that still emerges in Western magic today though in a different form and at times is heavily misunderstood. That pattern is one of *creation, stasis, and destruction,* and all three of those dynamics are considered to be within the natural order of balance, or in Egyptian terms, governed by the rule of Ma'at: balance. Outside of that balance is chaos which destroys order. In Western magic, destruction, death etc. are often considered 'bad' or chaos, this is expressed through modern terms like white/black magic.

The second dynamic that is foundational in Egyptian magic is 'seed' and 'harvest.' This dynamic runs through everything in Egyptian magic: something is 'seeded,' it grows, does something, and then its actions are harvested and weighed. The harvest is then 'judged' (weighed or counted) and what is good of the harvest is then renewed.

This not only applies to the actions of the magician/priest/individual but to their life also. We see aspects of this in Egyptian funerary texts where the deeds of the person (the harvest recorded by the heart spirit) are weighed[1] and if the harvest is sufficient, the soul of the person is considered 'developed.'

There is a deeper octave of this dynamic where the dead priest/magician/king is tested in death to *become* the scales.[2] If they pass this test, they are considered justified in death.

The most important dynamic of Egyptian directional magic is time. With time, and seed/harvest as two foundational dynamics, the Egyptian magician stands in the flow of time and operates through the input/output dynamic, with themselves as the vehicle through which the magic develops and flows.

The deity/spirit involvement is not the same as Western magic, though it can appear so on the surface to an untrained eye. In Western magic, the deities, spirits/beings are called to the magician and asked, forced, or instructed to do something: the magician as

---

[1] e.g. in the *Book of the Dead*, an Egyptian New Kingdom funerary text.

[2] e.g. in the Fifth Hour of the *Book of Gates*, an Egyptian New Kingdom funerary text.

A. The directions in Western magic

controller. In Egyptian magic, the *nṯrw*[1] (pronounced by modern Egyptologists as "NETCH-er-oo" or "NE-tyer-oo"), are the 'gods,' and the Egyptians looked upon the 'gods' in different ways to how we perceive them today.

Where modern magic has hierarchies of angels, demons, planetary spirits and so forth as well as deities and God, the Egyptians did not differentiate in the same way. For the most part, excluding things like hungry ghosts, almost everything was *nṯr*. This is a subtle but important difference in directional work: the Egyptian did not see the gods as the Greeks did (the basis of Roman and subsequently Western view) as squabbling Divine humans (i.e. human behaviours) in a literal sense, but more as powers and dynamics that manifested in everything around them (powers and creatures of nature) and this was played out in stories which were surface presentations of much deeper power dynamics.

By the end of the Dynastic era, the Persian and Greek ideas of the gods as squabbling Divine humans had integrated itself into Egyptian thought and we see this manifesting in the Ptolemaic period and beyond in Egypt.

This is all important to understand, as it shifts how the magician views power, works with power, and how that all relates to the directional work. And please bear in mind I have simplified this complex dynamic view right down, so that this article does not digress too much from the subject at hand.

The directional pattern

The Egyptian directional pattern, which governed everything in magic *and the magician themselves* is as thus:

> East: input, birth, seed, rising, left.
>
> South: future, in front, life, tomorrow, the new day.

East and south are inextricably linked to each other in a poetic sense: east is a 'gate' and south is a 'path.' The same is true for west and north:

---

[1] *nṯr*: singular deity, *nṯrt*: singular female deity, *nṯrw* plural 'gods'.

West: output, threshold of death, dusk, harvest, descending, right.

North: past, behind, dead, yesterday.

Centre: fulcrum/heart spirit.

The most important thing to think about, reading that list, is the understanding that mostly the directions were viewed as dynamic powers, not geographical points. For example in sacred (and thus magical) texts the term 'south' can often denote an inner/non-worldly state or location, not an actual physical one. South can also mean moving forward, the future and the path ahead.

The directions in Egyptian text are also identified with the body. Remember, with Egyptian texts one thing can have various meanings *all at the same time.* It was a similar way of approaching sacred information that was later used by Jewish Kabbalists (PaRDeS) and that Kabbalistic method most likely had its roots in Egypt.

The directions

The words/hieroglyphs of east and west are used to denote a geographical location, a sacred/inner location, a state of being, a goddess, the side of a body or object and the hand/foot on the body. Here are the emblems, transliterations and meanings for east and west in Middle Egyptian:[1]

 East:

iȝby (adj): left side, east, eastern. Will have suffix of an arm or foot to denote left/east side of the body, or a suffix denoting place.

iȝbt: The East (i.e. the power of the east) personified as the goddess Iabet, She of the sunrise.

---

[1]Raymond Faulkner. *A Concise Dictionary of Middle Egyptian.* 1962 Griffith Institute Oxford.

A. The directions in Western magic

 West:

imn (adj): right side, west, western. Will have suffix of an arm or foot to denote right hand/foot, or a suffix denoting place

imnt: The West, (i.e. the power of the west) personified as the goddess Imentit, She of the necropolis.

You start to see how the directions are inextricably linked with the body, with powers, inner locations and also physical space. With the left-hand default position as being east, you can then begin to understand the concept of south being forward, and north being behind.

Let us just looked briefly at how these body directions played out in statues and painting. Once you understand the directional qualities of east/left/life, and west/right/death, you can then begin to understand any underlying narrative presented.

Seti II

This 19th Dynasty statue of Seti II shows him with his left leg forward, which tells us it was made while Seti II was alive: he is striding forward into his reign. Also note the utterance is to the left of him.

As an aside, when you look at statues of some Egyptian kings, some scribes, and priests, you will notice that their hands are often curled around something. For years Egyptologists have hypothesized that they are holding scrolls, and sometimes they clearly are, and often have a tool in the other hand. But there are many times when it is clearly not a scroll, rather they are depicted as holding the *prow ropes of the barque.*

There is a whole narrative that appears in some of the funerary texts, where the Justified living and dead pull the Barque of Re in the Duat, and they are considered developed ones or developing ones: people of great learning where their heart speaks a truth, and they are considered 'Justified' before the gods. Pulling the prow ropes of the Barque of Re was a great honour and also a terrible burden. This is clearly outlined in the New Kingdom text *The Book of Gates.*

A.7. Dynastic Egypt

Figure A.1: Statue of Seti II, 19th Dynasty, Egypt. Displayed at the Museo Egizio, Turin, Italy.

A. The Directions in Western Magic

In this smaller image below, from the tomb of Tuthmosis IV, note how the king has his right leg forward, as he is in death, and is receiving *life in death* from Hathor, and *life and dominion* from Osiris.

Figure A.2: Tuthmosis IV tomb KV43, Valley of the Kings.

Now let us look in depth at a particular and famous funerary text, often called the *Egyptian Book of the Dead*. It is littered with imagery and texts that give us various insights into how directions were used to signify powers, places and actions.

Papyrus of Ani: The Book of Coming forth by Day

So many people look at these texts through a cultural lens of Western thinking which involves issues like monotheism and geographical location, and that immediately locks them out of the understanding of the text. A good example would be a section of the Papyrus of Ani,[1] the funeral text of Coming Forth by Day for Ani, spell seventeen:

> I go on the road which I know in front of the Island of the Just. *What is it?* It is Rosetjau. The southern gate is in Naref, the northern gate is in the Mound of Osiris; as for the Island of the Just, it is Abydos. *Otherwise said:* It is the road on which my father Atum went when he proceeded to the Field of Reeds.

When you look at this from a point of geographical location, the eye is drawn to Abydos which is an ancient sacred enclosure and temple complex. It is one of the oldest settlements in Ancient Egypt and is the eighth nome[2] of Upper Egypt. From that, many people, both lay readers and some academics have tied themselves in knots trying to figure out where Naref is geographically, using Abydos as a location indicator. This is how a modern Western person would think, but to an ancient Egyptian, a sacred inner location, a person, and a state of being can all be the same thing.

Naref and Osiris[3] Naref are mentioned numerous times in funerary texts, stelas, statues and tombs certainly in the New Kingdom through to the Late Period. The words can be used for a location, a person or a state of being. Here is an example from the 30th dynasty, titles found on a statue of a priest at Herakleopolis Magna:

> Revered before Heryshef, king of the Two Lands, ruler of the Two Banks, Revered before Osiris Nareref.[4]

If we go back to spell seventeen and look at it from a magical Egyptian perspective, we can hypothesize that Naref being *southern*

---

[1] Raymond Faulkner (translation 1974) *The Egyptian Book of the Dead* (spell 17) Chronicle Books USA 1994 first edition.

[2] Territorial area of Ancient Egypt.

[3] Osiris is not only a god, but a term for someone who is dead and has passed many of the trials of the Duat.

[4] Díaz-Iglesias Llanos, L. (2016). *Naref and Osiris Naref. A Study in Herakleopolitan Religious Traditions.* Berlin, Boston: deGruyter

A. The directions in Western magic

is before the dead person and the *northern gate* is behind the dead person.

When you then think about Rosetjau and that it is a *desert* pathway through one of the deepest sections of the Duat, and the gates of the Duat open for the dead traveller according to their 'harvest' or life deeds/state, then you start to understand that Naref as a gate is a state of being (i.e. the gate is within that state of being): by passing successfully through the gate of Naref they stand a good chance of safe passage to the next stage of their development journey.

When the text says "the northern gate is the Mound of Osiris" it is referring to a state: where the body has been embalmed and wrapped, and the dead spirit has gone through the first stages of the process in the Duat. The *northern gate* is the gate behind, it is in the past, the spirit is now moving away from one stage of death/destruction process, and is preparing to move forward into renewal and the 'afterlife.'

> I have established offerings in Abydos. Open the way for me in Rosetjau because I have relieved the sickness in Osiris. I have painted his perch. Make way for me so that he might shine in Rosetjau.[1]

The northern gate as the Mound of Osiris talks in terms of the Osiris mythology of death, dismemberment, reconstituting the body parts, and resurrection. In the process of the Duat's challenges as outlined in the funerary texts, a similar theme emerges of death, trials that take the person apart/the destruction of their self-image, the healing of wounds, the judgement/weighing of the heart, and the path to resurrection.

There is also a dynamic in which the dead person heals/reconstitutes Osiris by *becoming Osiris*: as the person emerges, so does Osiris. This mythology is heavily interwoven with the themes of seed, grain, threshing, harvest and weighing the harvest.

If you wish to look deeper into the magical aspects of the Inner Desert paths of Rosetjau, I suggest you read hours four and five of the

---

[1] Ogden Goelet. A Commentary on the Corpus of Literature and Tradition which constitutes the Book of Going Forth By Day. (San Francisco: Chronicle Books, 1998)

Amduat.[1] If you are familiar with Egyptian magical concepts, these two sections can be interesting.

Before we move on, here is another extract from spell seventeen of the Papyrus of Ani that has a directional fragment in it. In the spell it is talking about an image which we will look at in a moment:

> *Who is he?* It is Re who created his names and his members, it means the coming into existence of those gods who are in his suite.
>
> I am he who is not opposed among the gods.
>
> Who is he? He is Atum who is in his sun disk. *Otherwise said:* He is Re when he rises in the eastern horizon of the sky.
>
> To me belongs yesterday, I know tomorrow.[2]

Note that the action is east–west. The passage of the sun, and the time is yesterday (north) and tomorrow (south) which are the names of the Aker, the two guardian lions of the horizon which we will look at in a moment.

To summarise briefly, for Egyptians the directional pattern from a mythic (not geographic) perspective was born/east, lived/south, died/west, passed into history/north. The same pattern also unfolds in the Duat, the Egyptian Underworld.

A good example of the east–west, south–north dynamics in Egyptian thought can be found in the Old Testament (or the Jewish Book of Prophets) in *Isaiah* 43-5/6:

> Fear not, for I am with you:
>
> I will bring your seed from the east, and gather you from the west:
>
> I will say to the north: 'Give (them) up,' and to the south: 'Keep (them) not back.'

---

[1] Warburton D, Hornung E, Abt T. (2014) *The Egyptian Amduat: the Book of the Hidden Chamber.* Zurich. Living Human Heritage Publications.

[2] Faulkner Dr Ramond (translation 1974) *The Egyptian Book of the Dead* (spell 17) Chronicle Books USA 1994 first edition.

A. The directions in Western magic

This extract from Isaiah is sometimes used by magicians today in order to establish and protect the path ahead.

You see the similar concepts straightaway, and when you look closely at the first section of chapter 43, if you are familiar with the processes outlined in the Egyptian funerary texts you will also recognize what is going on in that first section, and where that imagery comes from.

The east/left is life (that moves south) and in life we 'do,' we act, think, create, destroy and so forth: we participate in all the trials, lessons and joys of life. The east is the seed that grows and flourishes as we move forward (south) through life: hence the command in Isaiah "I say to the south keep them not back" is protecting the person's future.

If we learn well, evolve from our mistakes, and develop/mature, then we are said to be 'winnowing our harvest' while in life: we take the best of the grain and discard the stones, husks and stalks. This leaves our harvest lightweight. In terms of the seeds that remain, there is a whole mystical magical rabbit hole you can vanish down when it comes to the depiction of the weighing of the harvest (the heart) and how much seed is left (must be lighter than a feather of Ma'at).

Upon death that 'harvest' is examined, and weighed upon scales. This concept appears to have emerged in New Kingdom Egyptian thought, and also appears in different ways in Judaic scriptures. Here is a good example from *Proverbs* 21:[1]

א פַּלְגֵי-מַיִם לֶב-מֶלֶךְ, בְּיַד-יְהוָה; עַל-כָּל-אֲשֶׁר יַחְפֹּץ יַטֶּנּוּ.	**1** The king's heart is in the hand of the LORD as the watercourses: He turneth it whithersoever He will.
ב כָּל-דֶּרֶךְ-אִישׁ, יָשָׁר בְּעֵינָיו; וְתֹכֵן לִבּוֹת יְהוָה.	**2 Every way of a man is right in his own eyes; but the LORD weigheth the hearts.**
ג עֲשֹׂה, צְדָקָה וּמִשְׁפָּט-- נִבְחָר לַיהוָה מִזָּבַח.	**3** To do righteousness and justice is more acceptable to the LORD than sacrifice.

The root תכן is widely used in second temple literature in the context of weights and measures,[2] and its use in Proverbs, applied to

---

[1] https://www.mechon-mamre.org/p/pt/pt2821.htm Proverbs 21. Retrieved 17/4/2019.

[2] Shupak, N. (2015). *Weighing in the Scales* Fs.Talshir. From Author to Copiest: Essays on Composition, Redaction and Transmission of the Hebrew Bible in Honor of Zipi Talshir

human ethical conduct, is strikingly similar to the Egyptian concept. Also note, "The king's heart is in the hand of the LORD": in the Egyptian pattern, the heart of the individual is the voice that speaks the truth upon judgement: the heart speaks to the scales upon judgement, telling the gods what this person has done in life. Note that the 'LORD' is holding the king's heart in his *hand* to weigh/judge. This is mirrored in the magical use of the right hand to weigh, complete and compost a magical action.

In New Kingdom and subsequent funerary texts[1] it appears as a judgement scene where the heart of the individual (the spirit of the heart that speaks truth) is weighed against a feather of Ma'at. In Egyptian thought the heart spirit listens and watches, and recounts our actions and lessons to the judge when we are being 'weighed.'

What remains of the harvest becomes our *west*. If the harvest has been winnowed in life to a great degree, there are little or no seeds left, the heart passes judgement and the soul moves deeper into the process of the Duat, later to rise with the sun and be in the company of the gods.[2] Remember that the west is also the right hand/right side.

Just to move briefly from history and into esotericism, the right-hand harvest contains seeds (new potential: the fruit of the harvest) and also learned wisdom from experience: the light of evolution. That is the lantern held in the right hand by the adept, depicted as the Hermit in the tarot. The light of our evolution guides us forward in life, and in death lights our way through the darkness of the Underworld/Duat as we navigate its trials on our journey.

This esoteric understanding which flows from this ancient pattern is also likely the root of understanding behind the 'right hand of God.' Remember that many of the philosophies and thinking behind early Christianity was partly seeded in Egypt,[3] as was a fair amount of Jewish philosophy.

To qualify that statement adequately would take an essay on its own. But there is enough archaeological, historical and textual evidence to demonstrate Egyptian thought and ideas mingling with

---

[1] *Book of Gates* hour five: the dead appear *as* the scales. See also Book of the Dead spell 30B.

[2] *The Book of Gates*: New Kingdom text.

[3] Choat, M. "Christianity." 2012. In: *The Oxford Handbook of Roman Egypt* edited by C. Riggs. Oxford: Oxford University Press.

A. The directions in Western magic

Hellenistic Jewish communities in Egypt (along with Greek and Roman communities in Egypt) to the point in which long fading Egyptian influences were taken up by the newer communities and absorbed into their mythology, philosophies and magical/religious thinking.

The continued adventures of Ani in the Underworld

A good example of learning to decipher images and text, specifically for these fragments of magical concepts in Dynastic Egyptian funerary texts and literature is spell 17 from the Papyrus of Ani, which we have already briefly looked at. Now we will look at an image from that papyrus and apply what we know of Egyptian concepts of time, state and direction to decipher a specific famous picture.

In Egyptian sacred imagery[1] everything has meaning, from the stance of the person, to the banners, flowers, animals and hieroglyphs. And remember that Middle Egyptian hieroglyphs in important literature, sacred/funerary texts and important stela often had layered meaning not only with the words, but also actual images, and the pictograms of the hieroglyphs.

Aker: yesterday and tomorrow

Aker is a power of the horizon between the otherworlds/Duat and the physical world. Aker is most often depicted as two lions sat back to back, and between their backs the sun is depicted either rising or falling. The sun, Atum (Ra/Re upon rising) is nestled between two peaks in a stylized hieroglyph named Djew.[2]

The two peaks are east and west, the two positions where the sun rises and falls. The image of the sun nestled between the two peaks is called the Akhet.[3] Akhet means the place the sun inhabits just before it rises over the horizon to flood the world with light. Interestingly the same word is also used for the inundation of the Nile.

---

[1] Statues, funerary texts, tomb walls.

[2] The two peaks of the primordial mountain are Djew are Manu in the west, and Bakhu in the east.

[3] ȝḫt, "horizon."

A.7. Dynastic Egypt

Figure A.3: Image from the Papyrus of Ani, Spell 17.

A. The Directions in Western Magic

So we have an image of Atum that also combines both east and west (Djew). Above the Akhet is the hieroglyph *pt* for sky or heavens. The image of the Akhet can depict the sun either rising or setting.[1]

On either side of the Akhet, also under the *pt* sign, sits the two lions: Aker. The image of Aker is one of the most misunderstood ones when people get interested in Egyptian images and symbolism, and the internet is rife with misunderstandings in articles that are then copied on *ad nauseam*. To look at the directional keys of the Aker, you need common sense and a basic knowledge of hieroglyphs and symbolism.

The names of two lions are Duaw and Sef, who together make up the Aker, *He who guards the Akhet*. Duaw can be a difficult hieroglyphic word to translate at times, as it can mean today (as in the day ahead) or tomorrow, and is translated in correlation to the context. And this is where you have to be careful about how language can shape thought: Duaw is a word that denotes moving forward, and would not be used in its context of 'today' as we would use it. For us, we would say, now, today, meaning this present moment in time. Duaw is always moving ahead, and the Middle Egyptian word for 'now' would be *3t* (at).

In the context of Aker, Duaw means tomorrow and Sef means yesterday.[2] Aker as a collective of the two lions was at times titled *He who is looking forward and behind, Yesterday and Tomorrow*, or *He who is beneath* (the horizon).

When you look at images of the Aker lions in funeral texts, also look at what is around them. In the papyri of Ani[3] the lion Duaw which is to the left in the image, has before its nose, two lotus flowers which are symbols for Upper Egypt/south.[4] Beyond the lotus flowers are the *ba* birds of Ani and his wife standing on top of their mortuary

---

[1] Magli, G. (2013). The lords of the horizon. In Architecture, Astronomy and Sacred Landscape in Ancient Egypt (pp. 57-104). Cambridge: Cambridge University Press

[2] Faulkner, Ramond (translation 1974) *The Egyptian Book of the Dead* (spell 17) Chronicle Books USA 1994 first edition.

[3] A copy of the Book of the Dead for Ani, Theban Scribe 1250 B.C. 19th Dynasty Egypt

[4] McDonald, J. Andrew. 2018. "Influences of Egyptian Lotus Symbolism and ritualistic Practices on Sacral Tree Worship in the Fertile Crescent from 1500 BCE To 200 CE," Basel: *Religions* 9

shrines, and beyond them is an image of Ani playing Senet: the game of Passing.[1] Ani is depicted sitting playing the game in his 'shrine' or 'enclosure,' which means he has passed the trials of judgement and is now 'eternal.'

On the right of the Akhet is Sef, yesterday. Before Sef is the Benu bird, *He who came into Himself*.[2] In the Heliopolis[3] creation myth, the Benu bird flew over the waters of the Nu before creation. He landed on the emerging Benben stone and the cry of the Benu broke the primeval silence, determining what was or was not to unfold in creation. He is connected with Ra/Atum and Osiris, a symbol of the early beginning of regeneration (the midnight before the dawn) and likely the source of the later mythic Phoenix.

The text of the spell includes the words:

> I am that great Benu bird which is in Heliopolis, the supervisor of what exists.

Before the Benu bird is the lotus flower of the south attached to the south end of the shrine, and beyond the flower is Osiris Ani in his shrine, flanked by Isis and Nephthys (the two birds) guarding the embalmed body of Ani.

The whole line of images for spell seventeen run right to left, and signify the transition from Osiris Ani to the resurrected Ani. The images tell of Ani as Osiris, his body 'healed' and wrapped (embalmed) in his shrine protected by the two goddesses, and the lotus flower signifying 'south,' i.e. the direction in which Ani is to go in his travels through the Duat. Notice that 'north' of Osiris Ani is Nephthys who is the goddess of the death process, and south of Osiris Ani is Isis, goddess of life.

> Ascend and descend: descend with Nephthys, sink into darkness with the Night-bark. Ascend and descend: ascend with Isis, rise with the Day-bark.[4]   — PT 222

---

[1]Dunn-Vaturi AE, deVoogt A, Crist W. (2016) *Ancient Egyptians at Play*. Oxford: Bloomsbury Academic.

[2]Hart, George (2005). *The Routledge Dictionary of Egyptian Gods and Goddesses* (Second ed.). New York: Routledge. pp. 48–49.

[3]Iwnw (Iuna)

[4]Faulkner R.O, 1969. *Ancient Egyptian Pyramid Texts*. Oxford University Press

A. The directions in Western magic

Egyptian summary

What does all of this tell us about the Egyptian magical directions? By careful study of the texts, wall images and texts, and looking at them through the eyes of a magician, we start to see a pattern emerging that reflects the foundation of a lot of magical approaches today.

Like most western magical directions, one element of the pattern is solar: the sun rises in the east, peaks in the south, sets in the west and is the weakest in the north. The Dynastic Egyptian magic, as opposed to later Greco-Roman Egyptian magic, was centered around the individual: the directional pattern was an operation of the human passing through time, not an operation of interaction with the geography around them.

The passage of the sun into the Duat through the western gate and rising the following morning through the eastern gate is a pattern of death, trial and resurrection, where the magician in life and in death forges forward into the south for the future.

The left hand/east as a life/action direction and right hand/west/harvest direction shows clearly a method of operating in which the magician in the centre of all things, and walks a path of triggering life, action and consequence, and simultaneously a path of ending, completion, harvest, the judgement of that harvest, and evolution. All of this is under the influence of Ma'at, the striving to keep balance, justice and order.

In Ancient Egypt, if the actions and intent of the priest magician were necessary in order to reestablish balance or Ma'at then the powers would work with and flow through the magician. This is not about only doing 'good' magic, but *necessary* magical actions, which could at times be violent or destructive if that was needed to defeat Isfet and re-establish Ma'at. Note how this centre of balance uses both creative and destructive magic in order to maintain balance and suppress chaos.

A.8 Right hand path, left hand path

In modern occultism/magic, people often identify themselves as either right hand path or left hand path. The RHP path was considered 'good and holy' and the LHP was considered 'bad' and

A.8. Right hand path, left hand path

evil. This duality was introduced (as far as I can tell) by Madame Blavatsky, who founded the Theosophical society in 1875, and who coined the terms in her book *Isis Unveiled* (1877).[1] She drew upon Indian Tantra for the ideas and posited the concept that LHP magicians/practitioners were followers of Black Magic and were a threat to society.

I find it ironic that someone who drew upon East Indian concepts, and named her book after an Egyptian goddess, did more to separate future magicians than anyone else from the powerful and complex pattern that had emerged out of Egypt.

When you mix Blavatsky's duality with the Christian understanding of 'The right hand of God' as being good/just, you can see how quickly this not only distorted an ancient magical pattern, but also contaminated magical thinking from that time onwards.

She didn't just get it from Tantra, the right hand/good, left hand/bad had already been kicking around for a thousand years in Christianity and Islam, and she would have grown up with the concept as it is in the New Testament. But it is far more glamorous to say you got the concept from Tantra, and it was familiar to people in the west: you accept something far more if your consciousness has already been exposed to its essence. Here is it mentioned in the Gospel of Matthew, written sometime between A.D. 70–100.

> All the nations will be gathered before Him, and He will separate them one from another, as a shepherd divides his sheep from the goats. And He will set the sheep on His right hand, but the goats on the left.[2]

In Islam, it also appears in the ninth-century writings of Abi Dawud[3] in *Sunan Abi Dawud*, one of the *Kutub al Sittah* (six major Hadith collections):

> It is narrated that 'Aa'ishah (may Allaah be pleased with her) said: The right hand of the Messenger of Allaah (peace and blessings of Allaah be upon him) was for his

---

[1] Evans, Dave 2007. *The History of British Magick after Crowley*. Hidden Publishing
[2] *Matthew* 25:31–46.
[3] Abi Dawud was a Persian Islamic scholar based in Basra. Died A.D. 889.

A. The directions in Western magic

> purification and food, and his left hand was for using the toilet and anything that was dirty. Classed as saheeh (which is narrated by men of good character) by al-Albaani in Saheeh Abi Dawood.

And yet, to give Blavatsky her due, what she was expressing and that she discovered in Tantra and would have echoed Christian thought, were ideas that also appeared in the old religion of Iran[1] and were also found in the Indian Vedas.[2]

When you merge the two concepts of the Persian and Egyptian together (remember the Persians conquered Egypt in 525 B.C.) you get a weird mix that right hand/death/harvest is good, and left hand/life/action is bad. This weird meld indeed emerged in esoteric and religious thinking in early Christianity and spread out across Europe during the first millennia A.D..

Now think about how that strange union of ideas affects magic and directional magic to this day, and how it locks the magician out of a sense of time, and of union with everything around them. It also causes a conflict within the magician not only in their magical thinking, but also their day-to-day lives. It separates the magician from their own magical sovereignty, and as a result, the magician can only draw from around themselves, not from within themselves, as there is a constant inner subconscious battle going on between what should and should not be.

This can then spill out into magical ritual action in which it can define which base direction the magician faces to work, how their use their hands and thus their tools, and how it locks them out of the stream of time. Instead it locks them into a battle of either good or bad, as opposed to the balance of creation, destruction and chaos. The RHP magicians sneer at the unravelling and destruction work of the LHP and the LHP magicians sneer at the self-righteous smugness of the RHP magicians.

When a magician works within a ritual or space, mostly they are actively working directional power in one form or another, whether it is to 'face east' which has become the default position in magic, or to

---

[1] Zoroastrianism 6th century B.C. Persia
[2] 1200-200 B.C. for present form, introduced into India by Aryans

circle the directions, also usually starting in the east. When you think about the long directional attributes list of Agrippa in the fifteenth-century which was uptaken by nineteenth and twentieth-century magicians, add the dualism, and also the seasoning of the soup that was provided by Luria, you start to understand the problems that many modern magicians find themselves in.

Luria, interestingly, picks up on the south/tomorrow, north/past in his attributes of power for the Sefirots Chesed and Gevurah, but that has largely been missed or ignored by later magicians.

All of these ingredients that have been drawn together, serve collectively to lock out the magician from their power within as they seek it outside themselves ritually. By not rooting the magician in the flow of time, and creation/destruction, the magician becomes reliant upon the powers around him or her, and not the ones within.

Instead, the internal power/Divinity of the magician becomes something that must be psychologized, or striven for in a semi-religious way without rooting it firmly into the magical practice as an anchor. This is not to say that the powers, beings and patterns that flow from the directions are not to be used or be a major component within magic, they are. However, if the magician is not first rooted within their own fate, time, and divine self, they are essentially trying to use software without an operating system.

When you add the concept of the duality/hand paths, you further limit the magical potential for power and balance within the magical work. The simple act of always facing east, which predominates in some magical systems, locks the magician himself out of time: why? Why does not a created pattern work when by rights it should?

If the facing east system was created around the inner power flowing out into the physical world from the 'inner east,' and the ritual system and physical actions of the magician were a holism designed to take that power and used it across their system, then yes it would work. But that is not what has happened.

Instead you have a patchwork of ideas and concepts stitched together, where related systems flow through those concepts: so for example you end up with a magical system where Egyptian, Greek, Romano-Christian, Persian, and Kabbalistic concepts are thrown into rituals and systems *without understanding what each component is*

A. The directions in Western magic

doing and why. Every single part of an old system that you use brings with it all the rest of the system into the magic, if it is not filtered. When you have clashing components inserted without real magical understanding, you also end up with whole clashing systems flowing into a ritual act.

This is not to say that you cannot mix components from different sources: you can, and it can work brilliantly—but only if those components are complementary and the mixing is done with true gnosis of all the different systems and their power flows. This is where the magician is anchored in a particular format, and weaves the power flows while limiting/filtering the rest of the various systems' 'idiosyncrasies.' They become the composer, the source and the landscape, as opposed to an operator who doesn't understand the machinery that they work on.

Before I finish, I want to just demonstrate how easily something ancient ended up in much later magical texts, but its knowledge was lost.

Remember when we looked at the nineteenth-century, Eliphas Levi and the Grand Grimoire, I asked you to take note of the forked staff?

> On the eve of the great undertaking you will search for a rod or wand of wild hazel tree that has not yet born fruit, at the highest point of the sought-after branch there should be a second little branch in the form of a fork with two ends: its length should be nineteen and a half inches.[1]

The forked staff has its roots in Ancient Egypt as the Was sceptre/staff, which magically is used to 'pin' the head of the serpent Apep and his fellow serpents, and is used in iconography and hieroglyphs to denote 'power of dominion.' That is, by pinning the serpents of chaos, the gods and magicians have power and control over the land. Incidentally this concept of pinning Underworld powers also emerges in Tibetan Buddhism.

The forked staff (without the head of Set on the end) is still used to this day in Egypt to pin and catch troublesome snakes: it has

---

[1] Grand Grimoire aka the Red Dragon: (early 19th century) Chapter III Book One

practical, magical and symbolic uses that have spanned thousands of years. In a practical sense, if you look up modern steel snake-catching sticks, the handles often have a Setian shaped handle for a good angle grip, and the forked bottom to trap the neck of the snake. So it is possible that the Was staff head (Set's head) not only had a power/magical/deity function, but also a practical one. Holding the Was staff by the head allows the holder to angle the staff in a way that gives maximum distance and maximum control.

Going back to the mention of the forked staff in the *Grand Grimoire*, yes there were venomous snakes in Europe (the common European viper) and the forked staff could have developed independently in Europe, but when you pay attention to the instructions on how to make the forked staff, it does not say 'make it like a snake-catching staff,' or a similar terminology that would have been used if they were familiar to the people of the time. Rather it has to give detailed instructions including looking for the fork in the branches, as if it were something unknown. I did look through images from the Middle Ages and Medieval period looking to see if a forked snake-catching staff was depicted anywhere, and most images were of spears, and usually in religious icons.

Now have a look at these images. The first is from scene thirty-four of the sixth hour in the *Book of Gates*,[1] a New Kingdom funerary text that it packed within magical and mystical meaning.

Figure A.4: The forked staff as depicted in the Book of Gates.

---

[1]McCarthy J, Sheppard M, Littlejohn S. 2017. *The Book of Gates: A Magical Translation.* Quareia Publishing Exeter, UK.

A. THE DIRECTIONS IN WESTERN MAGIC

The inscription with the image says:

> Receive for yourself your mortal grapples which you hold fast in your arms. What is yours is in the Absorbing One: Dispute you what should be in him, that what is best in him may come forth, and he retires.[1]

Think about what the inscription is saying, and in context of the power of the Was staff and what it does. Note it is not depicted as a Was with the head of Set, it is simply a snake-catching staff.

This image is the Was Sceptre, with the head of Set (the suppressor of Apep, Chaos) and the forked bottom. It appears frequently in Egyptian tomb wall paintings, and with temple statues and images/statues of the king. It denotes the power to suppress chaos and thus help the land, area or person maintain their Ma'at and protect Ma'at.[2]

Figure A.5: Was staff

And finally, in this Middle Kingdom stela[3] the Was sceptre/staff in the hand of the Goddess Isis (Aset). Note how the staff is held in the left hand, which means 'power of dominion in life,' and the Ankh in the right hand which means 'I give life in death.'

I hope this essay has been of use to you, to help you think about where things come from, how they are passed through time, and how ideas form and change over millennia, and as they move from one culture to another.

---

[1] Translation by Michael Sheppard, 2017.

[2] Ma'at: truth, balance and justice: the underpinning concept of the Dynastic Egyptian religion

[3] Stela showing "Isis the Great Goddess" sitting and holding a was-sceptre. A man, the head of necropolis workers, adores her. From Egypt, Middle Kingdom. The Petrie Museum of Egyptian Archaeology, London. With thanks to the Petrie Museum of Egyptian Archaeology, UCL.

A.8. Right hand path, left hand path

Figure A.6: Stela showing "Isis the Great Goddess" sitting and holding a was-sceptre. A man, the head of necropolis workers, adores her. From Egypt, Middle Kingdom. The Petrie Museum of Egyptian Archaeology, London. With thanks to the Petrie Museum of Egyptian Archaeology, UCL.

A. The directions in Western magic

Figure A.7: *Geb and Nut: The Gods of the Egyptians* (1904) by EA Wallis Budge

Appendix B

The Book of Death

by Josephine McCarthy, 1999

Foreword

Throughout the history of magic, one of the most powerful ways to transmit magical knowledge through the river of time was to put that magical knowledge into a story. Following that tradition, here is a magical story centered around the topic of dying and death: it looks at the inner beings involved in the process of death and beyond, and also touches upon some of the deeper aspects of the Western Mysteries.

Stories embed themselves within us in a different way to how nonfiction information does, and we can draw upon that difference to allow magical stories and myths to permeate our deeper selves. This in turn serves as a bridge between us and the Mysteries: magic without stories is no magic at all.

Part I

Margaret brushed the stray hair from her face and looked out over the washing line. Her tired arms drooped onto the thick line and rested there for a second. Hanging washing always hurt her arms and today it was worse than ever. With a groan, she bent over and tried to pick up a peg that she had dropped on the damp grass. Her toes gripped the earth as she tried to balance, but to no effect. She tipped forward from the weight of her body and landed on her knees.

"You should squat, it's much better for you than bending."

B. THE BOOK OF DEATH

The interfering voice cut through Margaret's wet maternity shirts that hung haphazardly to the line and moved slowly with the light breeze. The voice jumped over the fence and parted the damp washing. "Here, come on, up you get."

The young man from next door put his hands under Margaret's arms and heaved her onto her feet in one swift movement. It was too fast for Margaret, causing her to become dizzy. She clung onto him, trying to stop herself from swaying. How dare he tell her what to do and then stick his hands in her armpits. Her face reddened with embarrassment and the cursed panic crept upon her.

She felt sick. She did not want to throw up in front of this idiot, so she clung to him, gulping for air.

"Excuse me for asking, but how far on are you? You look pretty big, are you carrying twins?"

That finally cured Margaret of her nausea. She wanted to launch into him for being so rude, but she knew she would not be able to pluck up the courage. Deep within her she knew that he was just trying to be friendly, and he had helped her. What had got into her just lately? Everything annoyed her, everything frightened her, everything made her want to scream. Her chin jutted out as she looked up at the bright teen face that smiled back at her.

"I'm 35 weeks, 5 more weeks to go, and no it's not twins, I'm just big." Her voice had just a tad too much venom in it as she spat the defensive words into his face, something she regretted immediately.

The young man became uncomfortable. He slowly realized that he had probably insulted her by saying that she was big. It was beginning to dawn on him that women did not like things like size pointed out to them. He had often wanted to talk to her, not for any, well, sexual reason, but because she always seemed so alone.

Her husband only seemed to come home one or two days a week and even then he would arrive, park up his large truck and then go out in his car. He never seemed to take her anywhere and she never seemed to go out very much. As he looked closer at her face, it became clear to him that she was not that much older than him. Probably only a year or two. She looked around twenty and his eighteenth birthday was only a month away.

"Well, I'll leave you to it then. Please call over the fence if you need anything."

The young man smiled awkwardly before jumping back over the fence and vanishing into his house. Margaret placed her hands under her armpits where he had gripped to lift her. Now that she had recovered from the indignity of being a beached whale flapping about on the ground, she savoured the moment of human contact.

That night, as in all nights just recently, her dreams came harsh and unrelenting. She tossed around in her bed, entangling herself in the soft blue cotton sheets and her black hair mingled with the blue in the still silent darkness. Her arms twitched as she recoiled away from something: a dark fear slowly tiptoed towards her, taunting her. Beads of sweat and panic broke out on her forehead as she inched away from the unseen, her closed eyes darting this way and that in an effort to find safety. The sound of her breathing punctured the silence as it became more urgent, her breath labouring against the inner terror.

She lay rigid and motionless for a few seconds before her hands flew to her face, her fingers trying to fight something off. Margaret's voice called out into the darkness and her eyes opened suddenly. Her body was paralyzed. Her hands were still by her face, unable to move. The darkness took shape and moved towards her. Her body prickled against the fear as the presence moved ever so slowly to her side. She could not turn her head, nor could she cry out.

It approached her, growing until it extended beyond the ceiling. Each hair on her body told her to run. The droplets of sweat that ran down her face and breasts told her to scream. But her body lay motionless against the horror that moved slowly in a deliberate path towards her. She struggled to move her eyes from side to side. The being had filled the whole room and she knew in her heart it was something that she could not escape. Its hand reached out to touch her.

It was aiming for her forehead. She knew she had to stop it but she did not know how. The child in her womb lay motionless, as though waiting for the inevitable. Her instincts were to put her arms around her swollen belly and protect the little child snuggled up within her, but her arms remained glued around her head.

B. The Book of Death

Just before it reached her forehead, she knew, from somewhere deep within her, that if it touched her she would die. She did not want to die. She wanted her baby. She began to cry helplessly, for herself and her unborn child. The tears touched her face and something snapped within her.

Her eyes opened and an inrush of air to her lungs made her jump: when she thought she had been awake, she had actually still been dreaming. Sleep fell away from her as she sat up in bed, covered in sweat and tears. Her hands cupped her face as she wept, unable to cope with yet another night of the same nightmare.

Part II

"Okay, that's it Mrs. Kingsley, is there anything you want to ask?"

The doctor stood smiling at Margaret but she could see from the look on his face that he really did not want her to ask anything. But she knew she had to say something. Margaret smiled at the nurse seated beside the doctor, who had done her weekly observations, checking Margaret's blood pressure, urine and a mountain of other seemingly useless things.

"Well...there is one thing."

Her voice was unsteady as she began to redden. She felt overpowered by this professional man who held life and death, and her health in his hands. The doctor looked briefly at the ceiling and then back at Margaret before smiling. He had spent three minutes with this woman and now it was time for her to go. He hated women who asked questions. Why could they not just come in, be examined and get lost? His words came out with thinly disguised impatience, making Margaret go even redder.

"Go ahead, ask."

Margaret fiddled with her thumbs and tried to sound as confident as possible.

"Well, I feel that there is something wrong. The feeling gets stronger everyday but I don't know what it is. I just don't feel right."

She dropped her head and looked at her hands. She felt such an idiot for blurting that out. The doctor looked at the rotund, red-faced, raven-haired young woman sitting in a lump before him. He could see that she must have been quite pretty before she got pregnant, but they all faded after the babies started. It was always the same. That, he thought to himself, is why he would never marry.

"Mrs. Kingsley, there is nothing wrong with you. Your blood pressure is a little high, but that's okay. Now stop worrying, it will do baby no good at all if you worry. All will be well."

The nurse got up and stood by the door with it open and smiled at Margaret.

"Good-bye, Mrs. Kingsley."

The nurse continued to smile until the smile became fixed. Margaret slid from the chair and heaved herself up. Her body felt more than heavy, it felt poisoned. Her whole being seemed to be under a cloud and no one wanted to help or listen. As the nurse closed the door behind her, Margaret heard her voice filter through to the hallway.

"God, some of these women are such hypochondriacs."

Margaret wanted cry. She felt violated and humiliated, and she could not find within her the strength to challenge these people. Her mother had always told her that when she was twenty-one, she would find her voice. But it had not happened. Here she was, twenty-one, and she dare not say boo to anyone.

She cursed herself all the way home as she trudged back up the steep hill that led to her house. The road was dirty and smelly, full of rubbish that people had thrown from their cars. That was how she felt. Just a piece of rubbish that someone had thrown from a car.

She leaned heavily on the door when she finally arrived home. She had to wait a moment to summon the strength to get the key in the lock and when she finally let herself in, she knew she would have to go to bed for the afternoon to recover from the walk and the insults. Her nights were full of terror and she awoke every morning full of fear and exhaustion. At least she did not dream when she slept during the day.

She lay back on the bed, fully clothed, staring at the ceiling. She placed her hand on her enormous belly and caressed the child within her. Tigger, her secret name for her baby, had not moved in days. The doctor said it was normal. She felt that something was wrong. Tigger was named Tigger because of Tigger's amazing ability

B. THE BOOK OF DEATH

to do back flips at the most inconvenient moment. Tigger kicked, squirmed, hiccupped, pushed, stretched and generally gave a little joy and humour to Margaret in her loneliness. But now Tigger had stopped communicating with her. She felt the child was still alive, there were tiny little wriggles here and there, but nothing like what she had grown used to.

Slowly, Margaret drifted into sleep, her body twitching as she descended down into the Underworld, leaving her conscious mind behind. The dark stillness swallowed her until her jaw finally relaxed. The sleep was delicious. It drank its way through her body and the softness of the bed became deeper, kinder and full of a warmth that she had not felt in a long time.

When her eyes finally began to open, just as the sun was going down, her body snuggled into the comfort, laying and enjoying as she slowly surfaced from a rest that had not been plagued with terror and pain. In fact, for the first time in a long time, she felt no pain at all. She moved her legs to stretch and became aware that the bed was damp. She moved her leg back, and yes, there was dampness.

She stretched her arm out to turn on the lamp and she sat up in bed. As she sat up, a pain from hell shot through her, causing her to scream suddenly and fall backwards back onto the bed. She lay panting for a moment. Surely it was too early for her waters to break and the labor to start? She eased herself back up, slowly this time, allowing the pain to build rather than to attack. She pulled the bedcovers back, and cried out. The bed was soaked in blood.

Her hand reached calmly for the bedside phone and she dialled the emergency ambulance number. She talked so calmly that she could hear the disbelief in the dispatcher's voice. She replaced the receiver after being assured that an ambulance was on its way.

Laying back on the bed, she felt no panic, no fear. Everything was okay. Everything would be fine. There was no problem, it was all under control. She slowly sat back up and tried to stand. She felt dizzy but not too bad.

Methodically and calmly, she peeled off her bloodstained clothes and looked for fresh ones. The bleeding appeared to have stopped and she began to feel silly for calling an ambulance. Maybe she really did not need one. By the time the ambulance arrived, she had dressed herself, packed a small hospital case and left a note for her husband. She had also left a message on his work answer machine, just in case someone managed to get a message to him.

The ambulance man helped her into the vehicle and an ambulance woman wrapped a blanket around her. There was no sign of blood, no stains, no new fresh blood. Just a tired heavily pregnant woman who was slightly embarrassed at the fuss. They set off and as they travelled to the hospital, the ambulance woman took some details. She looked Margaret up and down, looking for signs of bleeding, shock, anything. Nothing.

"Are you alone, I mean, when will your husband get back from work? Is there anyone we can call?"

Margaret shook her head. The woman nodded and eyed Margaret again. Another lonely one looking for attention. She wrote that down as a side note on the admittance paper and circled it.

At the maternity unit of the hospital, Margaret eased herself onto the bed and retold what had happened as the nurses listened quietly. They nodded without comment and then asked Margaret to undress and put on a hospital gown. One of the nurses picked up Margaret's underwear and stated to the head nurse that there was no sign of bleeding.

"But there was a lot of blood in the bed, honestly there was."

Margaret was beginning to despair. It seemed that no one ever believed her. She looked from face-to-face as they all smiled patronizingly at her.

"Well, Mrs. Kingsley, we will link you up to a monitor to see what's happening and we will listen to baby. You say he hasn't been moving? Well, that's natural at the end of a pregnancy, don't worry about it. We will also do some tests to see what's happening. Just lie back and relax, doctor will be with you shortly."

Margaret lay on the hospital bed in a long and packed ward, staring out at the other women who all lay staring at her and at the wall. The place was depressing: no one was talking and no one was smiling. She lay there for over an hour and was just dozing when a brusque nudge of the bed brought her back to the gloomy ward.

She groaned inwardly when she recognized the clinic doctor who stood before her. She could also see from his face that he was

B. The Book of Death

groaning inwardly too. Another hypochondriac had dragged him away from his golf practice in the doctors' locker room. He sat on the side of the bed and looked her over. He asked why no baby monitor was being used, and the nurse informed him that there was not a low priority one available until the morning. He nodded and asked Margaret to "scoot" down the bed. She looked at him blankly.

"Please lie down and I will check your cervix to see if it is dilating. To see if you are in labor."

She lay down and the doctor pulled the bedclothes back. She did not register his face change at first, nor did she think it strange that the nurse had scurried off. She felt warm, relaxed and comfortable. Another nurse appeared with a large pad which she slipped under Margaret's buttocks. Margaret looked at her in question.

"For the blood."

The nurse did not elaborate and Margaret peered between her legs. Blood oozed out of her, slowly building into a pool between her legs. 'Strange,' thought Margaret, 'I didn't feel it this time.' In fact, as she plopped her hand on her leg to lever herself up, she had not felt that either. She wiggled her toes and breathed a sigh of relief that she could move them, except she could not feel her right leg or foot. Monitors appeared seemingly from nowhere and wires were soon growing out of every nook and cranny of her body.

"I'm going to break your waters and we are putting up a drip to help speed up your labor. We would normally do a caesarean section on you, an operation, but we have no spare operating theatre for nearly four hours at least. There is no emergency and all is well, the drip will really speed things up and he will be out in no time."

The doctor tried to sound as confident as possible. He hated working in this inner city hell hole and as soon as he was able, he wanted to leave England for ever, maybe to work in one of the Arab states where all the money was. Margaret caught hold of his wrist and looked into his eyes.

"Is my baby okay? It's a little early, isn't it?"

Margaret wanted to panic, but she could not. She felt calm and safe but she knew she had to ask. The doctor looked at her wearily. He tried to sound as strong as he could as he answered her searching question.

"No, lots of babies are born at this time, all will be well. Now you relax, you have a busy night ahead of you."

She lay back on her pillow and smiled at the nurse who had been stationed to watch over her. There was also someone standing behind her. But Margaret was not able to make out the figure who stood silent and unmoving.

She drifted off, unaware of the painless tightening that was stirring in her belly. The bleeding had stopped yet again, allowing everyone to breathe a sigh of relief. The warmth spread around her and pulled her deeper and deeper into a semi-sleep, the regular beeping of the machines singing her into oblivion.

The pain rose like a submarine surfacing from deep water, catching her unawares and making her gasp. The monitor sounds became uneven and somewhere, someone was shouting. Margaret opened her eyes and looked through the haze of pain. The doctor's face peered back at her, along with the nurse's and her midwife, who had just arrived and looked a little flustered. Behind the nurse and midwife stood two other people, but the shadows seemed to hide their features. It never occurred to Margaret that the ward was in full light and that there were no shadows. More and more people pushed around her, whispering to her, coaxing her.

Margaret, Margaret, come see the flowers, come see the lilies, they are so beautiful.

Margaret wanted to tell the voice that she was too busy having a baby to look at flowers, but her lips did not seem to work. The pain rose again, filling the space that she breathed and clearing out of her mind any thought other than pain. Endless, ceaseless pain. It got stronger and stronger as she groaned, the noise coming from deep within her. Someone touched her belly and Margaret wanted to pull the hands away but her arms were too heavy to pick up.

Sounds rushed past her, hands touched her, faces peered through the fog in her mind, staring at her intently. Someone told her to roll onto her side, but she did not know what that meant. What is a side?

She felt her body being pushed over onto her left side. The pain grew tentacles and seemed to grab her around her throat. Her breath became shorter until all she could do was grunt. Her thoughts became her world as she bathed in memories punctured only by pain as it passed through her on its way to somewhere.

A pressure began to build up in her head. At the same time, something solid moved down from her belly into her pelvis. The fullness became a centre point for the pain which was now exquisite as she bathed in it. Someone shouted her name, again and again. Margaret, Margaret.

She stood and looked at the chaos that was happening in the room. She found it much easier to breath now that she was no longer laid on the bed. Someone else was laid there. Margaret edged closer and froze when she recognized the woman on the bed. She looked at herself laying there, with her legs flayed and her lower body covered in blood. One of the nurses was crying as she carried something wrapped in a green cloth that the doctor had handed to her.

Margaret peered to see what it was. The body of a stillborn infant lay in the nurse's arms. Margaret was confused. She did not know why she could see herself on the bed when she was standing up and she did not know why they had a dead child. She hoped her child would not be born like that. She shuddered and thought about her own child. Should not she be busy with her labor?

With that thought she found herself back on the table and felt a warm wet cloth being wiped over her face. The warmth of the cloth punctuated the deep cold that had rolled into her body like a spring sea tide. She heard beeping and alarms. She heard conversations and regrets. Margaret wanted to comfort the nurse who had been crying. She wanted to say, "don't be sad, my baby will be born soon and you will see how beautiful she is. She will make you smile."

But she was too cold to speak. It had crept quietly upon her and wound its way into her bones, lodging itself there. The warmth from the cloth that was washing her down did not seem to penetrate her cold and she wanted to ask a nurse for a blanket. But her lips would not work. She tried to lift her arm to catch their attention, but she could not move. So she lay there while she was washed and thought about her child to come.

The daydream was shattered by a voice that cut through her cold and her thoughts. The doctor was speaking into a tape machine. He mentioned her name. He mentioned haemorrhage and torn placenta.

He described the condition of the dead child. He listed a date and time of Margaret's death. Feb. fourteenth, 3.45 a.m. Margaret screamed. The cry rolled through her body yet it could not escape. So it turned inward, digging deep into her soul and tearing her into shreds. It dug and dug until there was nowhere else to go. And then came the blackness.

Part III

Margaret moved in the darkness. Her thoughts reached out through the nothing and yet that nothing was full of everything. Someone called her. They did not use her name, or so she thought. But it was a sound that identified her and, in her fear and loneliness, she moved towards that sound.

The sound got louder until she found herself before a door. There seemed to be no door, but she knew it was there. She also knew that she had to go through that door. And yet, she was not sure about who or what she was. What part of her was going to go through that door?

The urge to move forward grew stronger and stronger until, using thought, she passed through the doorway and felt a power of transition, a shift, as she crossed the threshold. It was like waking from one of her terrible dreams. Her eyes scanned the horizon of a seemingly never-ending desert shining in the noonday sun.

In the far distance was a range of mountains and Margaret set off walking. The sun tore into her flesh as she walked, her feet stumbling as her legs got heavier and heavier. At first, it did not seem strange to her that she should be in a desert. But the further she walked, the more her memory of the hospital bed came back.

She remembered the pain and her child. She remembered her ever-absent husband and she remembered, finally, the voice of the doctor dictating his notes into a tape recorder. Margaret Kingsley, date and time of death: Feb fourteenth, 3.45 a.m. What a shame, he had said, to die birthing your first child on Valentine's day. The knowledge of her death washed over her and she began to weep. Her feet dragged over the dry earth and her tears fell, joining with other tears to form a stream that trickled on into the distance.

B. The Book of Death

Without noticing, she had come closer to the mountains, and Margaret looked up into the distance. The stream of tears ran ahead of her and joined into a river that sliced through the landscape. Up to now, she had felt no thirst. But on seeing the river, her throat began to burn with the fire of the desert: thirst consumed all of her thoughts.

As she came close to the river, she realized that she was not alone in the desert. People wandered about at the river's edge. Some stared into space while others lay weeping with their hands covering their face. The sorrow of the people blew past her like the wind: the strength of their emotions caught her off-guard. The emotions of the people flowed through her like a never-ending river, joining with her own deep sorrow and creating a deep pool of pain within her heart.

The loss of her own child began to swell within her and instinctively she placed her hand on her abdomen. Her husband's neglect of her rose to greet her along with the scorn that her father had always directed at her. Memories of her childhood surfaced, memories of pain and of joy. Things that she did not want to let go of rose into her mind: her cats and her house paraded before her, and Margaret began to feel homesick. She wanted to go home.

Immediately she found herself standing in her lounge. But it was full of people. Her husband sat in his usual armchair with his head cradled in his hands. Beside him sat his mother with her arm, as always, protecting her son. Margaret felt instant, overwhelming jealousy. His mother always had to interfere, always had to side with him to protect him, even when he had done wrong: *Mummy would always make it better.* The bitterness simmered in Margaret as she stared at the plump, overdressed woman.

Another man walked into the room, her husband's brother. He had hated Margaret on sight and the feeling had been mutual. He walked up to her husband and squatted on the floor beside him.

"We all will miss her, we all loved her."

His voice quivered as his younger brother looked up in thanks for the kind words. Margaret wanted to be sick. Not only did she know he was lying, but she could see the lies floating out of him. She saw the smugness nestled next to his heart and she wanted to tear it out for all to see.

Someone sniffled behind her, prompting Margaret to turn around. There, sat in black with deep rings under her eyes was Tanya, her best friend. Tanya had been working abroad and had flown back for the funeral. Margaret felt the horrendous pain that Tanya carried within her. She could hear Tanya's thoughts as she mulled over the fact that Margaret would probably be alive today if she had not moved away, but had stayed close to be with her friend during her pregnancy. Tanya had, right at the beginning of Margaret's pregnancy, a premonition that something was going to happen, and she had ignored it. The guilt tore into Tanya and Margaret wanted to ease that.

She moved next to her friend and placed her arms around her. She whispered into her ear while stroking her hair. How would she ever let go of her deepest love, her friend from childhood? All that remained of her memories of childhood happiness was Tanya.

At first, she did not notice the man who stood silently in the corner of the room. He was dressed strangely, with a black hat and a long beard. Margaret wondered if he was a vicar. She did not recognize him. Then he looked straight at her. Margaret was startled: how could he see her? He stared and stared at Margaret until she spoke to him.

"Who are you, how can you see me?"

The man did not answer but walked towards her and when he got to the table, he walked through the table and straight to Margaret. She tried to run.

"Daughter, you have no legs, how can you run? and where to? Come, follow me, I want to show you something."

He held out his hand and she grasped it without question. They were back at the side of the river and Margaret became angry with the man.

"Why have you brought me back here? I don't want to be here, I want to be with my friend."

She struggled against him, but her held her firmly with his eyes.

"You do not belong there, that is not your world anymore and that is no longer your friend. It has all gone and will never return. You must let go and cease to be Margaret Kingsley. You must now be yourself."

B. THE BOOK OF DEATH

Margaret cried out through her fear: "I *am* Margaret, what are you talking about?"

She wanted to flee, but she could not move and she did not know where to flee to. Instead, she flopped down to the ground beside the river, putting her head in her hands. All around her, people sat with their heads in their hands. Fear swam around them, lapping at their feet and refusing to go away.

Whenever she was in pain, Margaret always remembered her mother and the pain would go away. Her mother had died when she was a little girl, but Margaret had clung to the threads of memory that had remained with her.

Instantly she found herself back in her old childhood bedroom with her mother perched on the end of the bed, her golden hair shining from the hall light that reflected around her. Her mother smiled and Margaret snuggled down into bed. At last she was safe and warm, no one could harm her.

But something was wrong. Her mother did not change her expression and did not read her a story like mothers are supposed to. She just sat and smiled the same smile that Margaret had always remembered: the only memory that she had of her mother. The memory played itself over and over until Margaret finally understood that she could not hide in her memories.

She was back again, by the river, with her head in her hands. She looked up and scanned the desert with her eyes. People were constantly arriving out of the wilderness and sitting down by the river. Most ran to the river to drink, throwing the water over themselves and laying down to sup their fill. But Margaret did not want to do that. Yes, she had been thirsty, but something within her drove the thirst away.

People panicked around her as they reached the river: some cried out, some curled into a ball like terrified children, and others became violent. But the man who had frightened her with his words sat without emotion, looking out over the river with an expression of peace on his face. Margaret was intrigued. She walked over to him and sat quietly down beside him.

He did not react at first, but just allowed Margaret to be still with him as he watched the mountains. Finally, she turned to look at him.

Margaret wanted to introduce herself properly, but for the moment, she could not remember her name.

"That is good," said the man.

"What is good?" said Margaret.

"That you do not hold to your name. It is time it was no longer with you. It was just a tool and now you have finished your job, you no longer need the tools."

The man's voice was beautiful, but she wasn't sure she understood what he said. She tried to change the subject.

"Who are you, and how come you are not so afraid?"

Margaret was curious, this man was like no other she had seen anywhere: he was full of peace and his face seemed to shine like a thousand lamps. And yet, he just looked like a rather crumpled old man.

"Oh, I am myself. I remember this place, it holds no fear for me, and you will remember next time around, because you were wise enough not to drink of the river."

Margaret opened her mouth to ask about his answer, and then shut it again. Maybe she should not ask.

"So, what did you do, you know, before, well, before you died?"

She tried to be polite, but the question came out sounding rude and she wanted to be angry at herself, except she could not remember how to. The old man smiled and pulled on his beard thoughtfully as he looked out over the mountains.

"Hmm, well, I was supposed to be recognized. But no one recognized me, so here we all are and here we go again. They say, when you recognize a Tzadik Nistar, it is because that potential is also within you, and that when two come together and join, then our world becomes the Garden again."

Margaret frowned in confusion. She had no clue what he was talking about and yet, something deep dawned within her. Rather than ignore it like she would normally do, she allowed it to rise into her thoughts.

She saw the man in a beautiful city, like the pictures she had seen of Jerusalem. He was walking the streets and he shone like a full summer sun. But no one seemed to notice. Everything he touched

B. THE BOOK OF DEATH

became beautiful, every word he spoke took shape and travelled around him, echoing sacred sounds out to the world. But no one heard. No one recognized the grace that poured from this simple rather crumpled man. Therefore no one could partake of that grace.

"I see."

Margaret felt sadness for the man, that no one had recognized him. But then, she felt that he had no sadness, so why should she? What purpose would it serve? Why would it have a place here?

"You learn quickly!" said the man, as he smiled at her.

"Come, come with me and we will walk through some of this together. I can show you some wonderful things on the way. It's much better than walking on your own."

For the first time in a long time, Margaret was happy. She really wanted to be near this man and she knew that it would be good for her to walk with him. He held her hand as they walked along the river bank. He asked her about her life, her family and friends. As she talked about them, they seemed to get further and further away until she could no longer understand why they were talking about them.

They began to feel like distant characters from a book that no one wanted to read anymore. Eventually, she told him that she did not want to remember anything else because it all seemed so pointless.

"Why do you think it is pointless?" Asked the man.

"Well, I'm not sure, but that is how it feels. I suppose that just before I died, I had pulled away from people, I don't know. I do miss the feeling of the child within me though. It was wonderful having someone so close whom I could love.

"Although I do remember the anger and love I felt when I found myself back in my house and they were all there for my funeral. And yet, I cannot feel those feelings now. Why is that?"

Margaret posed the question to herself and the man waited for the answer.

"Maybe," she continued, "it's because they are there and I am here and *there* doesn't really matter anymore. Does it even exist anymore?"

She looked at him intently and he smiled.

"Not for you. It does for them. Love, anger, hate, joy, these are all things unto themselves. You have to learn that they are not yours to give and take. The love you had for your friend is never lost, ended or to be wept over. Every face that you see is potentially your lover, child, mother, or friend. You have all, as souls, interacted at one time or other. The love that you shared must be itself, unconditional and timeless. It flows through all being."

Margaret scanned the horizon silently. She was confused about many things, and the more she talked, the more confused she became. She turned back to the man, a question itching to be asked.

"Okay, one last question. Where is God? And Jesus? I don't see any of the stuff we were taught about at school. Where are they? Do they exist?"

The man laughed loudly and then turned Margaret around. She did not know what she was supposed to be looking at for a second. She watched a man walking towards the river and he was weeping uncontrollably. She could see pain all around him. Loss and regret fell as tears into his hands as he walked.

He reached out in all directions for something, anything to guide him. A being, like a thread of light appeared and began walking towards the man. As the being got closer, it began to take human form. It formed itself into the image of Jesus and held out its arms for the man. The man saw Jesus and ran weeping towards him. The being enveloped the man and held him in compassion until the man was ready to be released.

Margaret blanched. She had not led a religious life, not really. But she had been raised a Catholic and here she seemed to be seeing that Jesus was just a masquerading being? Her new friend heard the thought and shook his head.

"No, Jesus was a person who lived in time and then did not live in time. He was who he was, a Justified One, a Righteous One, but he was not a crutch as people would like to wish that he was. But when people die, they often die in fear and they cling to whatever memory they have of something greater than themselves. So the beings who are responsible for the transition of life and death, the doorways, often have to appear in a form taken from the human mind."

B. THE BOOK OF DEATH

"These doorways, you know them as angels. Not long blond-haired men with wings, but beings who are a part of the Divine order: they are doorways, thresholds, enablers."

His words made sense to Margaret, and yet thought was becoming difficult for her. She did not want to learn, or think. She wanted to do something, to move forward. She had started to feel uncomfortable, as though she did not fit anymore. Her body shape had started to break up and she was finding it harder to think of herself as a human shape.

She turned to ask the man about this feeling but as she formed the question, she already knew the answer. Her earthly body had been cremated. She had no material pattern left that she could connect to in solid form.

In the distance, a bridge appeared over the river. It was a bridge of light, shape and movement, like a strong shimmering rainbow that drew Margaret instinctively towards it. She wanted to ask about the bridge, but the man had vanished. She turned, looking all around her, but he was nowhere to be seen.

The bridge pulled harder and harder until she could not bear it any longer. She broke into a run, pulled by a deep urge that coursed its way through her, driving every other thought out of her mind. On reaching the threshold of the bridge she stopped suddenly. Something blocked her. She leaned against it, trying to break through.

The sound of a whirlwind whipped around her pushing at her from all directions and she became frightened. Out of the whirlwind peered many eyes, focused intently on her and probing deep into her thoughts. Memories flooded into her mind. Memories of her childhood, her early love affairs, her night terrors, her baby, and finally her death. But somehow, these memories did not evoke anything within her anymore. They seemed like lead weights that pulled her farther and farther away from the bridge. She did not want them, she no longer needed them, so she let the whirlwind take them.

It tore into her, dismantling from her everything that she knew. It tore at her thoughts, her ideas, the concepts she had learned with the man on the river bank. It pulled away all her emotions and beliefs until she stood naked before the eyes.

The whirlwind stopped. All was quiet. It felt so wonderful to be rid of all the baggage she carried for so long, and with that lightness, she stepped forward onto the bridge. The moment her foot touched the surface of the bridge something powerful and beautiful passed through her. For each step she took, she felt a joining with something, a communing, as though she had become aware of her presence within a huge web that spread into infinity.

It felt good, it felt natural, as though this was her real self. The crest of the bridge drew her onwards and passing over the centre of the bridge, a nothingness enfolded her. The nothingness had all the potential of everything in it. Every thought, deed, word, and universe were held like a breath in that nothingness.

She knew she had a choice. Stay in the nothingness, or move on. The nothingness beckoned to her. She could drink of the union with all that is Divine, being at one with the Void: the source of all creation. But something else pulled her in the opposite direction. Service. To be in a world, in a life and to allow life to flow through her. The act of being within substance. She chose substance.

Immediately she was back on the bridge, stepping through the connections of all worlds as she journeyed towards the other side of the bridge. With each step that she took, her awareness expanded to enfold each soul who had ever walked the path she was now walking. She felt the deep connection with each individual as they passed through and over the bridge in their own time and space. Like the web, they were all one being.

On reaching the other side, an angel stood in silence, pointing into the distance. Rising out of the earth was a huge range of mountains. The angel indicated that she must climb the biggest mountain.

Her heart sank. It was so far away and so high, she would never get all the way up there. The angel started to walk with her, placing one foot in front of the other, and she copied. One step at a time. As she walked, she felt things fall off of her, things she had not realized were there. She did not know what they were, but something deep within her knew it was good to shed whatever it was. She felt lighter, more balanced and with a fuller sense of freedom.

B. The Book of Death

At the foot of the mountain, the angel vanished without any warning or communication, leaving Margaret to stare up at the clouds which covered the summit. A pathway was worn by many footfalls as it snaked up the side of the mountain, vanishing into the mist. Margaret stepped on the path and began to climb. She heard voices whispering and mumbling as she climbed. There was nothing specific said, no words that she could grasp, just noise. But the higher she climbed, the clearer the voices became.

She heard the texts of the gospels being read and the words mingled in with recitations of the Qur'an. Over the top of that was a speaking of the Torah, the Gita, and beyond that a whispering of Fire incantations. Words in languages she had never heard were chanted in the background as she climbed, their sounds dragged at her feet, weighing her down. All the sacred words that had ever been written and uttered whispered around her, making it harder and harder to reach the top of the mountain.

Other voices joined in the chorus, voices raised in political anger, voices speaking out against beliefs, voices calling for war, and voices crying for peace. And then came the loudest: the cry of beings as they were slaughtered: human voices, animals, birds, every creature she could imagine, the sounds of their voices raised in terror in their last moments of life drove itself into her like sword piercing her soul. The cry broke through all others and imprinted itself on her. It followed her wherever she turned. She could not escape it: the sound of life, of death, the sound of the living world of creation and destruction.

Margaret climbed and climbed in an attempt to escape the noise. As she neared the top, the sounds suddenly stopped. All was quiet, all was peaceful. The mist hid the summit from her and the atmosphere around her had become cold and damp. She knew she had to walk into the mist. She knew she could not turn around and return back down the mountain. There was nowhere else for her to go but into the unseen.

Her thoughts stilled as she prepared for what was beyond the mountain mist. The weight of her previous life had all but fallen away. It had become some dark distant memory that she had managed to finally shrug off like a disease. Now she was herself. Timeless.

With that stillness, she moved into the mist and was immediately enveloped in a dreadful weariness. Her mind forcibly pushed her onwards until she could go no further. The mist had begun to thin ever so slightly: just enough to see back down some of the mountain and to see ahead. Before her lay many people, all fast asleep. Beyond them, the mountain top fell away but the horizon was obscured by the mist. The tiredness ate into her and she fell to her knees. Motionless, she stayed in that position briefly, before finally laying down. Each position that she took felt uncomfortable until a voice passed through her.

Remember, the voice said.

Remember what?

Margaret could not remember, *but the body that she no longer had remembered.* Its human imprint, that was stored deep within her, remembered. The memory played out through her and she shifted into the remembered position. On her stomach, left arm outstretched, right arm behind her back. Right leg outstretched, left leg bent and tucked behind right leg. Finally, she knew she was in the correct position. With that knowledge came sleep.

The keepers of the dead wandered in and out of the sleeping bodies, maintaining the sleepers' inner balance as they slept. Some that they came across still had residual patterns from their last life that needed removing: the sleepers' bodies twitched from deep nightmares, or moaned quietly as if in pain. The keepers took pity on the sufferings of the sleepers. In their pity, the keepers lay beside those who slept and sang songs that would settle in the minds of the sleepers and guide them during the darkest hours of their next incarnations.

They stroked the sleepers, filling them with balance and power, tools they would need for their journey ahead. And finally, before the dawn broke, the keepers cupped their hands over the sleepers, holding the deep eternal inner flame of each sleeper and giving it temporary sanctuary.

As the dawn broke, the mist cleared and the keepers called to the dawn with a conch shell: the labyrinth of the ocean that carries the wind. The noise awoke the sleepers who looked out in awe as the light and darkness of the Void shone upon them.

B. The Book of Death

Margaret turned in the blackness, at one with the nothing. Not wishing to move or be. Silence.

Out of the silence, the sound of a loud horn vibrated through her, calling her back to existence. Margaret wanted to fight the call, she wanted to stay within the stillness but the call became more and more urgent.

She awoke to find herself lying on the top of a mountain. She looked up just in time to see someone bend over and push her down the far side of the mountain. She wanted to cry out in panic but her breath was taken as she rolled and tumbled down what felt like a grassy hill. During the rolling, she became more and more aware that she was feeling with senses and shape: with limbs, eyes, ears, even though she had none. The strangeness of such thoughts tumbled with her as she cascaded down the hill.

The scent of the fresh grass and dust awoke her awareness of the world and of being in human form. She ached for such life again and just as the ache became unbearable, something slowed her to a stop.

She unravelled herself at the foot of the hill and stood up. Before her was a large rupture in the ground: the Abyss. Behind her was the mountain. Looking up, she could see others tumbling down, just as she had done.

They all slowed, seemingly of their own accord until something nudged her from behind. The nudge seemed to alter her vision and she slowly became aware of a giant hand reaching out to each person and carefully slowing them down. She turned back to look at the Abyss and before it stood a being that made Margaret afraid.

Before the Abyss stood an angelic being that reached up to the stars. She had many arms and wings that stretched out to prevent people from falling into the Abyss. Many other arms reached out to slow those who tumbled down the hill. Her hair flowed in all directions, scooping up those who had lost their way. Her eyes turned to each person as she looked at them intently, one by one.

Her eyes finally looked into Margaret, and Margaret began to cry. Every failing that she had, became apparent to her. Every cruelty, ignorance, indifference, stupidity and thoughtlessness paraded before her. Behind it came every goodness, every drop of love that she had shed for others, every hand she had outstretched, every gift she had given.

The angel weighed it all in the palm of her hand. The balance was presented without judgment back to Margaret and Margaret became aware of what she needed to achieve to better that balance.

The angel turned her head to look out over the Abyss to the Desert beyond and Margaret's gaze followed. In that Desert beyond the Abyss Margaret saw many lives paraded in front of her, all happening at once, all lives that would give her the skills to achieve what she needed. Some were more tempting than others, but Margaret could see that the tempting ones might not yield all that she needed in a balanced way.

She saw one life that she felt she recognized. It was a difficult life and yet was rich in learning. Her heart lurched towards it and Margaret followed. The angel withdrew the protective arm from Margaret's centre and Margaret pitched forward into the Abyss. A whirlwind came up to greet her and whipped her into its centre. Her thoughts were flung around and around the directions as she fell, its wind flowing through her and adjusting her for what was to come.

Part IV

The angel stood impassive as the couple joined in love. The emotions that they released for each other joined and created a rising vortex, spinning throughout the worlds. The vortex connected with a whirlwind that whipped down out of the Abyss and the roar of the whirlwind echoed around the room where the couple lay. Still the angel did not move.

At the moment of connection between the vortex and the whirlwind, a light shone through the darkness and the angel began to awaken from its stillness. A soul tumbled through the worlds, twisting and turning within the whirlwind as the soul passed from wind to vortex. The whirlwind withdrew and the soul completed its journey into the world as it slowly passed, guided by the angel, into the body of the woman lying in the arms of her lover.

On contact, the soul spread out, joining with the soul of the woman and the angel took its position by the woman's head. A beautiful web pattern appeared, the pattern of human shape. The angel gently teased the newly arrived soul into the pattern and wove it in deftly within the pattern of the mother.

The woman's body shone with the intricate connections as her soul upheld and gave sanctuary to the new being that would eventually be her child. When the angel was satisfied that the connection was complete, it withdrew and vanished into the Void.

Margaret turned in a swirl of warmth and love. A regular heartbeat punched out a sense of rhythm for her as she lay in silence and light. She was at one with being in substance and yet she was in the stillness, in the deep. The stillness was full of Brightness, a light that was home. It was a place she did not want to leave, ever.

But there came a time, a turning within her. The sense of connection was lessening, and her sense of being was growing. She became aware that she was not her surroundings, that they were separate to her, and yet were still a part of her. At that point, the moment of awareness of separate, something shifted with her. She knew she had to leave. But to where?

The urge for a journey became overwhelming. It tore at her, forcing her to make the move to leave. Once the thought was accepted, her world began to contract and change. Pressure built up all around her, forcing her, squashing her into a battle for life.

She tried to fight back at times, until a deep knowing within her surfaced, telling her to relax. She felt herself leave the safety and comfort of her world. There was only forward into the unknown, there was nowhere else to go. It was terrifying. Her mind reached forward as her body was propelled on until she broke free of the warmth and safety, and was pushed into a dull light full of external noise and coldness. She took a breath as her thoughts vanished with the Brightness, and the loneliness of separation and dull light hit her without mercy.

The angel hovered around the woman's body as she arched her back against the pain. Other beings that were connected with the process of birth and death hovered, ready to be of assistance, their presence unseen by the people assisting the woman with the birth of the child. The child's head appeared and rotated. All the beings waited in silence as the woman screamed. And then came the final push.

The child slithered out and immediately the angel bent over the woman and cut the inner cord that passed from mother to child. The child's pattern became locked in its separateness at that moment, no longer integrated with that of the mother. The angel then stroked its fingers through the mother to rebalance her before turning to the child. As the other beings, and the humans in the room tended to the mother, the angel focused on the new life before it.

The child lay still and silent as the angel looked into the eyes of the child. In the communion, the angel sought the thread of the child's soul and when he found it, he tied a knot in it. A small, delicate knot of remembrance. The child and the angel passed visions of recognition before the angel bent over and listened to the child whispering something on its first breath. The child then turned its gaze to a bright harsh lightbulb hanging above it: all the child could remember was the Brightness, and the child longed to be within that Brightness once more. It searched for the Brightness in the lightbulb, but could not find it.

The angel went to the mother and whispered in the mother's ear. He whispered the words spoken by the child, the Divine breath made word and the word was in flesh. The words travelled around the mother before settling deep in her heart. The words transformed themselves into sounds and joined with the mother's thoughts. They, together, became a name. The mother bent over and whispered the child's name in her ear. And the angel withdrew.

Only in death can the light of the Sun truly fall upon our slumbering faces

Quareia
a New, Free School of Magic
for the 21st Century

*Advancing education in Mystical Magic
and the Western Esoteric Mysteries.*

www.quareia.com
schooldirector@quareia.com

Quareia is a practical magical training course founded by Josephine McCarthy and Frater Acher. It is a complete and freely available course designed to develop a student from a complete beginner into an adept. There are no barriers to entry: the course is accessible regardless of income, race, gender, religion, or spiritual beliefs.

Quareia is aligned to no particular school or specific religious, mystical, or magical system; rather it looks at and works with various magical, religious, and mystical practices that have influenced magical thinking in the Near Eastern and Western world from the early Bronze Age to the present day.

The entire course is free and openly available on the Quareia website.

www.ingramcontent.com/pod-product-compliance
Lightning Source LLC
Chambersburg PA
CBHW071725080526
44588CB00013B/1899